Open Source Projects - B

A blueprint for scalable and sustainable open source projects

John Mertic

BIRMINGHAM—MUMBAI

Open Source Projects - Beyond Code

Group Product Manager: Gebin George

Publishing Product Manager: Akash Sharma

Content Development Editor: Rosal Colaco

Technical Editor: Pradeep Sahu

Copy Editor: Safis Editing

Project Coordinator: Manisha Singh

Proofreader: Safis Editing

Indexer: Hemangini Bari

Production Designer: Shyam Sundar Korumilli

Developer Relations Marketing Executive: Sonia Chauhan and Rayyan Khan

First published: March 2023

Production reference: 0240323

Published by Packt Publishing Ltd.
Livery Place
35 Livery Street
Birmingham
B3 2PB, UK.

ISBN 978-1-83763-688-4

www.packtpub.com

To my amazingly supportive wife, Kristy, and children, Mallory, Carter, Yin Bai, and Zarah, always there for encouragement and love, especially for all the zany things I get myself into, like writing this book.

– John Mertic

Contributors

About the author

John Mertic is the director of program management for The Linux Foundation. Under his leadership, he has helped ASWF, ODPi, the Open Mainframe Project, and R Consortium accelerate open source innovation and transform industries. John had an open source career spanning two decades, both as a contributor to projects such as SugarCRM and PHP, and in open source leadership roles at SugarCRM, OW2, and OpenSocial. With an extensive open source background, he is a regular speaker at various Linux Foundation events and other industry trade shows each year. John is also an avid writer and has authored two books, *The Definitive Guide to SugarCRM: Better Business Applications* and *Building on SugarCRM*, as well as publishing articles on IBM developerWorks, Apple Developer Connection, and PHP Architect.

I would like to first and foremost thank my loving and patient wife, Kristy, and children, Mallory, Carter, Yin Bai, and Zarah, for their continued support, patience, and love throughout the long process of writing this book. Thanks also to all the open source projects I have had the privilege to work on over the last two decades, as I wouldn't have had any of these experiences without them.

About the reviewer

Guy Martin is Director of Open Source and Standards at NVIDIA, where he works with the Omniverse team to help them utilize and contribute to important open 3D projects and standards such as **Universal Scene Description** (**USD**), **Material Definition Language** (**MDL**), PhysX (a real-world 3D physics engine), and many others. He also serves as an internal consultant on open source and standards to the rest of the organization.

He brings a unique blend of 30 years of experience as both a software engineer and open source strategist to NVIDIA. He previously served as Executive Director for OASIS Open, an internationally recognized open source and standards consortium. He has participated in building numerous open source and standards bodies for technologies ranging from visual effects to the Internet of Things.

Table of Contents

3

Open Source License and IP Management   37

4

Aligning the Business Value of Open Source for Your Employer   53

Part 2: Running an Open Source Project

6

7

8

9

Part 3: Building and Scaling Open Source Ecosystems

10

11

12

13

Transitioning Leadership   183

14

Sunsetting an Open Source Project   193

Preface

Open source has become not only the most dominant software development methodology but also a preeminent strategy for rapid innovation, decentralized collaboration, ecosystem building, and career growth. You can't go anywhere these days without interacting with open source. Open source is in your mobile phone, car, and refrigerator; it enables the distribution and production of your favorite show or movie, keeps planes in the air, and helps impoverished sectors of society leap forward to being a part of the digital world. It's even responsible for helping write this book (thank you, Neovim and Pandoc!).

With the vast amount of open source out there comes immense variety. While one big part of that variety is the technology stack being used, another just as important part is how open source projects operate. There has been a cornucopia of **intellectual property** (**IP**) strategies, hosting and governance models, community structures, commercial engagement, and growth trajectories. While the technology stack of an open source project tends to be more of a science, the operational end is more of an art. No two projects are alike; what works for one project may not work for another.

This is precisely what this book is focused on; the art of how open source projects work. *Chapters 1* and *2* will give you the base knowledge of an open source project, why you would participate in or create an open source project, and the characteristics of a good open source project. From there, you will dive into multiple aspects of an open source project; think of *Chapters 3* through *14* as a *cookbook*. One big difference from what you might expect from a *cookbook* is that there is not a clear answer on "the right way" for any of the topics covered; you will learn from the examples of many projects that have been successful (along with ones that haven't been as successful). These examples will hopefully resonate with the focuses your open source project might have and give you more of a framework for working through a focus. After all, open source is an art and not a science.

Who this book is for

This book is for anyone with an interest in open source, particularly those looking to launch an open source project or currently running an open source project and looking to gain knowledge on how better operate their project or scale it for growth and sustainability.

What this book covers

Chapter 1, The What's and Whys of Open Source, digs into what open source is and the history of open source. From there, you will learn about how open source is used and some example projects that showcase different motivators for open source.

Chapter 2, What Makes a Good Open Source Project?, identifies the core characteristics of an open source project. You will learn the difference between "open sourcing code" versus "creating an open source project," along with exploring various patterns and anti-patterns in open source projects.

Chapter 3, Open Source License and IP Management, will explore the various aspects of licensing, copyright management, contribution sign-off, and brand and marks management, although coming from a non-lawyer.

Chapter 4, Aligning the Business Value of Open Source for Your Employer, will help you build the case for having your employer contribute to open source or start an open source project. This will cover why a company would want to open source code, getting support and building the business case for open sourcing code, and how to execute the open sourcing process and measure success.

Chapter 5, Governance and Hosting Models, explains how open source projects can structure governance. You will learn about the various governance models, the roles in open source projects, documenting your project structure, and getting financial support for your project.

Chapter 6, Making Your Project Feel Welcoming, provides guidance and best practices for creating an inclusive community. Topics will include setting up your project for newcomers, supporting end users effectively, and engaging your community when it grows beyond the scope of your project.

Chapter 7, Growing Contributors to Maintainers, covers why it's important to convert contributors into maintainers and then looks at the process of identifying contributors who could become maintainers and how to know when they are ready to become a maintainer.

Chapter 8, Dealing with Conflict, approaches understanding how humans think and their motivations as a way to better deal with conflict in open source projects. You will also learn about inclusive decision-making and how to remedy toxic behavior in your project.

Chapter 9, Handling Growth, is all about measuring growth, assessing areas of your project with low growth, and figuring out how to remedy them. You will also learn about how to scale project leadership to manage their time better and focuses as a project grows to help them avoid burnout.

Chapter 10, Commercialization of Open Source, will review the importance and value of open source projects being used commercially. You will learn about commercialization models for open source projects and how to set up your project for commercial usage.

Chapter 11, Open Source and the Talent Ecosystem, will look at the intersections between open source projects and talent. You will learn about personal career growth using open source, how to find talent using open source, and how to recognize employees who contribute to open source.

Chapter 12, Marketing for Open Source - Advocacy and Outreach, discusses the need for marketing for open source projects. You will learn about how to develop the base marketing materials open source projects should have, and then explore broader ways to drive engagement in your project through marketing.

Chapter 13, Transitioning Leadership, tackles the topic of succession planning for open source project leadership. You will learn how to build a transition plan and how leaders can step back comfortably to let the next generation of leaders take the project forward.

Chapter 14, Sunsetting an Open Source Project, will prepare you to identify when an open source project is approaching its sunset. You will see how to sunset an open source project, both in terms of the work to be done before sunsetting and the considerations post-sunsetting.

To get the most out of this book

This book isn't a technical book, but more of a guide to the art of open source projects. While there aren't any prerequisites per se, it's best to have a base knowledge of what open source is before reading this book. You don't need to have a technical background to be able to get the most out of this book.

Download the color images

We also provide a PDF file that has color images of the screenshots and diagrams used in this book. You can download it here: `https://packt.link/FZrJq`

Conventions used

There are a number of text conventions used throughout this book.

`Code in text`: Indicates code words in text, database table names, folder names, filenames, file extensions, pathnames, dummy URLs, user input, and Twitter handles. Here is an example: "The simplest way is for the project to have an `ADOPTERS` file in its code repository."

Bold: Indicates a new term, an important word, or words that you see onscreen. For instance, words in menus or dialog boxes appear in **bold**. Here is an example: "The backend of the life cycle is **Sustain...**, which sometimes means the project is just maintained over time."

> **Tips or important notes**
> Appear like this.

Get in touch

Feedback from our readers is always welcome.

General feedback: If you have questions about any aspect of this book, email us at `customercare@packtpub.com` and mention the book title in the subject of your message.

Errata: Although we have taken every care to ensure the accuracy of our content, mistakes do happen. If you have found a mistake in this book, we would be grateful if you would report this to us. Please visit www.packtpub.com/support/errata and fill in the form.

Piracy: If you come across any illegal copies of our works in any form on the internet, we would be grateful if you would provide us with the location address or website name. Please contact us at copyright@packt.com with a link to the material.

If you are interested in becoming an author: If there is a topic that you have expertise in and you are interested in either writing or contributing to a book, please visit authors.packtpub.com.

Share Your Thoughts

Once you've read *Open Source Projects - Beyond Code*, we'd love to hear your thoughts! Scan the QR code below to go straight to the Amazon review page for this book and share your feedback.

https://packt.link/r/1837636885

Your review is important to us and the tech community and will help us make sure we're delivering excellent quality content.

Download a free PDF copy of this book

Thanks for purchasing this book!

Do you like to read on the go but are unable to carry your print books everywhere? Is your eBook purchase not compatible with the device of your choice?

Don't worry, now with every Packt book you get a DRM-free PDF version of that book at no cost.

Read anywhere, any place, on any device. Search, copy, and paste code from your favorite technical books directly into your application.

The perks don't stop there, you can get exclusive access to discounts, newsletters, and great free content in your inbox daily

Follow these simple steps to get the benefits:

1. Scan the QR code or visit the link below

https://packt.link/free-ebook/9781837636884

2. Submit your proof of purchase
3. That's it! We'll send your free PDF and other benefits to your email directly

Part 1: Getting Ready to Go Open Source

In this part, you will get an understanding of what open source is, why open source is chosen as a model for software development, and what makes a good open source project. Additionally, we will cover some of the important parts of starting an open source project, including licensing and IP management, aligning business value to get your employer to participate in open source, and the myriad of governance and hosting models for open source projects.

This part contains the following chapters:

- *Chapter 1, The Whats and Whys of Open Source*
- *Chapter 2, What Makes a Good Open Source Project?*
- *Chapter 3, Open Source License and IP Management*
- *Chapter 4, Aligning the Business Value of Open Source for Your Employer*
- *Chapter 5, Governance and Hosting Models*

1
The Whats and Whys of Open Source

When I've explained **open source** to people who aren't in tech or related areas, I often find myself in a conversation that goes something like this:

Person: "So what is this open source thing?"

Me: "It basically is a way that multiple people and organizations can collaborate on building software out in the open."

Person: "So, it's free?"

Me: "I mean yes, but there are licenses involved that set the terms of reuse."

Person: "Is this stuff valuable? If it was, wouldn't someone sell it?"

Me: "Well, yeah, it is, but it's often the software that is a base technology that people would build a product from. Or it's something enough people feel strongly about being out there in the open for anyone to use."

Person: "Okay, so people get paid to build this software?"

Me: "Often, yes, but sometimes people just do it because they want to."

Person: "So, why would someone do this?"

Me: "Well, it could be a lot of reasons. Maybe they like the technology. Maybe the group of people they are working with is interesting and fun to work with. Maybe they are trying to get a foot in the door in software development."

Person: "Okay, yeah, uh, sounds fun."

And this conversation aligns with one you might have with someone in business; I have had similar ones with friends and family, and they walk away worried about my future job prospects and how I would support my family ;-).

In all seriousness, describing open source requires some nuance. It is part licensing, part development methodology, part culture, and part *ethos* – and it is something that continues to *ebb and flow* over time. Despite millions of open source projects having been successful and just as many (if not more) not having been, there is no one right way to do it – thus, the point of this book!

This chapter will cover the following topics:

- What is open source?

- A brief history of open source

- How is open source used?

- Open source projects and why they are used

I believe that to understand a topic, you must understand its origin. In this chapter, we will do that by describing what open source is, how it came to be, how it's used, and examining some open source projects to understand why they are open and where they are used.

What is open source?

Wikipedia (`https://en.wikipedia.org/wiki/Open_source`) defines open source as follows:

> *Open source is source code that is made freely available for possible modification and redistribution. Products include permission to use the source code, [1] design documents, [2] or content of the product. The open-source model is a decentralized software development model that encourages open collaboration.*

If you search online, you will find a number of definitions used:

- **Red Hat** (`https://www.redhat.com/en/topics/open-source/what-is-open-source`)

- **IBM** (`https://www.ibm.com/topics/open-source`)

- **Opensource.com** (`https://opensource.com/resources/what-open-source`)

While the definitions are certainly different, some common themes align here.

The first is the concept of source code being made freely available, allowing anyone to view, modify, and share the source code with others. This is often where people will start with open source, thinking of it as software one can get for free. However, open source takes that one step further; it's not just making software available for free (better known as *freeware*) but also giving the user the ability to see the source code, modify it for their own use, and share it with others.

A good way I've heard the difference described is to imagine that you have a car, and the hood is sealed shut. Sure, you own the car and can drive it, but what if something breaks? What if you want to upgrade a component? What if something becomes out of date and needs to be changed to work for the future (such as changing from standard gasoline to E87)? The car with the sealed shut hood means only the manufacturer can change it – the one with the hood that can open is *open* and can be changed by the user. That's where the difference lies – it's, as is often said, not *free as in beer* but *free as in freedom* or *libre*.

The second theme focuses on **open collaboration**, meaning that anyone can participate in how the code is built. This is an area you see in open source that isn't always adhered to; many projects that are sponsored by a single organization can be a bit of a challenge to contribute to, and even single, individual maintainer projects struggle here. I've seen this most often due to maintainers being overwhelmed and not having a ton of time to dedicate to a project. Other times, it's due to the project being more of a *proof-of-concept* and being somewhat abandoned by the maintainer, or occasionally a maintainer not really wanting any help. I'll dig into this more in later chapters as I cover governance and growth, but as we talk about what open source is in this chapter, open collaboration tends to be a key tenet of the expectations we have.

Finally, there is the theme of a **decentralized community**. This means open source projects are truly global; while a maintainer might start a project to solve a problem they have and pull in a few others who they know with similar goals, both the model of licensing (the code can be freely viewed, used, modified, and shared by anyone) and the distribution (thank you, internet!) mean that literally anyone in the world who finds this code and uses it is part of a community. This likely feels daunting and intimidating at first glance, but this is one of the best parts of open source; it is a connective thread across locales, cultures, genders, backgrounds, ages, and abilities. Again, a topic that we will chat about a bit more in later chapters, and one that is often a struggle point with projects, is that with this great ability to connect people globally comes the responsibility of supporting them.

The **Open Source Initiative** maintains **The Open Source Definition** (source: `https://opensource.org/osd` (Creative Commons BY 4.0)) and is considered the standard definition of measuring whether a piece of code or project is truly open source.

The definition really focuses on the concept of open source from a licensing perspective and for many, is where the definition of open source starts and stops. Licensing is what many would consider as the table stakes for what open source is (and have no fear, we have a whole chapter dedicated to licensing – *Chapter 3, Open Source Licensing and IP Management*). What truly makes open source transformational is *open collaboration* and a *decentralized community*, bringing together a diverse group of persons to build something that is greater than any one of them. In other words, the license choice enables building community and collaboration, which, in turn, makes open source projects successful.

Now that we have defined open source and learned more about what the key parts of it are, let us look back at how we got to where we are today. In the next section, we will go back to history to trace the roots of open source.

A brief history of open source

Open source as a term dates back to February 3rd, 1998, but the ethos and ideals date back decades before that. Let's take a look back in time.

The concepts of viewing, modifying, and sharing, along with open collaboration, can be traced to way before the internet and computers. Much of this was commonplace in *hacker* and *maker* cultures, both rooted in artisan spirits. For hundreds and thousands of years, new technologies and innovations were born out of the sharing of ideas with each other, each time seeing the next effort built off of that of others before. The challenges were only the ability for ideas to travel, where Gutenberg's invention of the printing press began the acceleration of knowledge that became the Renaissance.

There has always been a natural tension between the collaborative spirit and commercialization. The establishment of the system of patents in the 1400 and 1500s had the intention of protecting inventors but in many cases, created monopolies that stifled open collaboration. A classic example is in the automotive space, where a patent on the two-cycle engine was filed by and awarded to George B. Selden. Henry Ford challenged that patent and won, which opened innovation and formed an association in which automotive engine knowledge could be shared amongst competitors (and had one of the first patent agreements, where members would agree to share patent licensing freely with one another). This change sparked the automotive boom of the early 20th century.

Tracing the roots of open source to the mainframe community

In computing, the traces go back to 1955 in a room in the Los Angeles, California area. **International Business Machines (IBM)** had released what is considered to be the first mainframe a few years earlier – the **IBM 701 Electronic Data Processing Machine**. Early users of this machine came together to collaborate on how to use it, sharing information, insight, code, and knowledge with one another – very like what open source communities do today, but instead of sharing over the internet, it was punch cards and magnetic tape. Thus was born the **SHARE** community – named most eloquently after its motto: *SHARE – it's not an acronym, it's what we do.*

These user group meetings continued for years, creating a commons known as the **SHARE Operating System**. This culture of sharing outgrew these commons, and there was a need for a place to collect this code not just for sharing but also to have a central repository to track it. In 1975, Arnold (Arnie) Casinghino, then with **Connecticut Bank and Trust (CBT)** Company, began collecting this code and distributing it on tape to anyone who requested it. Additionally, if someone wanted something added to the tape, they could send it to Arnie, and it would be added. You could call this an early example of an open source project, complete with a maintainer (Arnie), open collaboration, and a decentralized community. Interestingly enough, this project continues to this day; Arnie has long since retired, but others in the mainframe community have stepped up to maintain the tape. It is now downloadable over the internet, but you can also send the maintainers a few dollars in the mail and they will send you a tape.

In the 1950s and 1960s, with computing so new and generally focused on science and research, along with use in academia, collaboration and decentralized community were the norms. At the same time, the cost of developing software for these computers was increasing as these computers became more complex. This is the point at which we saw the birth of software companies, which were at odds with hardware manufacturers such as IBM who bundled software with hardware at no cost, as they saw it as a necessity to sell the hardware. The United States government saw things differently, filing an antitrust case against IBM in 1969. While the case was eventually withdrawn in 1982, what it did set in motion was IBM *unbundling* software from hardware, which was a boon for software companies. This was aided by the 1974 US **Commission on New Technological Uses of Copyrighted Works (CONTU)** deciding that software was copyrightable, and later cases such as Apple versus Franklin, saying object code was copyrightable in the same way literary books are – thus, the idea of free, public domain, sharable software seemed to be a thing of the past.

The emergence of free software

The late 1970s into the 1980s saw the rise of **Bulletin Board Systems** (**BBSes**) where enthusiasts, now able to acquire computers to use in their own homes, began sharing software back and forth as was done in the 1950s and 1960s. Two individuals in particular were important at this time.

The first was Richard Stallman, who launched the **GNU** project in 1983 with the aim of writing a complete operating system free from constraints on the licensing commons with source code from software companies. Probably the most noteworthy of the projects launched include the following:

- **GNU Compiler Collection (GCC)**
- **GNU Debugger**
- **GNU Emacs**

All of these projects are hugely popular to this day. This also kicked off one of the earliest open source licenses, called the **GNU Public License**, which captured the ideals Stallman had of creating a commons of software. Stallman has been quite outspoken over time and, at times, controversial within the realm of free and open source software, as he has leaned toward a more free software approach (meaning the license should ensure the code and derivative works remain free software), rather than more permissive licensing approaches. I'll dig more into these differences later in *Chapter 3, Open Source Licensing and IP Management*.

The other individual is Linus Torvalds, who released a **UNIX** clone in 1991 called **Linux** (more on the history of UNIX at `https://www.redhat.com/sysadmin/unix-linux-history`). While Stallman's work created the space in which open source today was built, Torvalds' work brought open source and free software into the mainstream. It also opened up revenue streams and economic development in the order of billions of US dollars, from vendors such as Red Hat and SUSE creating distributions of Linux, IBM, Sun, and Oracle to birthing commercial applications and today's cloud and infrastructure vendors such as VMware, Amazon, Google, Microsoft, and many others. What has been unique is that alongside commercial application and success, the hobbyist and enthusiast community has been just as strong; Debian Linux and Slackware were early distributions, still to this day having large user bases.

Open source is coined as a term

In 1997, one of the main free software influencers, Eric Raymond (known by his initials ESR), penned an essay, *The Cathedral and the Bazaar*, which spoke to his experiences as an early free software project maintainer and his observations of the Linux kernel community. This was one of the first pieces of writing about the hobbyist and hacker culture and ethos, drawing visuals to the then two models of free software development. One model was called the *Cathedral*, where software was developed behind closed doors and then released publicly (used with the various GNU projects). The other model was called the *Bazaar*, where software was developed in the open over the internet (then still a new concept) in the view of the public (the model of the Linux community). I will dig into the insights and learning from this essay throughout the book.

From a historical perspective, this was considered the nudge for the **Netscape Communications Company** to release the source code for **Netsuite Communicator** and launch the **Mozilla** project in January 1998 (read more about the browser wars at `https://thehistoryoftheweb.com/browser-wars/`). Companies releasing their commercial products open source is commonplace today. Still, back then, it drew the eye of the technology world (this also happened during the first browser wars, so there were additional factors that drew interest). Those involved in these early open development projects saw that they had an opportunity to start to build a larger movement and define this emerging effort from the free software movement of the 1980s.

This brought together a meeting on February 3, 1998, in Palo Alto, attended by Todd Anderson, Chris Peterson (of the Foresight Institute), John "*maddog*" Hall and Larry Augustin (both of Linux International), Sam Ockman (of the Silicon Valley Linux Users Group), and Eric Raymond. One thing this group strived to do was to make this movement distinctive from free software and more inclusive of commercial software vendors – the ethos and licensing around the free software movement were considered off-putting and, by some, hostile for commercial use. As the brainstorming and discussion occurred, the idea to label this software as *open source* came from Chris Peterson, and everyone in the room aligned around it – open source was officially born.

Giving open source a vendor-neutral home

In 1994 and 1995, as Linux was starting to get some early commercial traction, several companies were attempting to trademark the term *Linux*. Torvalds fought these as best he could and later would be awarded the trademark for Linux. Torvalds then partnered with Linux International to be the organization to hold the marks.

This raised an important question – how can open source projects be best legally protected? I'll dig more into this in *Chapter 3*, *Open Source Licensing and IP Management*, but we saw the rise of non-profit entities to become vendor-neutral homes for these marks (and, in some cases, copyright holders). The initial motivation for these foundations focused on fiduciary homes for marks, copyrights, and other key legal assets but over time, grew to provide professional services for these projects, including but not limited to development and collaboration infrastructure, marketing and outreach support, fundraising, and event management.

One of the first open source foundations was the **Apache Software Foundation** (**ASF**), which was established in 1999 as a US 501(c)(3) charitable organization. The ASF had a funding model to accept corporate and individual donations and sponsorships, which supported legal support for projects, along with extensive development and communication infrastructure. It is predominately an all-volunteer effort, and one of the big innovations it brought was *The Apache Way*, which set a clear governance structure for hosted projects built from the experiences of the more *Bazaar*-style open source projects from the 1990s. Quickly many of the other key open source projects launched foundations, including **GNOME**, **KDE**, **Eclipse**, and one around the newly open source Netscape Communicator source code called the **Mozilla Foundation**.

In the years that followed was recognition that many of the functions of these foundations had overlapped, and there could be some efficiency and cost savings by having joint infrastructure. This is where the Linux Foundation innovated by creating the *foundation-of-foundations* model, which bore key foundations such as the **Cloud Native Computing Foundation** (**CNCF**). In addition to the CNCF, the Linux Foundation has also enabled smaller foundations such as the Academy Software Foundation, Hyperledger, LF Energy, Open Mainframe Project, and others to have top-notch professional staff supporting the growing communities with more efficiency, requiring less cost on the staff overhead and, instead, this saving being invested in the communities themselves. I will dig more into these foundation models in *Chapter 5*, *Governance and Hosting Models*.

With a good background of the history of open source in hand, let's look forward now to how we see open source used.

Implementing open source

You can see that there has been a long and winding history of open source, which has predominately been driven by enthusiasts who were passionate about the technologies they worked with and, over time, brought in commercial investment while staying true to form with the ethos that grew these communities.

With those years of effort came many patterns of success and patterns that did not pan out as well. We have seen the concept of open source applied to different areas outside of computing, including quilting patterns, the home brewing of beer, genome patterns, and more. From these efforts we have seen a few patterns in how open source has been used with a degree of success – let us look at those.

Information sharing amongst enthusiasts

The earliest use we've seen of open source (and arguably most pervasive) is just being able to share information and knowledge with others with a common problem. It generally is the underlying motivation for open source generally and aligns with the historical ethos of open source being based on hacker and maker cultures.

When it comes to information sharing, what is shared comes in many different forms. While in open source we generally think of code, often, it can be a design, documentation for a tool or process, diagrams, datasets, or some other sort of medium. I will cover how licensing works in these non-code settings in *Chapter 3, Open Source Licensing and IP Management*, but know that there are licenses out there for just about every type of work and expectation of the community.

Some projects that focus on information sharing include the following:

- **Ubertooth** (`https://github.com/greatscottgadgets/ubertooth`): This is an open source wireless development platform for Bluetooth experimentation. The project both builds a software stack for the hardware, as well as providing hardware designs that others can use to build the actual hardware for the software stack (and cultivates an indie community that offers hardware kits, as well as fully-built dongles to use).

- **PiFire** (`https://github.com/nebhead/PiFire`): This provides a smart Wi-Fi-enabled controller for a pellet smoker or grill, including software design as well as hardware designs based on the Raspberry PI platform.

- **SecurityExplained** (`https://github.com/harsh-bothra/SecurityExplained`): This provides informational content for the software security community.

- **Darwin Core** (`https://github.com/tdwg/dwc`): This is a standard maintained by the Darwin Core Maintenance Interest Group, which includes a glossary of terms intended to facilitate the sharing of information about biological diversity.

Various **Awesome Lists** are ways for communities to collaborate on some of the best resources in a given topic area. A few that I've run across include the following:

- **Awesome 3D Printing** (`https://github.com/ad-si/awesome-3d-printing`): This provides links and resources for those into 3D printing

- **Awesome Interviews (list of job questions)** (`https://github.com/DopplerHQ/awesome-interview-questions`): This is to help interviewees prepare for job interviews better and for interviewers to be able to screen and assess the talent applying for roles in their organization better

- **Awesome lists relating to programming languages and frameworks**: For example, **NodeJS** (`https://github.com/bnb/awesome-awesome-nodejs`), **Erlang** (`https://github.com/drobakowski/awesome-erlang`), and minimalist frameworks (`https://github.com/neiesc/awesome-minimalist`)

- To be fully meta, **Awesome List of Awesome Lists**: There are several, such as `https://github.com/t3chnoboy/awesome-awesome-awesome`, `https://github.com/emijrp/awesome-awesome`, `https://github.com/icopy-site/awesome`, and many more.

Underlying technology

There is a concept called either *the UNIX way* or sometimes *the UNIX philosophy*, which describes a minimalized and compartmentalized approach to software written about by several individuals, including Doug McIlroy, Peter H. Salus, and then popularized in the writings of Ken Thompson and Dennis Ritchie. While there are several variations to the philosophy, one could largely boil it down to one phrase: *Do one thing and do it well*. As the open source software communities come from more of a UNIX background, open source projects take on this mantra. Many of the basic command-line tools contained in Linux and other UNIX-derived systems that we depend on are taking this approach, such as the following:

- **grep**: This is a command-line utility for searching plaintext datasets for lines that match a regular expression

- **sed**: This stands for **stream editor**, which parses and transforms text

- **cat**: This is a tool for taking the output from one program and writing to standard output for input into another

Modern software has multiple layers of libraries and frameworks that build a complete solution and are built with this same minimalist and integration-focused mindset. Here are some of the open source projects we see often used:

- **Android Project** (`https://source.android.com/`): This is the underlying operating system that powers over 3 billion active devices as of 2021 [1]

- **Ruby on Rails** (`https://rubyonrails.org/`): This popularized the **Model-View-Controller (MVC)** approach for web development, which was a major influence on web development in the mid-2000s, with over 1.2 million sites globally using this framework as of 2022 [2]

- **Pandoc** (`https://pandoc.org/`): This is the *Swiss Army knife* of document conversion tools, enabling the conversion of documents between dozens of different formats (and was super useful in the creation of this book).

- **Memcached** (`https://memcached.org/`): This is a distributed and high-performance key-value store used for speeding up web applications by reducing database hits for data that doesn't change frequently

You'll notice these projects are predominantly developer tools, and that isn't a coincidence. Open source has greatly reduced the cost of building software and, more importantly, made high-quality tooling, languages, and frameworks for software development accessible, which helped kickstart so many of the Web 2.0 era companies such as Google, Facebook, Netflix, and hundreds more.

Establishing technology ecosystems

There are some projects that fit into the previous category of *underlying technology* within a classification of where they would fit in an application stack, but the formation of and motivations behind the project are more related to ecosystem building in nature. In other words, they are created with the intention of both open and commercial solutions to be built from them and have expectations of a certain level of interoperability or skills alignment between the various solutions. This might be done for a multitude of reasons, such as setting a standard in an industry horizontal or vertical market, trying to establish a new area of technology, or maybe bringing together competing for solutions where the active value and investment are higher up in the stack and this level of the stack has become commoditized.

We will talk a bit more about technology-ecosystem-building through open source in *Chapter 4, Aligning the Business Value of Open Source for Your Employer*. Here are some of the projects that fall into this category:

- **Kubernetes** (`https://kubernetes.io/`): This is an open source system for automating the deployment, scaling, and management of containerized applications. It has built the **Certified Kubernetes** program (`https://www.cncf.io/certification/software-conformance/`) for solutions that use Kubernetes with over 130 offerings, along with the **Kubernetes Service Provider Program** (`https://www.cncf.io/certification/kcsp/`), with over 250 vendors providing support and services. These programs are built by the Kubernetes community and managed by the CNCF staff.

- **Anuket Assured** (`https://lfnetworking.org/verification/`): This is an open source, community-led compliance and verification program to demonstrate the readiness and availability of commercial cloud-native and virtualized products and services, including NFVI, cloud-native infrastructure, VNFs, and CNFs, using Anuket and ONAP components.

- The **Zowe Conformance Program** (`https://www.openmainframeproject.org/projects/zowe/conformance`): This establishes requirements for interoperability between solutions building or integrating with the Zowe (`https://www.zowe.org`) open source project. Again, this is a community-built program managed by the Open Mainframe Project staff, with over 70 unique solutions and service offerings as of 2022.

One thing to note is while these programs intend to establish technology ecosystems, it has no impact on the open source licensing and reuse of the code base. The terms of the license itself are what establish the rules for the reuse of the code, and other implementations. Programs such as these are purely to provide a vendor-neutral and community-run program for recognizing implementations. There will be more to come in later chapters as I discuss the commercialization of open source in *Chapter 10, Commercialization of Open Source*.

Providing high-quality free software

While many of us are fortunate to have been born into and/or living in an environment where software is easily affordable and accessible, that isn't true for everyone. Even for those in wealthy regions, the costs of some software are prohibitive to being able to provide for groups of people. Think of a startup company where you might be trying to keep costs low, or maybe a school where you might need hundreds or thousands of copies of a piece of software; free software makes this accessible when it otherwise wouldn't be.

However, one angle that is of equal importance is free not just being *free as in beer* but *free as in freedom*. Having high-quality software that users can make changes to in order to support their needs and workflows, or keep updated when the upstream project might have gone stale, are key tenets of the free software movement.

Linux distributions such as Debian, Fedora, Ubuntu, Arch Linux, and many, many more have paved the way for the free desktop environment to let users have increased flexibility on how they work with their computers; and in many cases, have made it possible to reuse outdated hardware with modern software, which is especially valuable in areas of the world that lack easy access to modern hardware. On top of that we've seen, most of the key desktop applications have vibrant and active open source equivalents; here is just some of that list:

- **LibreOffice** (`https://libreoffice.org/`): This provides a full office suite comparable to **Microsoft Office**

- **GNU Image Manipulation Program (GIMP)** (`https://www.gimp.org/`): This enables image editing and manipulation similar to **Adobe Photoshop**

- **Inkscape** (`https://inkscape.org/`): This is an open source vector graphics editor much like **Adobe Illustrator**

- **Mozilla Firefox** (`https://www.mozilla.org/en-US/firefox/`): This draws its heritage from the 1998 open source release of Netsuite Communicator, providing a modern and secure web browser

The list goes on and on and is one area that is more widely recognized when we speak about open source software. It's also an example of where the community has often grown larger than just developers; with the projects in the preceding list, you see experienced project managers, user interface experts, and individuals with domain-specific knowledge and productivity expertise coming together to build high-quality software to be used in professional environments.

Now that we have seen how open source is implemented, let's take a look at a few projects themselves and understand the motivations for why they have used open source as a model.

Open source projects and why they are used

Now that I've walked through the *what* of open source along with its historical roots and *how* open source is used, to complete *The Golden Circle* [3], let's look at the *why* of open source.

I heard Alan Clark of SUSE once describe open source as "*the ultimate scratch-your-own-itch model*," meaning that participation is tied to whatever motivates the participant. As you can imagine, this makes the steering of an open source project challenging (another topic we will dig more into in later chapters, covering governance, bringing in new contributors, and growing contributors into maintainers in *Chapter 5, Governance and Hosting Models*). Still, it also makes answering the *why* open source question not one with a clear, universal answer.

The best way to answer the *why* is by looking at a few projects and understanding the motivations of those communities. Let's take a look at some that hopefully will give you an idea of the value of and motivations behind open source projects.

PHP

If you did any sort of web development in the 1990s, you'll be familiar with the concept of a CGI script (long live the `cgi-bin` directory!). Web pages were largely static, and any interactions such as sending a form required a CGI script to process it on the backend. Most of these scripts were written in Perl and others were actual executable binaries written in C. Yes, the web was a much simpler time then!

Rasmus Lerdorf wrote a number of these for maintaining his personal home page while he was a student at the University of Waterloo, releasing his implementation as **Personal Home Page/Forms Interpreter (PHP/FI)**. These scripts grew over time, and with the help of Zeev Suraski and Andi Gutmans, were rewritten and renamed to a recursive acronym, *PHP: Hypertext Preprocessor* (one of many examples of maintainers with interesting senses of humor in naming projects in the early days of open source) [4]. As a project, this was a huge shift in web development, moving away from separate form processing displaying content on web pages to being able to embed things such as database calls and complex logic right into a web page as it was being processed.

What this also did was *scratch the itch* of making interactive web pages much easier to build, helping anyone with basic programming skills be able to build a web application (although PHP is often known for building web applications with what is known as *spaghetti code*, but that can be the cost of progress).

One other thing I find fascinating about PHP is that Lerdorf, when asked, will humbly admit that he never had the intention of creating a programming language when he started with PHP/FI. I've also heard interviews from him in which he expressed that he felt the weight of being the single maintainer, with many individuals coming to him requesting new functionality to be added or help to get it working. This same pressure falls on open source project maintainers today and is something I will explore more in a later chapter on handling growth in *Chapter 9, Handling Growth*.

Blender

Computer graphics and other interactive display technology are one of the largest areas where open source is strong. In fact, most of the movies you see today or the video games you play all have open source underpinnings.

Ton Roosendaal, a Dutch art director and self-taught software developer, started his own 3D animation studio, NeoGeo, in 1989. One of the software tools he wrote was called **Blender**, which was a combination of various scripts and tools to enable 3D creations and visual art to be built. It was software specifically targeted toward so-called *creatives*, and Roosendaal understood the struggle they had in delivering rapid changes to a 3D project following complex customer requirements. Blender as software exchanged hands over the years to follow until in 2002, Roosendaal formed the Blender Foundation and released the code under the **GNU Public License** (**GPL**) to ensure the work would forever be in the commons for creatives to use. To this day, Blender is used throughout special effects and visual effects workflows, as well as by others who do 3D model animation and development.

The *why* for Blender is very clear—creating a tool for and built by *creatives*. What is interesting about Blender is its model; while there is a foundation that sponsors grant work and has a small staff to manage operations for the project itself, the vast amount of development is done by volunteers from around the world. I will dig more into this model later in the book when I talk about governance models for open source projects in *Chapter 5, Governance and Hosting Models*.

Zowe

There is a joke amongst those in the mainframe community that every technology that is considered novel today was done by mainframes decades ago. For example, virtualization was introduced in 1972 with IBM System/370 but popularized in the early 2000s by VMware. And as I discussed earlier in this chapter, much of the roots of open source is derived from early mainframe computer operators and developers. As is often said, *what's old is new!*

One challenge the mainframe community was having is that the methodology for interoperating with mainframe applications and data was rooted in technology that was quite different than what modern developers were accustomed to using. Where a developer in 2018 might use Java, Node.js, or Python for building an application or integrating various applications, mainframe applications were often built on decades of COBOL or FORTRAN code. Some interfaces may use **Representational State Transport** (**REST**), but others may be custom-coded or interact with an IBM 3270 terminal. This created a divide in organizations depending on mainframes, where there would be one set of individuals and skills maintaining the mainframe environment and a different set for the rest of the IT infrastructure.

Zowe was founded as a project with initial code contributions from CA Technologies (which was bought by Broadcom in 2019), IBM, and Rocket Software, which provides a framework for integrating mainframe applications and data with other applications and tools using development tools and methodologies more common to a developer not in the mainframe world. The *why* for

Zowe was twofold; one motive was solving the problems of mainframe users having separate teams and approaches to managing mainframe applications and data from the rest of those organizations computing infrastructure. Additionally, there was a growing skills gap where the skills you needed to be successful in the mainframe industry were quite different from those needed to develop software for other systems.

Open source projects that come out of companies can often have a bit of a learning curve as they adapt to the open source development methodology, and this is one project that went through that curve and has begun to embrace that model, even though the initial participants were not well versed in open source. I've often seen this in projects from vertical industries as well, and a topic I will dig into in later chapters is all about getting your organization to launch an open source project, governance models, and growing committers into maintainers.

PiSCSI

I grew up in a time when Apple Macintosh computers were commonplace in schools. These were innovative at the time, both on the basis of their capabilities but also their iconic design. There is a whole enthusiast community around these beige- and platinum-colored machines, who painstakingly restore these machines to working order to preserve an important part of computing history. I happen to be one of those folks, currently working on restoring an Apple Macintosh IIsi circa 1990.

Apple Macintosh computers of that era, and also those from other manufacturers, used hard disk drives with the **Small Computer System Interface (SCSI)** interface that was popular in those times. Over the decades, not only have hard drive sizes increased from the 20-megabyte or 40-megabyte drives of that era to the 1-terabyte drives of today, but the technology interface has moved on from SCSI to Parallel ATA and now Serial ATA, meaning that finding replacement hard drives that are more than 30 years old are hard to come by. A developer under the name of *GIMONS* built a solution called **RaSCSI** for use with the Sharp X68000 computer, which enabled the use of an SD card and specialized adapter connected to a Raspberry PI to take the place of a SCSI hard drive. A group of enthusiasts who saw the use case for applying this to other computers by using SCSI hard drives took on the project and built the PiSCSI project. This project was created to expand on the work and add additional functionality, such as the ability to emulate an Ethernet interface, provide multiple disk images for a computer that could be managed using a web interface, and other useful functionality to enable these computers to be used even if they had a failed hard drive.

Figure 1.1: My Mac IIsi

This is a great example of a community motivated by enthusiasts trying to solve a common problem; emulating SCSI hard drives using common, lower-cost components but over time, grew to *scratch more itches* for these enthusiasts in being able to connect vintage computers to modern networks. It provides both software built for running on the Raspberry Pi itself and also diagrams for building the custom hardware needed (if you don't want to go to that trouble, you can buy kits to assemble or fully build devices). This being done open source helps bring together this large community to improve and provide feedback, creating commons that everyone can benefit from.

Summary

Open source, while being driven by a multitude of motivations and a diverse group of enthusiasts, is tied together by a common spirit; the idea of being able to freely share code and knowledge with others openly and do so through open collaboration in decentralized communities. Open source has been built on decades of collaborative spirit, with the ideal of sharing information to advance humanity. I've often seen open source described as the next Renaissance, harking back to the same outpouring of knowledge and innovation that advanced society but if you look at the last 3-4 decades, you can truly see how much our society has advanced in technology (which we could agree has opened up a new set of problems, but that is one of the aftereffects of progress, and we've tended to see society respond to and correct it over time).

This chapter was intended to give you a good foundation of the *what* and *why* of open source, which then lets us dig into the next key topic – what makes a good open source project.

Further reading

[1] https://www.theverge.com/2021/5/18/22440813/android-devices-active-number-smartphones-google-2021

[2] https://iwanttolearnruby.com/how-many-ruby-on-rails-developers-are-there/#1

[3] https://fourweekmba.com/golden-circle/

[4] https://www.php.net/history

[5] https://en.wikipedia.org/wiki/Hardware_virtualization#Hardware-assisted_virtualization

2
What Makes a Good Open Source Project?

We talked in *Chapter 1, The Whats and Whys of Open Source*, about the *whats* and *whys* of open source and looked a bit at the *how* in the context of existing open source projects. In this chapter, we will look at what makes a good open source project. We will look at some of the key characteristics of what a good open source project looks like, some of the pitfalls I've seen when open source projects aren't created with the idea of building community, and, finally, some patterns and anti-patterns for open source projects.

The concept of a *good open source project* is by no means a trivial one. I get asked this question routinely, usually in a conversation that goes something like this:

Person: "So, how does my project compare to other projects you work with?"

Me: "Well, that's a hard comparison to make."

Person: "Why is that?"

Me: "Each project is different; different work being done, different participants, different velocity of development, and so on."

Person: "So, how do I know whether it's a good project?"

I'll pause this dialog to not tip my hand too much on how to answer the what makes a *good open source project?* question, but I do want to highlight that it's not a cut-and-dry answer.

We'll cover the following topics in this chapter:

- The core characteristics of an open source project
- Open sourcing code versus creating an open source project
- Patterns and anti-patterns for successful open source projects

Before we dig into what that good open source project looks like, let's back things up and correctly characterize what an open source project is.

Core characteristics of an open source project.

Early on in the free software movement, the characteristics of a project being *open* were simply tied to the licensing aspect of the code – is it under a license where one could see, modify, and distribute the code or not? At that time, that was novel in and of itself; recall from *Chapter 1, The Whats and Whys of Open Source*, the main challenge was proprietary software growth being antithetical to a *hacker* and *maker* culture.

I reread *The Cathedral and the Bazaar* [1] as I was writing this chapter, and when I did, I could sense the *aha* moment that Eric Raymond had as he looked at the early development of Linux. A given piece of software, in general, up to that point, was developed by a single developer or a small circle of developers, carefully built and aligned with what you would think of today as obsessive-compulsive tendencies; carefully constructed code, nothing other than perfected code released, and while feedback was appreciated, code contributions were under a lot of scrutiny.

Before you look at this with ire, consider the time and place. Much of software development was still heavily academically rooted. The tools were still out of reach for many due to the hardware being quite expensive (in 1990, the average cost was nearly USD 4,000, adjusted for inflation [2]). Picking up programming wasn't something you could do in a six-week boot camp; it was years of post-secondary schooling. You can't blame the early project maintainers for the approach that they took; it was largely pragmatic, and many of those projects are the cornerstones of free and open source software today.

However, Raymond saw something novel in how Linus Torvalds approached Linux, namely the following:

- It wasn't all code he wrote from the ground up; instead, there was a fair amount of code borrowed from Minix (along with concepts and ideas)
- The first version of Linux released was effectively *beta*-quality code
- He openly encouraged others to give feedback and participate in the work

If you look at Torvald's post announcing Linux on 25 August 1991, you can see his humility in approaching the community. If you look at some of the most popular open source projects today, they model the approach Linus took intentionally with Linux; Linux is looked at as one of the best examples of what an open source project is. What are those characteristics? We'll look at them in the following sections.

Users are part of the development process

This is something we'll dive deeper into in later chapters when we talk about roles in open source, but one thing that is evident with open source is the intention for users to have a path to be part of the development process.

Recall the anecdote I shared in the previous chapter about the car's sealed-shut hood, making it nearly impossible to see or modify its internals. Without that constriction, the user can now learn more about the car, how it works, where some of the weak points of the design are, and areas where an upgrade might be easy to do versus others where it will be more complicated.

This is something you see quite often in car enthusiast groups; one I have an interest in is the enthusiasts around the Buick Grand National. The peak years for this vehicle were 1986 and 1987 (and the drivetrain was used in the 1989 Pontiac Trans Am Pace Car). In the years since, we saw the enthusiast community take the vehicle much farther than General Motors intended. They saw the air intake as limiting, so they added larger air intake systems. They saw the possibility of larger turbos, injectors, and exhaust systems and built them to fit. Now, they are making the car modifiable to the new fuel types, with many converting the car from using 93 octane fuel to E85. All of this was driven by real-world requirements, whether that be performance, adaption to modern needs, or just general technological improvements, and those were made involving those who owned the cars, as well as the vendors and mechanics.

There's a saying in open source that says, *a rising tide lifts all boats*, which is evident in the user's involvement in the development process. While it seems obvious from where we are sitting, the idea that there would be new ideas beyond the core developers was a bit novel at the time, but encapsulates exactly how Torvalds approached Linux and what we continue to see decades later.

Release early, release often

Getting users involved in the development process requires a way for users to be able to get involved. Generally, in open source projects, individuals start as observers (or what some might call lurkers, but let's keep things positive). These individuals are often thinking less about being a contributor and more about whether the project will be useful to them, asking questions such as, does it solve my problem? How does it compare to other solutions? How would I get started? Over time, they progress to being a user, then someone interacting on mailing lists and forums. However, as discussed previously, in an open source project, the intention is not to keep the user far away from the development process but instead to see how they could integrate into the process.

In the work I currently do with open source projects, I often help set up their code repositories. One invaluable tool for me has been **repolinter** (https://github.com/todogroup/repolinter), which is a tool that checks your code repository for common issues, such as finding missing license files, ensuring there is a contributing guide, and alerting you if there were any build artifacts (such as binary files, test files, or build logs) that were accidentally checked in.

When using the tool, I found a bug with how it detected pull requests and issue templates. The tool did great if you used a single file, ISSUE_TEMPLATE or PULL_REQUEST_TEMPLATE, but GitHub also had support for adding multiple templates if you named the directory ISSUE_TEMPLATE or PULL_REQUEST_TEMPLATE, and the repolinter tool didn't recognize that. This being an open source project, I was easily empowered by the project to not only submit a bug report but also a guide on how to fix it:

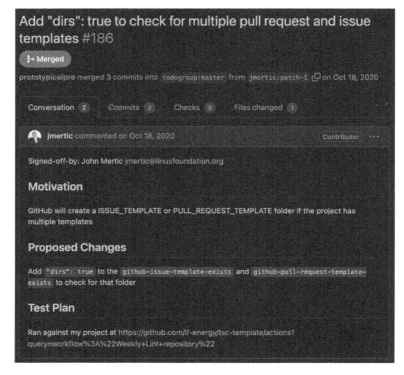

Figure 2.1 – Pull request against repolinter (https://github.com/todogroup/repolinter/pull/186)

Quickly, a project maintainer looked at the pull request and approved it coming in, and that fix made it into the **0.10.0 release** [3].

This is the exact model and rationale behind "release early, release often." The project, having version numbers starting with *0.*, was still in active development, and features needed to be added. Regular releases in that timeframe that rolled up the fixes coming in got into the hands of users quickly for them to try out. Additionally, a user could pull a version right out of the code repository at the given point in the main branch (at that time, named master, although it is now named main) to start trying it right away (which is exactly what I did). This enabled the feedback loop to move faster, as users could test these features before a release and potentially catch edge cases and other hard-to-reproduce issues that come out of extensive testing; fortunately, my contribution was quite simple, so there weren't any.

We will dig into users becoming contributors in later chapters as we talk about making a project feel welcoming and contributors becoming maintainers, but know that the cornerstone for this is a development model that empowers and encourages users to take part.

Transparent and dynamic decision-making

One unintentional trend I often see in groups outside of open source that I work with is it's hard to understand how the group works and where you can take part. I say *unintentional* because when I talk to those leading or taking part in those groups, they will often lament that others don't want to join or help the group or that the questions they get about the group from outsiders are often basic ones that they answer with, "*well, everyone knows that!*"

As I write this book, I'm volunteering to lead our local school district's school levy campaign, where the goal is to renew an income tax levy, which is a major revenue source for the school district's operating budget. One of the frustrations that school administrators and those volunteering in the levy campaign have is the vast amount of disinformation out there; one particular piece of disinformation relates to the funding of the turf installed on the football field. Questions arose about why this was funded over other projects, which is a fair one to ask. With a void of what I call *intentional transparency*, many rumors have started that spread false information, such as "*this town only likes football and nothing else*" or "*the school board doesn't know how to spend money.*"

The truth was that the old field was in really bad shape, borderline unsafe to play any sports on, and when weighing up the options of repairing and maintaining the field versus going with turf, they saw turf as the better solution going forward. Additionally, going with turf made it possible to host more events on the field during the times of the year when the ground would be wetter, thus a greater revenue opportunity. It was also not just funded by the school district but also by private sources and fundraising done by the athletic boosters. Not to mention when a new school was constructed a few years prior, part of that new building included a state-of-the-art performing arts center, which to this day hasn't hosted an athletic competition.

The school board felt they had been transparent because all of this kind of decision-making happens in public meetings and the finances are made public, but there was a lack of intentionality in sharing the background on why the choices were made.

Open source projects thrive on both *intentional transparency* but also the ability to quickly and dynamically make decisions, which typically results in a higher development velocity and vibrancy around the project in general. Good open source projects focus on these aspects, typically with a strong written culture in writing down all the processes in the project, such as how releases happen, what is required to make a code contribution, and how decisions are generally made.

Good open source projects also make all of the past discussions available and make current discussions transparent so that others can see how decisions are being made; for them, it lets them have a sense of the culture and dynamics of the group and impacts whether they might want to get more involved in the project in the future. We will dig more into these concepts in *Chapter 5*, *Chapter 6*, and *Chapter 7*.

While open source projects can be a mechanism for driving collaboration and innovation, we've also seen them as a way to push out code without an intention to build community. Let's look more at the expectations you should have when releasing code as open source.

Open sourcing code versus creating an open source project

The release of the **NetSuite Communicator** source code was the validation of the *bazaar* model that Raymond described. While that started the tidal wave of open source, as with any new trend, you see those pushing the edges of the trend to see what works and what doesn't.

One particular trend is companies seeing open sourcing code as a method for making source code available, but not necessarily wanting to build an open source project around it, as described in the previous section. This is an important distinction, and while in general, it isn't a great open source strategy, there are some cases where it is worth discussing. Let's look at them now.

Intelligent code dumps

You might have heard of the term **code dump**, which refers to when code that might have previously been a commercial product or otherwise not open is made available under an open source license, but the group contributing the code has no intention of maintaining it, let alone building a project or community around it. I've seen companies using this strategy over the years that have the thought *"if we release the code, people will come and build a project around it,"* which has rarely been the case.

That being said, there are some edge cases where it's not such a bad thing, such as when Microsoft open sourced the source code from **MS-DOS v1.25** and **MS-DOS v2.0** [4]; the rationale was more to enable research into operating systems and enable various retro-computing communities to support running older software on newer hardware and operating systems better. This is what is called an "intelligent code dump," as is quite useful if it is done for these reasons, in addition to any of these:

- Enabling companies who use older versions of the software that you no longer support to continue to support themselves

- Allowing others to build converters or connectors using obsolete file formats

- Showing goodwill by making software that is obsolete available for hobbyists and enthusiasts in the community

One thing important for an "intelligent code dump" is to be super clear about the intentions in the README file for the project. This has been done quite well by Microsoft in the release of the MS-DOS source code, as illustrated in *Figure 2.2*:

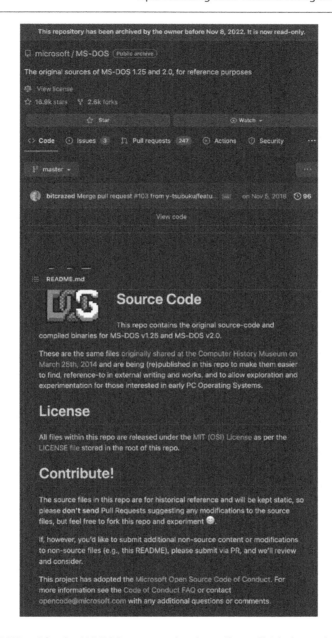

Figure 2.2 – README.md for the MS-DOS source code release (https://github.com/microsoft/ms-dos)

Sometimes, releasing open source code but not creating an open source project doesn't just apply to obsolete software but also to current software that hopes to gain a larger user base. Let's look at that use case now.

Open Core

One early business model of open source was called **Open Core**, meaning that a company releases a basic, stripped-down, yet functional version of the product as open source and then a more full-featured version as a commercial product under a proprietary license. This was an extension of the *shareware* model that started in the 1990s (also known as *nagware* because of the annoying popups that urged users to pay for a commercial version). You can see parallels with the code dump approach in that the code going out into open source is not where development is happening; instead, releases are *dumped* to the community for consumption. Often, you can contribute to these Open Core projects, but it typically is quite difficult, as the patches have to be incorporated into internal development.

Open Core as a model hit its high-water mark in the late 2000s. One particular software company that chose this approach was **SugarCRM**; they owned **Sugar Community Edition**, which in itself was a full-featured open source CRM (something new and exciting on the market at that time), and then **Sugar Professional** and **Sugar Enterprise**, which were commercially licensed versions, although the source code was made available to customers. For SugarCRM and companies such as this, the idea was growing a market share – that is, getting as many users as possible, with the strategy that as the use of the software grew in an organization, they would look at one of the commercial versions.

Many in open source viewed the concept of Open Core as a bit of a *black eye* in history, and frankly, there are valid arguments for why you would view Open Core that way. I've always looked at the trends in both technology and life, and seen that they often follow the pattern of a pendulum; swinging from one side to another and eventually coming to rest somewhere in the middle after lessons have been learned and experiences gained. Open Core came about as open source business models were still being developed, and you see some later open source companies who have led projects in open source, often within a vendor-neutral foundation, regarding the concept of downstream ecosystem building as an evolved way to help solve the monetization question.

Expectations when releasing code as open source

One thing that came to light as Open Core went through its life cycle is that open source has an ethical responsibility to downstream users and developers. The **TODO Group**, which is a project hosted at the Linux Foundation that provides a forum for collaboration around **Open Source Program Offices** (**OSPOs**), offers a great resource. This resource is their OSPO guides [5], which walk through the various aspects of being effective in participating in open source as an organization.

One guide in particular focuses on starting open source projects as an organization [6], which speaks not only to the responsibilities and due diligence an organization needs to bear in mind to release an open source project (much of which we will cover in *Chapter 4, Aligning the Business Value of Open Source for Your Employer*) but also, toward the end, to the post-release responsibility. Some key considerations include the following:

- Get other outside organizations and people with an interest in contributing or participating involved as early as possible. You'll want them to feel like part of the process and letting them contribute to governance, development standards, and marketing/outreach activities starts to build the comradery that sets the cultural tone in the community early.

- Get the collaboration infrastructure set up and out in the open. Things such as mailing lists, chat channels, code repositories, and issue trackers out in the open give people a sense of the activity of the project and the culture around it. Beyond that, having social media accounts engages a broader audience of more casual individuals that might track things from a distance and will inspire them to get involved in the future.

- Hold community meetings at a regular cadence, and also look for natural opportunities to meet, such as a part of an event or through local meetups. I really, really, emphasize the *regular cadence* part – this not only sets expectations for your community but also for you as a maintainer to keep these things at the forefront of your mind.

Again, much of this we will cover in later chapters, but the key thing to think about here is that putting out an open source project means you need to be intentional in supporting its success. This investment upfront will very likely be high, even higher than it was as an internal, non-open source project, but done right, that investment pays off and you will reap the rewards of lower investment and amazing technology that you can leverage (and others can too!).

Patterns and anti-patterns for successful open source projects

I started this chapter by ruminating on the challenge of defining what a good open source project is. The challenge with that definition is what works for one project may not work for the next one, as each project has its own people, culture, industry dynamics, and velocity. Because of this, I like to think in terms of patterns instead, and there are several patterns (and anti-patterns) I've seen that are good guideposts and ways to think about open source projects and how to approach and work with such a community.

Open communication (and over-communication)

The biggest challenge I see with open source projects, and often in other domains in life, is communication. As I described in my earlier story on my work in my local school district's levy campaign, communication gaps lead to confusion, misunderstanding, and in the worst case, things being taken the wrong way. I often hear the saying that *"if you don't define yourself on the market, the market will gladly do that for you."* Open source projects are no different and require the same intentionality.

One challenge I often see with communication comes from those in a project being frustrated that someone who is not in the project doesn't know something that they think should be obvious. For example, they might ask, "Hey! Do you support doing CSV export?" As a maintainer, you might respond with, "Did you read the documentation?" In my experience, this is a surefire way to turn someone off from ever contributing anything else or asking another question (we will cover other surefire turn-offs in *Chapter 3, Open Source Licensing and IP Management*).

This is not to say it's entirely the maintainer's fault either; I'm a firm believer that a breakdown in communication faults both the communicator as well as the recipient. This is why I recommend *over-communicating*, meaning communicating multiple times, in multiple ways, and in multiple different places, such as via a mailing list, discussion forum, and chat channel. As a maintainer, you might take this as some sort of *millennial placating* exercise, but instead, I'd recommend thinking about the contributor or user. Each of them is likely super busy, has tons of priorities, and, with the constant rate of technological change, is probably overwhelmed (which doesn't even account for factors in their personal life). As a maintainer, you can likely relate; the list of to-dos is endless, the demands are constant, and users often give you grief. Having a bit of mercy for these folks goes a long way, but more importantly, gives you clues on the best way to engage your contributors and users.

So yes, over-communicating is much more work on the front end, but it saves you the time of answering questions later and potentially helps you reach users you might never have connected to. Keeping communication open adds transparency and insight for users and potential contributors. Often, you can gain interest from the so-called *drive-by* audience. We will dig into this more in *Chapter 6* and *Chapter 7*.

Benevolent dictatorship versus leading by committee

Linux has famously been led by Linus Torvalds for over 30 years at the time of writing, and he has been the poster child for the *benevolent dictator* style of leadership. This style mirrors similar national governments of the same style, such as Singapore from the 1960s through the 1990s. Benevolent dictatorship puts a heavy burden on the individual, both from a project management standpoint and from a cultural, ethical, and growth standpoint, meaning the person has to be able to move the project forward while bringing contributors and users along, enabling them and empowering them for the growth of the technology.

Beyond Linux, we've seen other projects adopt this in their early years as well; examples include Rasmus Lerdorf for PHP, Guido van Rossum for Python, and Ton Roosendaal with Blender. Linux is a bit unique in that it's largely maintained this model throughout its life, but like the other projects I just mentioned, it's slowly transitioning away from it, as maintainers are looking at ways to bring in new maintainers to carry Linux into the decades to come.

Benevolent dictatorship as a pattern generally falls into the narrow category of "*generally doesn't work well, but in some cases, with the right benevolent dictator and the right community, it works*." Often, it's a good choice in the early days of the project, where there are several opinionated choices to be made that set the course for the future. However, the challenge is having the right individual to lead; as described earlier, they need to be visionary, organized, thoughtful, and able to bring people together to make it work. With this being quite a demand, it can be stressful and consuming, which is often why you see the model akin to a start-up, which then transitions to the next stage as a critical mass forms.

Leading by committee solves the problems of the benevolent dictator model by spreading the decision-making and responsibilities across multiple people, which enables a project to drive efficiency and get diverse contributors and contributions over time. It also forces a project to involve better communication; a benevolent dictator can ruminate on key decisions in their head, while a committee approach forces each person to externalize their thoughts to get a consensus.

That's not to say leading by committee is perfect; it can often slow down development and project velocity because of the work needed to get alignment. That can be a good thing in one sense, as it makes decision-making more thoughtful, but at the same time, it can lead to overthinking and the dreaded *bikeshedding* [7] that stagnates a project.

Thinking about both approaches with a pattern mindset, most often, an early-days project benefits more from a benevolent dictator whereas a more mature project benefits more from a committee approach. We will explore this more in a later chapter when we dig into governance.

Forks

Forks are one of the inherent rights one has in open source and are at the heart of every open source license out there. They give the user the freedom to take a code base any way they want, customize it to their specific needs, and use it to solve their unique problems. The downside of forks is the cost to that user, namely in continued maintenance and the upkeep of a fork, as it can become long-lived (meaning a fork that is intended to persist for several project releases, or even indefinitely), including bringing changes from the project code base back into the fork as it changes over time.

That overhead is often a headache, and why generally long-lived forks are an anti-pattern. The better approach is known as **working upstream**, which means that as you make changes to the code base, you contribute them back into the project rather than maintaining them separately. In open source communities, working upstream generally is the best approach; it gives you the benefit of your changes being tested more broadly, saves you time in not having to merge them into later versions, and showcases you as a steward of the code base. There are cases where that isn't always possible due to technical or licensing issues; for example, what you might be modifying breaks other use cases, so it can't be upstreamed. Another example is changes that include code licensed in a way that is incompatible with the upstream project.

Other times you will see forks are when there are differences of opinion on the direction of a project or a project may have slowed down in its development, and certain individuals want to break away from that and increase its velocity. Another case is when cultural or personal clashes happen. These are often problematic forks, and in open source, almost always end up with one of two outcomes:

- One fork ends up getting all the momentum, and the other fork dies off
- The forks merge back together into one project

Conflict in communities is healthy, as it gives people a voice and ensures there can be cohesion and space for different opinions. At the same time, if that conflict gets to the point where a fork happens, then you see long-term scars that are hard to repair. In a later chapter, we will dig into dealing with conflict so that your community doesn't face this dilemma.

Over-governance

Someone once told me that if you run into a law or rule that seems a bit crazy, then there is an even crazier story behind its origin. That is not to say there isn't validity in the law or rule, but often the context is missed or the problem it was meant to solve is no longer relevant.

Governance is something I've tended to see open source projects over-engineer. This isn't done maliciously, but details that can be hard to predict may be over-indexed. One that I recently ran into is a project wanting to define exactly how long a vote via email should be open. The group forming the project had the right intentions; they had a concern that a vote taking too long to complete would slow things down or be a sign of disengagement with the group. However, the downside was that being prescriptive got in the way of several possible scenarios:

- What if a person was out on leave or vacation and didn't have access to email? That would be a clear barrier.
- What if there needed to be some more thought or internal company alignment on the item being voted on? Putting the vote out there forces the vote to happen, regardless of alignment within the project.
- What if the person had more sensitive concerns that were hard to address in the context and timeline of a vote?

The thought when building governance and looking at adding a given policy or rule should be, what is the goal the project is aiming to achieve? And then, what is the most lightweight way to accomplish that? If we look at the previous example, the goal is to conduct a vote efficiently. If not everyone has submitted a vote in a given amount of time, the factors in the preceding raised bullet points may come into play, as does how often we can expect this to happen. Generally, during the early days of a project, people are more engaged, so we would likely never run into this constraint.

Later on, that might change. Projects should always know their governance isn't written in stone or tattooed on the maintainers. Rather, it's a living document that can change easily over time to accommodate the concerns in that project stage. An example that I see come up in open source communities is, don't make rules to handle hypothetical situations, but rather ones for known concerns and revisit them over time. We will discuss this topic in *Chapter 5, Governance and Hosting Models*.

Competitors welcome!

One of the unique aspects of open source is that because the collaboration is open to all, anyone can participate – even if they are competitors. This probably seems like a scary proposition, but in reality, the right ground rules in place can make a very vibrant and high-velocity open source project.

Kubernetes, a project hosted by the **Cloud Native Computing Foundation** (CNCF), is the poster child for this in my view. Check out the chart from the following Kubernetes project journey report [8] that speaks to organizational diversity within the contributors to the project in its first 5 years:

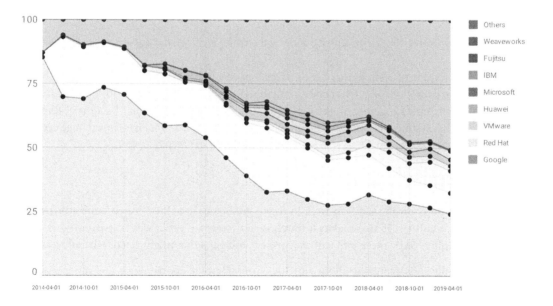

Figure 2.3 – Percentage breakdown of contributions by company since the Kubernetes project launch

You can see that while at the project launch, **Google** dominated contributions to Kubernetes, with well over 80% of contributions, that changed dramatically over the following 5 years, with **Google** making up just under 25% of contributions. We may infer that Google has stepped back from the project during that time, but rather it's been just the opposite:

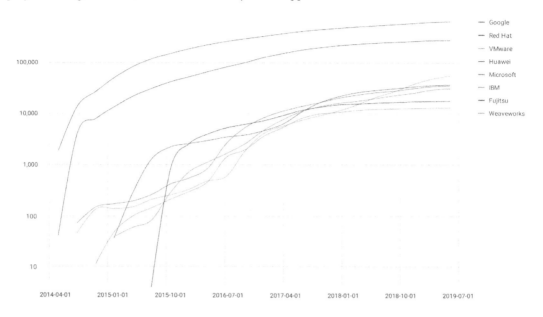

Figure 2.4 – Cumulative volume of contributions by the company since the Kubernetes project launch

This speaks to the value of competitors coming together in a project to collaborate; not only has this project seen huge overall growth from code contributions and contributor standpoints in its first 5 years but also by bringing together all the top cloud providers, Kubernetes has become a ubiquitous technology. This has resulted in a vibrant and growing vendor ecosystem that has driven huge economic value. I'll dig more into this in *Chapter 10, Commercialization of Open Source*.

Write everything down

This pairs with open communication well, in that a great way to achieve open communication is through a written culture. It also makes it much easier to repeat processes consistently, as well as identify opportunities to be more efficient as a project and gaps that might need to be addressed.

I have a large family and organizing all the activities from school to sports, work, and other groups we are involved with is an undertaking. Adding to that, my amazing wife and I aren't getting any younger, so juggling it all in our heads is a bit more challenging than it was in our youth. Like many of you, we established a family calendar using one of the major software and hardware vendors' family calendar solution, where we were keen to add all our kids' sports practices and games, any work events or travel, volunteer group meetings, activities, and other events we might be taking part in.

We also keenly decided to make it so that when an event was added or changed on the calendar, it sent notifications to everyone in the family and alerted them a day in advance, as we often add to the calendar when away from each other, which ensures that everyone else knows about these events. Of course, we aren't perfect at this and have run into the occasional double-booking of events due to someone not adding something to the calendar, but it's worked well overall.

What this written culture has given, in addition to coordination, is a sense of whether someone is overloaded or has the capacity to do more. For example, my oldest daughter has taken on the responsibility of cleaning our house once a week, which is something she balances, as I write this book, with taking a full load of college classes as a high school junior, year-round volleyball, and trying to have a social life as a teenager. The family calendar has become a great tool for her to look ahead on when she could do that cleaning and plan it into her schedule, which has helped her balance things and better communicate with us on when she can clean the house (or helped us as parents point out to her when she does have free time and should do the house cleaning).

This same concept works well in open source projects; writing things down helps make it easier to not only communicate externally but also coordinate and prioritize activities. For example, if a project aims to release once a month, writing down the release process ensures the project isn't scrambling to pull together code and run through all the building and other processes to get a release out of the door, while at the same time being able to prepare contributors and maintainers to submit their code by a certain point for it to be included in the release.

Writing things down, while sometimes seeming like an annoyance, helps make a project more efficient and organized. As a bonus, it helps your community scale and enables new people to come in over time to take over these responsibilities and consistently manage those tasks. We will talk more about this in *Chapter 9, Handling Growth*.

Embrace your community

The primary driver I see in creating an open source project is to get a diverse set of individuals to come in and offer feedback, contribute code, and help maintain the project. I've often seen that software engineers can be somewhat introverted or have social anxiety, which can make this daunting. Perhaps there is a degree of *imposter syndrome*, and the maintainer might be leery of engaging with community members or intimidated by them. While I can appreciate all of that, especially as somebody who has had to work through that in my career and still struggles with it from time to time, embracing your community is key if you want success in your project.

I won't dig too much deeper into this topic as later on in *Chapter 6, Making Your Project Feel Welcoming*, I'll discuss this more, along with strategies to help.

Focus on your strengths and use tools and other resources for your weaknesses

One of the hardest things we have to do as humans is accept our shortcomings and what we aren't good at. It becomes worse oddly enough as we become more successful in other aspects of our career, as we think success in one area translates across everything.

In the United States, we see this culturally in American football, where from time to time, coaches move from being highly successful college coaches to trying to replicate that in the **National Football League (NFL)**. More often than not, it isn't very successful [9]. Various factors are at play, such as the age and maturity of the players, the environment of college students versus paid athletes, and the greater demands on managing the various aspects of a longer season and often more talented athletes. Similar patterns exist in coaches transitioning from college basketball coaching to the **National Basketball Association (NBA)** [10]. What is interesting is that often these same coaches go back to the college ranks and become successful, which leads us to infer that it's not a question of somebody losing their touch as a coach but rather whether skills translate well in one environment more than another.

I often see open source projects try to run their events, do their marketing, or manage other operational tasks themselves. To be fair, I have seen projects do this well (and sometimes, this teaches me a few things). However, more often than not, these aren't skill sets that a software developer has, and frankly, that's okay, as that person has skills that an event manager, marketing person, or lawyer doesn't have. Technical documentation is a great example here; most software engineers feel they aren't great at it or have little affinity for technical writing, but there are people out there who *excel* at this and can partner with a project to produce stellar documentation.

On top of people, tools are another way to *work smarter, not harder*. Taking the technical documentation example, multiple tools can take code comments and build API reference guides or take plain Markdown files and build out beautiful-looking documentation that can be consumed in multiple formats. Scanning files by hand for the right license headers is a lot of work, but tools such as **FOSSology** [11] can do that for you and build out reports and the **Software Bill of Materials (SBOM)** at the same time. There are multiple tools for tracking contributor growth and project health, and collaborative work in projects such as the **CHAOSS Project** [12] that provide guidelines on metrics to measure based on the collective experience of millions of open source projects over the past few decades.

Summary

This chapter built upon the *what* and *why* of open source into the *how* – namely open source projects in which the work of open source is done. Additionally, I dug into the ethical expectations of releasing open source code and some of the patterns and anti-patterns I've seen in various open source projects.

One thing I want to stress is that there is no one way to run an open source project or one way a community should work; there are so many factors that come into play across cultures, industry verticals and horizontals, the pace and velocity of development, the maturity of a project, and the people involved themselves. Using a fruit analogy, apples and oranges are both fruit and will share some characteristics, and direct comparisons are equivalent to comparing apples and oranges.

This chapter also ends the so-called *101* level of education, as future chapters will delve into specific areas more. I've called out several of those chapters in this chapter and the previous one, and encourage you to jump ahead if one of those topics is specifically of interest – feel free. For those just starting this journey, simply continue on to the next chapter, where we will dig into one of the most debated and nuanced topics in open source – **licensing**.

Further reading

1. `http://www.catb.org/~esr/writings/cathedral-bazaar/cathedral-bazaar/`

2. `https://www.usatoday.com/story/tech/2018/06/22/cost-of-a-computer-the-year-you-were-born/36156373/`

3. `https://github.com/todogroup/repolinter/releases/tag/v0.10.0`

4. `https://github.com/Microsoft/MS-DOS`

5. `https://todogroup.org/guides/#ospo-guides`

6. `https://todogroup.org/guides/starting/`

7. `https://en.wiktionary.org/wiki/bikeshedding`

8. `https://www.cncf.io/reports/kubernetes-project-journey-report/`

9. `https://athlonsports.com/nfl/college-coaches-who-went-nfl-good-bad-ugly`

10. `https://www.espn.com/mens-college-basketball/story/_/id/26738229/how-college-coaches-fared-nba`

11. `https://fossology.github.io/`

12. `https://chaoss.community/`

3

Open Source License and IP Management

One of my favorite slides regarding open source license and IP management comes from my colleague Mike Dolan of the Linux Foundation:

Poor IP management is easy to spot...

◻ THE **LINUX** FOUNDATION

Figure 3.1 – Comparing good and poor IP management using illustrations in garage organization

I like this slide not only because of the stark contrast but also the focus it places on the importance of the details. The floor colors carry over to the stripe on the wall. The gas pump hose has space to bend around in a nearly perfect circle. The toolboxes all match. Even someone who might not notice that level of detail would certainly recognize the garage on the right as more appealing than the chaos on the left.

A good software developer will obsess about similar details in their code, such as indentations, spacing inside of statements, positioning of brackets, comments, and variable naming. Here, it's not a case of obsession, but it's because they view putting a bit of extra work upfront saves them time later in tracking down bugs or refactoring. This is similar to license and IP management; the aim is to add clarity, consistency, and documentation regarding all the details of how code can and can't be used, the expectations and obligations of that contributing code, and clarity on brand usage. Where code styling guidelines look to save time for both downstream users looking to extend the code as well as project maintainers down the road, it is the same for licensing and IP management, which both save time for those same constituents, making it easier for the code to be used downstream of the project.

> **Important note**
>
> Before we dig too much into this chapter, I want to add one disclaimer. While there are many things I am – a husband, father, author, and open source expert – one thing I certainly am not is a lawyer. Please do not constitute anything I am saying as legal advice; if you need legal advice, I would suggest contacting an attorney, preferably one with experience in open source licensing.

In this chapter, we will discuss licensing and intellectual property management for open source projects. We will cover the following topics:

- Permissive versus non-permissive licensing – why and what to pick?
- Copyrights and contribution sign-off
- Brand and marks management

By the end of this chapter, you will have a good sense of the areas of focus for open source projects concerning licensing and intellectual property management.

Permissive versus non-permissive licensing – why and what to pick?

If we boil down all the licenses out there, there is a general spectrum for the restrictions and responsibilities of the user of the open source code that spans from permissive usage to non-permissive or what is known as *copyleft*. More on what copyleft is can be found at https://copyleft.org/.

Richard Stallman, in defining what free software is, came up with several freedoms that were the cornerstone of defining the expectations of what free software is. After some evolution over time, the following four freedoms were established (starting its numbering from 0). The following work was adapted and modified from, under the CC BY-ND 4.0 license, https://www.gnu.org/philosophy/free-sw.html#four-freedoms:

1. The freedom to run the program as you wish, for any purpose (freedom 0).
2. The freedom to study how the program works and change it so it does your computing as you wish (freedom 1). Access to the source code is a precondition for this.
3. The freedom to redistribute copies so you can help your neighbor (freedom 2).
4. The freedom to distribute copies of your modified versions to others (freedom 3). By doing this, you can give the whole community a chance to benefit from your changes. Access to the source code is a precondition for this.

So much of how both free software and open source licensing philosophically build from those freedoms. These freedoms establish a general set of expectations you should have from open source.

From there, we get into a lot of nuanced details, which has led to extensive license proliferation. The Open Source Initiative, which is an organization created out of the meeting in 1998 discussed in *Chapter 1, The Whats and Whys of Open Source*, and is the steward of the definition of open source, has approved over 110 different licenses as of this writing [1], as does the Free Software Foundation [2]. The **Software Package Data Exchange** (**SPDX**) project has license identifiers for over 450 licenses [3] as of this writing. This doesn't consider the many variations of an existing license for a specific project. Choice in open source like this is a good thing, but with too many choices comes confusion. This confusion can come in a myriad of ways but generally falls into one of a few categories:

- Obligations of the license chosen. When we look at non-permissive or copyleft licenses in the following section, you'll see the many obligations that can be unclear on how to best stay in compliance.

- How the code under one license can be leveraged or used by code under another project with a different license. Depending on the license, this could result in code needing to be relicensed to be compliant.

- Differences in license variation and why you would pick one versus the other. The family of BSD licenses is a good example, with four different official variations and then numerous derivates from there. Each has different minor stipulations created to address different situations, but how important is each for a project?

Most organizations who use open source code in their internal tooling or projects have adopted guidelines that align with the most common licenses to avoid constant legal reviews, resulting in more open source code being able to be used. I'll dig more into this as we talk about getting your organization to let you launch an open source project in *Chapter 4, Aligning the Business Value of Open Source for Your Employer*.

Let's dig into what each end of the licensing spectrum looks like.

Permissive

Permissive licenses, as written, tend to be the simplest type of open source license, giving the user not only the four freedoms outlined previously but also the ability to use the code generally with minimal obligations on the user. Permissive licenses are typically quite short, for example, the MIT License [4] stated as follows:

Copyright <YEAR> <COPYRIGHT HOLDER>

Permission is hereby granted, free of charge, to any person obtaining a copy of this software and associated documentation files (the "Software"), to deal in the Software without restriction, including without limitation the rights to use, copy, modify, merge, publish, distribute, sublicense, and/or sell copies of the Software, and to permit persons to whom the Software is furnished to do so, subject to the following conditions:

The above copyright notice and this permission notice shall be included in all copies or substantial portions of the Software.

THE SOFTWARE IS PROVIDED "AS IS", WITHOUT WARRANTY OF ANY KIND, EXPRESS OR IMPLIED, INCLUDING BUT NOT LIMITED TO THE WARRANTIES OF MERCHANTABILITY, FITNESS FOR A PARTICULAR PURPOSE, AND NONINFRINGEMENT. IN NO EVENT SHALL THE AUTHORS OR COPYRIGHT HOLDERS BE LIABLE FOR ANY CLAIM, DAMAGES, OR OTHER LIABILITY, WHETHER IN AN ACTION OF CONTRACT, TORT, OR OTHERWISE, ARISING FROM, OUT OF, OR IN CONNECTION WITH THE SOFTWARE OR THE USE OR OTHER DEALINGS IN THE SOFTWARE.

Typically, permissive licenses try to steer clear of any liabilities on the project itself, granted software patents, and any other guarantees. The idea is that the project or author of the code just wants to get the code out there and for people to use it.

The **Apache License, Version 2.0** [5] falls in the general family of permissive licenses but adds a bit more in terms of guarantees to the downstream user. First off, it is an explicit copyright license from the contributors to the project to each downstream user; licenses such as the MIT license referenced previously more implicitly grant this. Additionally, the Apache License, Version 2.0 ensures that any software patents that the contributors have are granted a license to the downstream user, which often helps resolve concerns around adding explicit language for this in a contributor agreement (which we will discuss in the next chapter) or another document. For those two reasons, generally in open source areas, the Apache License, Version 2.0 has become incredibly popular as it is viewed as more *corporate-friendly*.

Non-permissive or copyleft

Where permissive licenses generally stay out of the space of defining specific responsibilities on the downstream user, **non-permissive** or copyleft licenses more explicitly set these expectations. Probably the most well-known license in this category is the **GNU General Public License** [6], which is the license used by the Linux Kernel project and many of the desktop applications built as open source, such as Blender, Inkscape, LibreOffice, and more.

Copyleft licenses are designed with the intent to ensure the code in the project, as well as any improvements made downstream, remain under the same license as the project. If you go back to the 1980s when free software was coming of age, as we talked about in *Chapter 1, The Whats and Whys of Open Source*, free software was a counter to the proprietary models dominating the software industry, and there were major concerns of free software effectively being absorbed by vendors and moved into becoming proprietary software. This licensing model was certainly critical as projects such as the Linux Kernel project, GNU toolchain, and others were becoming more popular.

The concerns about copyleft licensed open source code come down to the ability to incorporate it into other proprietary software. Depending on how that is done, there are arguments to state that the entire work (both the open source project and the proprietary software) is required to be licensed under the project license. This has generally driven product vendors to stay away from copyleft software – both in terms of incorporating it into the proprietary software they are building but also sometimes from using it altogether. This continues to be an evolving legal area.

With some copyleft licenses, such as the **GNU General Public License, Version 2**, there was a fair amount of creativity in how to use such licensed code in a proprietary offering. Tivo was one example, where the software for Tivo set-top boxes incorporated code from the Linux Kernel and the GNU toolchain into the software used. While Tivo complied with the terms of the GNU General Public License, Version 2, their hardware had **Digital Rights Management** (**DRM**) incorporated, which made it impossible to run modified code on the hardware. This was called **Tivoization** [7] and was permissive by the letter of the license, but not the spirit of the license, and drove most of the intentions in version 3 of the GPL.

Another case was around the use of open source by cloud providers. In these cases, the software wasn't distributed at all but used by a user on a shared system, which was a concept not popularized until the early 2000s. At that time, copyleft licenses didn't address this concept, but later, licenses such as the **GNU Affero General Public License** [8] and the **Commons Clause** [9] were developed to address this, requiring access to the open source licensed software running on those systems.

Which type of license makes sense for my project?

Here is the area where, once again, I will emphasize that I am not a lawyer and can't provide legal advice.

When I generally talk with projects about licensing, there are a few considerations that are part of the discussion:

- Who is the user, and how do you expect the user to use the code?
- Is there a need to set expectations of pushing code and development upstream (meaning to the primary code base of the project), or is that already in the culture of the community?
- Do you expect commercial usage, and how do you as a project maintainer feel about that?
- What type of project is this? A library? A ready-to-use application? A framework?

I have left out the question of a maintainer's personal view on software freedom intentionally. While there will be those biases that will be incorporated into the decision-making process, I generally advise that they not be part of the considerations. A good open source project put its users first.

What I generally see is open source projects and code that are part of the building blocks of an application, such as libraries, frameworks, and integration layers, work best under a permissive license. The reason for this is the intention of the code usage; it's going to be mixed with propriety code, so the copyleft obligations are going to be a major concern. Generally, we also see the primary users of projects such as these are software developers, and within that culture, there is a desire to upstream, mostly because of pragmatism – who wants to have to patch a dependency every time the upstream project makes a new release?

For more end user applications, such as desktop or web applications, the general trend is to go with a copyleft license. This is primarily to encourage development upstream and have a more consistent version and release cadence, as well as direct vendors looking to build a business model to focus less on selling a version and more on providing ancillary services such as support and training. There is also the argument that using copyleft is helpful when the software is encroaching on a highly competitive space with multiple commercial offerings exist. An example here is MySQL, which came to be when the market was dominated by commercial solutions. I would argue that this approach, if development is primarily done by one organization, can lead to the *Open Core* model described in *Chapter 2, What Makes a Good Open Source Project?*

If your project doesn't fit in either category, then start thinking from the perspective of your user – what expectations do you have of them and how much of a community are you looking to build? If you sense the culture of your community will naturally be more collaborative, and more software engineering focuses on open source leans this way, the additions of copyleft obligations might not be worth it. If that's not the case, then a copyleft license could be a better option.

One thing I will say is that once you pick a license, it's a lot of work to change it. The biggest factor that makes it hard is that to change a license, every contributor who owns the contribution made to the project (unless there is an agreement in place that provides a copyright license – this is something we will cover in the next section) must agree to relicense the code they contributed to. If there are only 3-4 contributors – it's fairly easy. But let's say there are 50 or 100 contributors, and some of them haven't contributed in quite some time and are hard to contact – that becomes a painful challenge. In the case that a contributor's agreement to relicense the code isn't granted, the project has to remove that code and potentially rewrite it. So, yes, pick your license wisely.

Now that we've discussed licensing, let's start to look into the next key part of intellectual property management – how to manage incoming contributions to an open source project and copyrights.

Copyrights and contribution sign-off

When people think about license and IP management, the conversation often focuses on outbound licensing – that is, what license the code from the project uses. But just as important (or even more important) are the terms that the code comes into the project under, because if it doesn't come in under the license and/or terms that will work with the license the code is released under, it makes it difficult on downstream users to use the code.

In smaller projects, this is often overlooked, as you often will only see a few contributors to the code base, so project maintainers tend not to pay much attention to contribution sign-off. But this can quickly get out of control, especially if you have someone come to the project and say, "Hey, that code looks like something someone pulled from my commercial product." It gets awkward quickly here at this point, as the project is suddenly scrambling to see who added the code, hoping that someone knows the person and it's not just someone with a random GitHub user account. Remember that picture at the start of this chapter? Don't be that project ;-).

There are generally two approaches seen in open source for a contributor to indicate their sign-off or approval for code to come into a project, and they, in some cases, are used in conjunction with each other. They are the **Contributor License Agreement (CLA)** and the **Developer Certificate of Origin (DCO)**. Let's look at them now.

Contributor License Agreement (CLA)

A CLA is a legal document executed by a contributor that provides an agreement between the project and the contributor on the terms and conditions for the contributions that the contributor makes to the project. CLAs can be agreements with either an individual or an organization, referred to as an **Individual Contributor License Agreement (ICLA)** or **Corporate Contributor License Agreement (CCLA)**, respectively.

For CCLAs, these will typically cover a set of named individuals from an organization or all employees and contractors for an organization. These agreements typically only have to be executed once to cover all contributions for a given individual or organization. However, if the terms in the CLA change, the individual or organization would need to re-execute the agreement before making future contributions.

A project will typically use a CLA for project contributors to specifically address the rights and obligations of contributors. Some examples of those situations include the following:

- Allowing organizations to provide a license to any software patents they own that are used in the project

- Letting an organization specifically identify individuals who may contribute on their behalf

- Requiring the contributor to provide a copyright or IP license to the project, or in some cases, entirely assigning copyright and IP rights to the project

CLAs terms tend to be a bit all over the place, and unless a standard template is used (such as the **Apache CLA** [11]), they will often require legal reviews for organizations to be comfortable with contributing to the project. Because of that, CLAs can add some friction to contributors, even on projects where there's a CLA with very lightweight terms. Some contributors will even refuse to contribute to a project with a CLA; sometimes, this is more idealistic, but other times, there can be a bit of fear and lack of trust in a project that implements a CLA.

We've also seen CLAs used in conjunction with the *Open Core* model described in *Chapter 2, What Makes a Good Open Source Project?*. This is because the organization needs to have the right to relicense the code under a commercial license for their non-open source products. But we've also seen this as a way an open source project could be taken to become a proprietary product or have added more restrictive licensing. Examples of projects where this has happened include the following:

- **MongoDB**, which changed from the **GNU Affero General Public License version 3 (AGPL v3)** [12] to the then new **Server Side Public License (SSPL)** [13] after concerns with cloud providers monetizing their customers using MongoDB without MongoDB, Inc. gaining revenue from that [14]

- Redis Labs added the Commons Clause [15] to its open source code due to similar concerns with cloud providers]16]

- SugarCRM initially provided its community edition under its own SugarCRM Public License [17], later moving to the AGPL v3 and finally moving to an entirely proprietary product

I know I've presented CLAs in a bit of a negative light, but that is not always the case. For some organizations, using a CLA helps address some of the ambiguities the license of an open source project might have. An example would be an open source project using the **BSD 3-Clause** license [18], which doesn't address an organization giving a license to any software patents they might own. Depending on the industries and circumstances in which the code is to be used, a CLA can cover gaps like these while enabling a project to use a more permissive license that might not address those gaps directly. On the other side, licenses such as the **Apache License, Version 2.0** [19] have provisions that often can make a CLA redundant and eliminate the need for one, which has been a factor in its popularity in open source projects driven by commercial vendors.

Developer Certificate of Origin (DCO)

At the height of the lawsuit where the company Santa Cruz Operation (which many will recognize by its acronym, SCO) was disputing copyright claims on code within the Linux kernel project [20], there was discussion on how to streamline the contribution signoff process without adding the perceived friction that implementing a CLA would bring. There was a culture within the Linux kernel project where contributions were owned collectively rather than by one group. Naturally, this made the Linux kernel project copyright ownership situation a bit of a spider web – but that is by design, as it ensured that the technology could progress openly and without any specific vendor taking the project in one direction without the consent of all the contributors. Think of it as making the project a *commons* of sorts.

While much of the legal basis for the SCO allegations was dismissed over two decades, the concept of making this model more streamlined into the contribution workflow was necessary for that community. Thus was borne the **Developer Certificate of Origin** [21], a simple declaration a contributor makes by adding a `Signed-off-by:` line to their source code commit message. This sign-off asserts the following:

Developer Certificate of Origin

Version 1.1

Copyright (C) 2004, 2006 The Linux Foundation and its contributors.

Everyone is permitted to copy and distribute verbatim copies of this license document, but changing it is not allowed.

Developer's Certificate of Origin 1.1

By making a contribution to this project, I certify that:

(a) The contribution was created in whole or in part by me and I have the right to submit it under the open source license indicated in the file; or

(b) The contribution is based upon previous work that, to the best of my knowledge, is covered under an appropriate open source license and I have the right under that license to submit that work with modifications, whether created in whole or in part by me, under the same open source license (unless I am permitted to submit under a different license), as indicated in the file; or

(c) The contribution was provided directly to me by some other person who certified (a), (b), or (c) and I have not modified it.

(d) I understand and agree that this project and the contribution are public and that a record of the contribution (including all personal information I submit with it, including my sign-off) is maintained indefinitely and may be redistributed consistent with this project or the open source license(s) involved.

In effect, the contributor asserts they're allowed to contribute the code to the project because either they created it, or they created it with someone or got the code from someone, and it's under the same license (or they have the right to put it under the license being used by the contribution). Additionally, they indicate that the personally indefinable information they submit along with the contribution will be maintained indefinitely with the project and redistributed with the project as any contributor information would be – something very important to address with the many data privacy regulations commonplace globally.

Version control systems such as `git` make it trivial to do a sign-off with a commit by issuing the `git commit -s` command when doing a commit. GitHub also has tools to automate adding the signoff as part of contributions made through its web-based interface. DCOs are quite popular with open source projects, with thousands using the DCO due to the simplicity of the mechanism.

All that said, because of its simplicity, this means some gaps are not directly addressed, which can cause concerns for organizations looking to contribute to a project, such as the software patent concern shared in the previous section. Sometimes, organizations see the actual open source license used as able to address the gaps. Other times, using the DCO in combination with a more lightweight CLA works. The latter approach was used by several of the open source projects hosted by the Academy Software Foundation until they shifted to using the Apache CLA [22].

Choosing the right approach that makes sense for your project lies in understanding the downstream users and organizations. We've seen the importance of code providence in the last several years – meaning organizations want to understand where the code they are using is coming from. Software supply chain attacks, as of this writing, are sharply on the rise. If a project cannot attest to where a line of code comes from, it poses a risk to every user of the code. On top of that, continued sensitivities on software patents, as we've talked about, add another dimension to the right level of rigor relative to risk management; in other words, you want to strike a balance between how much work it is for a new contributor to contribute and the right amount of legal protection in place for the project and its users.

Some good questions that can help guide you as a project maintainer on which path to go down include the following:

- Who are the users of the project? What industry are they in? What regulatory or other considerations are there?

- Who are the contributors to the project? Larger enterprises? Start-ups? Individuals?

- What license is the project using? Does the license have specific language around copyright or patent licensing?

- What are your intentions for the code to be used in a project? (the same question that was asked regarding picking a license ;-))

Generally, as a project, it's advisable to lean toward the lightest way for contributions to come in. Even CLAs, when used, can be executed using automated tools such as LFX EasyCLA [23], and sticking to a standard template keeps the friction low.

Managing intellectual property for a project is more than just the code since the brand, project name, and other assets are very important to an open source project's success. Let's look at best practices for brand and marks management.

Brand and marks management

One of the last considerations (you could argue it's one of the most critical for a project) is managing the brand. For a smaller project, this might not seem like such a big deal, but for a bigger project, this can be critical to its success.

We've seen examples of this many times in open source. One that comes to mind immediately is the PHP project, which in the early 2000s took off as the go-to web development language. From there, all sorts of projects were built using PHP. One such project was named **phpMyAdmin**, which is still a popular web application for managing MySQL databases. We saw all sorts of projects taking the same approach, naming themselves PHP, which could mean anything from a developer tool, end user application, or library. The only common thread was they were written in PHP.

On the one hand, that sort of publicity made PHP more popular. But on the other hand, it added confusion; for example, is phpMyAdmin from the PHP project itself? If this were a product company, a good product marketer would immediately recognize this as brand confusion. But as an open source project, this momentum can get away from the maintainers and, in some cases, is outside of their skill sets.

So, what should a project maintainer think about in the scope of brand management? Let's explore some areas.

Determining your project's name

A project should determine exactly what its brand is. Much of this is thinking about its distinctiveness to the user; namely, does the name connect to the project's purpose? A project such as OpenEXR makes that clear – it provides the specification and reference implementation of the `.exr` file format. Sometimes, projects use a name that, through a story, relates to the domain or the time and place the project was created. Debian's name is described as a portmanteau, combining the first name of the project founder Ian Murdock's then-girlfriend, Debra Lynn, with his name, Ian [24]. Apache HTTP Server was named as it was *a patch* (or rather a set of patches) to the original NCSA web server.

A project can get too clever here too. While researching for this book, I came across an article [25] talking about the open source project *Twisted*, which is an event-driven networking engine written in Python. While the space and problem being solved by the project made the naming appropriate, it did lead to some bad jokes (that is, *Twisted is so twisted*), metaphors that only make sense in a certain region (that is, naming a package `twisted.spread.jelly`), and a fun copyright infringement with a popular heavy metal band (`twisted.sister`).

As a project is considering a name, it's really important to make sure no one else is using it – if so, you run into not just confusion but potential trademark infringement. A good place to start is searching Google and GitHub for the term and seeing what comes up – if you see a few projects or commercial products, it's usually a bad idea to proceed with that name. The next step would be checking the various trademark databases, both with the **US Patent and Trademark Office** (**USPTO**) [26], as well as with the **European Union Intellectual Property Office** (**EUIPO**) [27]. If this comes back with no results, or none in the goods and services related to your project, generally, things are fairly safe. If not, either find a new name or discuss more with a trademark lawyer.

Brand consistency

Once you have a name, the next step is establishing its brand. A brand will usually have a few different aspects, such as the project name itself, a logo, and maybe a saying or descriptor. The big thing at this stage is ensuring you are consistent; let's take the example of a fictional project named *Zeus*:

- Is the project name *Zeus* or *ZEUS* or *zeus* (notice the difference in capitalization)?

- Is it Zeus Project? Zeus Framework? Zeus Suite?

- Is there a logo for Zeus? Is it distinctive, or just the word *Zeus* spelled out?

The importance at this stage is consistency across the board. Having one person call it *Zeus* and another *Zeus Framework* makes it confusing if they are the same project or something different.

The same is true for a logo; it should be the same colors, scale, and design. Take this example from the Linux Foundation Trademark Usage guidelines [28] as a guide – it speaks about the correct usage of the Kubernetes logo:

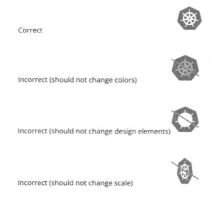

Figure 3.2 – Examples of correct and incorrect usage of the Kubernetes logo (source:
`https://www.linuxfoundation.org/legal/trademark-usage`)

These might seem like minor details, but they are critical in brand management, not just to help decrease confusion but also to showcase the project as a professional, well-run project.

Protecting the brand

In general, the best way to protect your brand is to use it consistently. Even if a project goes down the path of registering trademarks or logo marks, they become incredibly hard to defend if used inconsistently. This is a classic example of the adage that *an ounce of prevention is worth a pound of cure*; being intentional in how the project uses its name and logo set it up for success.

After that, the next level of protection is trademark registration. The USPTO describes the usage of trademarks "to identify and distinguish the goods/services of one seller or provider from those of others, and to indicate the source of the goods/services." By default, a project using its mark effectively gives it the protection known as a **common law trademark**, which is generally considered a valid owner of a mark by trademark offices globally. The next step up from there is registering a trademark, which, depending upon the term used, the popularity of the project, and the industry in which the project is used, can be an advisable step. All that said, it can get costly, both for registration and maintenance. This is often an area where we see projects look to move toward a vendor-neutral entity, such as the Linux Foundation, the Apache Foundation, or The Software Freedom Conservancy, all of which have deep experience and expertise in managing trademarks. We will discuss this a bit more in a later chapter when we talk about the role of foundations in open source governance.

Enabling others to use your brand

Apache Hadoop was a huge technology that gave birth to the entire big data industry in the 2010s, with billions of dollars of venture and product investment and many downstream products leveraging the project. With that, we saw the term *Hadoop* being thrown into the product naming for several offerings, with the term *Hadoop Distribution* becoming commonplace. There was one problem that end users had with this situation – what does being a *Hadoop Distribution* mean? Does it mean a certain version of Hadoop? Certain configuration? Does one *Hadoop Distribution* work with another? Does a product designed to work with Hadoop work with any *Hadoop Distribution*? Details like these seem minor, but in the realm of enterprise software, they are critical for growing an ecosystem.

Just like the PHP example earlier in this chapter, making sure your brand is used in such a way that communicates clearly with downstream users is critical to a project being able to grow an ecosystem. It's something to get ahead of, too; many projects start building trademark and branding guides to help clarify this. One example is the Open Mainframe Project, which has branding guidelines [29] to help make it clear how its projects can be referenced, including how an organization's role in a project should be established.

But coming back to the Hadoop example, there is value in a project establishing its downstream ecosystem and what it means to be compatible with the upstream project. This is an area where establishing a conformance program can be valuable. These programs let the project community set standards for products and offerings based on or leveraging the project in such a way as to develop an ecosystem. Some examples include the following:

- **Certified Kubernetes** [30], which ensures that every vendor's version of Kubernetes supports the required APIs, as do open source community versions
- **Zowe Conformance Program** [31], which aims to give users the confidence that when they use a product, app, or distribution that leverages Zowe they can expect a high level of common functionality, interoperability, and user experience

By being part of such a program, a project will grant the use of a special set of marks to the product or offering to indicate its alignment. Programs are managed using objective criteria, and often a third party will be involved in the evaluation process to ensure there is no vendor bias.

Note that conformance programs don't infringe on the ability of others to use the code – the code is still available under the project's license. This would just add a way to solve the end user concerns that a product using the term *Hadoop Distribution* would have had; now, there are both specific criteria of what that means, but also clarity on the project's brand.

Summary

This chapter scratched the surface of license and IP management in terms of open source but aimed to give you enough insight and knowledge so that you can start down the path of understanding this concept.

There are several resources to help guide you on this topic, namely **FOSSMarks** [32], some of the legal articles coming out of the Linux Foundation [33], and the Software Freedom Law Center [34]. For a lot of the basic needs of a project, this chapter is helpful, but I always encourage projects to seek legal advice as they get into more broad concerns and questions. As I stated at the beginning of this chapter, I am not a lawyer and cannot provide legal advice.

One thing you will note that I didn't speak about is license enforcement – and that was intentional. While there are some narrow cases where taking legal action against a license violator is advisable, in the vast majority of cases, reaching out to them is a much better solution. One comment I've heard that resonates here is "*The best way to ensure a person no longer contributes to your project is by sending them a cease and desist letter.*"

Additionally, license enforcement is something that the project maintainers and/or authors should be the center point of; after all, they are the people that this directly impacts. I don't often post on social media, but I did on this topic several years ago:

I see this article that covers Linus's thoughts as an insightful counterpoint...

https://www.zdnet.com/article/linus-torvaldss-love-hate-relationship-with-the-gpl/

Net-net, I struggle to get more worked up about GPL compliance than the author of the affected open source compliance.

Now that we've covered licensing and IP management, you are well equipped to be able to take the knowledge you've learned up to this point and get your company to start working in open source. In the next chapter, we will help you get your company to start or contribute to an open source project, and how best to measure the investment and recognize contributions.

Further reading

To learn more about the topics that were covered in this chapter, take a look at the following resources:

[1] https://opensource.org/licenses/alphabetical

[2] https://www.gnu.org/licenses/license-list.html#SoftwareLicenses

[3] https://spdx.org/licenses/

[4] https://opensource.org/licenses/MIT

[5] https://www.apache.org/licenses/LICENSE-2.0

[6] https://www.gnu.org/licenses/gpl-3.0.en.html

[7] https://en.wikipedia.org/wiki/Tivoization

[8] https://www.gnu.org/licenses/agpl-3.0.txt

[9] https://commonsclause.com/

[10] https://www.apache.org/licenses/contributor-agreements.html

[11] https://www.gnu.org/licenses/agpl.txt

[12] https://lwn.net/Articles/768670/

[13] https://www.mongodb.com/licensing/server-side-public-license

[14] https://commonsclause.com/

[15] https://lwn.net/Articles/763179/

[16] https://spdx.org/licenses/SugarCRM-1.1.3.html

[17] https://spdx.org/licenses/BSD-3-Clause.html

[18] https://en.wikipedia.org/wiki/SCO%E2%80%93Linux_disputes

[19] https://developercertificate.org/

[20] https://tac.aswf.io/process/contributing.html#contributor-license-agreement-cla

[21] https://lfx.linuxfoundation.org/tools/easycla

[22] https://opensource.com/article/18/3/how-11-open-source-projects-got-their-names

[23] https://codewithoutrules.com/2017/06/14/how-to-name-your-software/

[24] http://www.uspto.gov/trademarks-application-process/search-trademark-database

[25] https://euipo.europa.eu

[26] https://opensource.com/article/18/3/how-11-open-source-projects-got-their-names

[27] https://www.openmainframeproject.org/branding-guidelines

[28] https://www.cncf.io/certification/software-conformance/

[29] https://www.openmainframeproject.org/projects/zowe/conformance

[30] https://fossmarks.org/

[31] https://www.linuxfoundation.org/blog/tag/legal

[32] https://softwarefreedom.org/

[33] https://en.wikipedia.org/wiki/Tivoization

4

Aligning the Business Value of Open Source for Your Employer

If you've read *Chapter 1* and *Chapter 2*, you've hopefully come away with some concrete motivations for using open source and starting an open source project. And if you've made it to this chapter, you are probably thinking, "there is some great code at my company we should open source!" That's the right attitude!

However, there's a lot more than meets the eye when it comes to an employer seeing the value of contributing to an open source project, let alone starting one. As an individual deciding to contribute to open source or start an open source project, the justification is usually quite simple: you have something interesting to you that you want others to benefit from, or are using a project and you see something that you want to fix or improve – what is often referred to as the *scratch-your-own-itch* pattern. You may also find the work that a project is doing helpful and just want to help out – maybe writing some documentation or providing feedback on a pull request – more *itch-scratching*.

For companies, *scratching your own itch* is noble but not enough – they need to see how this benefits them as a business overall, which is often termed "enlightened self-interest." Software developers are considered less than business-savvy in many organizations, and due to that perception, the conversation on open source stops there. This speaks to the need to connect the value of open source to business value, which in the past few decades, we've seen come together. It has been a bumpy road at times to align business models with open source, which is no different from how the disruptive technologies of the past took time to find a suitable business model.

In this chapter, I'll lay the groundwork to help you get your company into open source, either contributing to or launching a new project. This is merely the tip of the iceberg, and we will look at further resources toward the end that can help you establish open source as part of your company's strategy.

Why would a company want to open source code?

Getting support for open sourcing code within an organization requires first understanding what the motivations are for even doing so. It requires you to think with a business mindset, which at the end of the day comes back to costs and revenue. Sometimes, this can be framed in more long-term thinking, but being persuasive when championing this kind of initiative also requires citing some short-term benefits. Let's look at what tend to be the primary motivators.

Lowering development costs

The bottom line is something every company thinks about, and this tends to be a major motivation in looking at open source. In software development, there are costs both in terms of initial development and maintenance, which includes new functionality, as well as fixing bugs and resolving security issues. Staying on top of this can be quite an endeavor.

One aspect of the development costs that companies don't often think about is the specialization involved in software development. If you go back to the early 2000s and before, the most common software developer was what is known as the *full-stack developer*, meaning someone who had broad knowledge and expertise in different technologies and languages. For example, a full-stack developer would be able to write the frontend code for a website in HTML, JavaScript, and CSS, the business logic in something such as PHP, Python, or Ruby, and manage the database backend using MySQL or PostgreSQL. If you are a software developer, you know there are technological differences not only between each of those but also in how you would approach scaling, performance, security, and maintainability with each of them. For the software developer today, those layers have become more complex, moving from simple JavaScript calls to complex frameworks such as Bootstrap, from monolithic applications to micro-services, and often not just one database backend but multiple ones that may involve different approaches and methodologies.

For an organization today, even a modest software development company, hiring software developers with expertise in each area is an endeavor. In some cases, there may only be a handful of individuals that have expertise in a particular tool. For example, if you need to build a largely static website that has some template logic to keep multiple areas of a website in sync, you could define a template language and build some scripting to automate it – or you could use something such as **Jekyll** or **Hugo**, which has all this ready to go. That way, you don't need a developer to maintain this script, which will undoubtedly break at some point, or the template language will need to be extended for different data types, but instead use the build functionality and templating language that either Jekyll or Hugo provides. This not only saves the company time and effort but also means they don't need staff with deep expertise, just somebody who understands how to use the tool itself. This simplifies hiring by looking at the skills around a project and lets them be more flexible with their developer resources.

Adding new features/functionality for customers

Let's say your company is building out a task management tool, and a customer comes in with this request: *It would be great if all of a user's tasks were listed on their calendar to help them plan ahead and coordinate with the other meetings on their calendar.* One route would be exploring how to build integration into a single calendar tool, such as Microsoft Outlook or Google Mail; another would be writing a custom iCal server that implements the **iCalendar** standard. Or, you could look for a library that is able to deal with the entire iCal standard. Which one would you choose?

This is exactly the kind of sweet spot where open source comes in, the ability to provide a piece of functionality to solve a particular problem that exists across a wide variety of use cases. You could argue it comes from the Unix and free software heritage, where each tool solves a particular problem (and does it well) and is designed to work in conjunction with other tools. As with the previous point on lower development costs, a company doesn't need staff to understand all the ins and outs of these libraries or tools; they just need to be able to use them.

Another piece of this equation is being able to improve libraries and tools to make the integration or customer experience better. For example, if we look at the iCal example, maybe the company's development team identifies a compatibility issue with a particular calendar client that uses the iCal endpoint (if you haven't worked with iCal before, note that clients can be incredibly picky on things such as whitespace and line endings). Not only could they report the issue but they could also provide a test case, and even fix it. If this wasn't open source, they would have to rely on the vendor's timeline and support team, which could take weeks, months, or even years; in open source, it's a question of submitting a patch and getting it merged into the main code base. As a bonus, the company then doesn't need to maintain a version of the tool with the fix – this is called **working upstream** (which was discussed in *Chapter 2, What Makes a Good Open Source Project?*) and makes it easier to introduce new features and functionality to your company's product without any work on your end at all!

Faster time to market

The previous two points on why a company would open source code focused on the developer alignment angle in using open source as a way to optimize a company's developer investments. Another part of that optimization is velocity – or better put, how a company can build software faster.

If we look at the classic **Facebook, Apple, Amazon, Netflix, and Google** (**FAANG**) companies (Facebook now being Meta), the differentiating factor for all of them was building their solutions on top of open source. Facebook heavily used PHP in its rise to popularity, Apple built Mac OS X using many parts of FreeBSD and the Mach kernel projects, and we've seen Amazon, Netflix, and Google use open source, as well as build a lot of open source for the larger open source community to use and contribute to. The same pattern has been used numerous times with other technology companies, with numerous start-ups forming from open source communities or starting open source communities of their own to drive innovation.

What is often a big question to those outside of open source is, "Why put technology like that out there for anyone to use? Couldn't open sourcing this code jumpstart a competitor in the space to overtake you?" It's a fair observation, but companies look at it as a trade-off; is there more value in owning all the code and IP, or is there more value in getting a solution to market faster? And furthermore, what layers of the stack have value?

Apple, when they made the move from Classic Mac OS to Mac OS X, realized that the value was at the user experience level, so building their own operating system kernel didn't make a ton of sense (it also didn't help they were coming off the heels of the Copland project, which is considered one of the biggest failures in software development history [1]). A big driver was the need to move quickly to achieve a more modern operating system, as the Classic Mac OS was aging and didn't include several key features, such as pre-emptive multitasking, protected memory, access controls, and multi-user management, so building on top of a kernel and operating system that had all of those things got them to market faster.

As we looked at in previous chapters with the value of open source being ecosystem building, there is a secondary benefit – not just getting to market faster but also establishing the market faster as well. Cloud Foundry comes from an open source project launched at Pivotal Software back in 2011, with the idea that starting this project would make it a standard for anyone building multi-cloud **Platform-as-a-Service** (**PaaS**) applications. This idea did come to fruition, with several vendors and cloud providers bringing support for Cloud Foundry, thus not only helping solutions come to market faster but at the same time establishing Cloud Foundry as the standard faster – and by proxy, Pivotal Software as a market leader.

The ability to focus investments

I will often chat with companies when they are looking at open sourcing some code that they have written and when the discussion moves to the value of open sourcing the code that they have, I draw the analogy to other services they might have for their business.

For example, you don't often see the CEO emptying the trash cans around the office; most commonly, we see that as a contracted service. Emptying trash cans is a *commodity*, meaning it's something a broad scope of people could do. Often, the cost itself of a commodity service is low because economies of scale kick in; for example, if a company shares a building space with four other businesses, one person could empty all the trash cans instead of four different people each cleaning different offices.

The same idea applies here as well – as I mentioned before, you don't have to have specialists for each layer of your application, just ones for the specific parts that are critically important to your business. It's similar to how cloud computing has reduced the need for each company to have a data center administrator; if you build your application on top of a framework such as Cloud Foundry, you just need experts in Cloud Foundry and not each of the underlying components. This makes it easier to focus a company's investments, attract talent, and generally execute better as a business.

With this background on why a company would participate in the open source ecosystem, let's now talk about how to build that support internally to open source code.

Getting support for open sourcing code internally

Now that you know why a company would open source code, let's walk through what we must consider as we go through the process of proposing to open source code. Note that every company works a bit differently, so many of the points I'll cover are at a higher level; however, the general concepts are key ones that any company will need solid answers to.

Reviewing what's out there already

Open source projects are consistently under-resourced. Even if there are enough developers, those developers might not have the bandwidth to write tests, build documentation, triage incoming issues, respond to questions, and deal with security issues. Working together helps make projects more efficient, have a larger impact, and address more features and use cases than working alone.

Before you start a new open source project, research other ones out there that might solve the same problem. As you review them, consider these questions:

- Does the project cover the same use cases as mine?
- Is it built using the same language, framework, or technology stack?
- Are there multiple companies contributing to the project, or just one?
- Does the project have a track record of accepting community contributions promptly?
- What license is used, what IP policies does the project have, and are they compatible with our needs?

If you answered *yes* to all those questions, contributing to that project is likely a better choice than starting a new one.

Even if there are some *no* answers, that doesn't necessarily rule out contributing to versus starting a new project. For example, if you are looking to distribute a product and use the open source project as a part of that product, and that project is under a GPL license, that might be considered a showstopper. Before you do that, reach out to the maintainers and see whether they would be open to changing to a more permissive license; often, maintainers aren't overly savvy in open source licensing or might not realize the challenges a license might have regarding adoption. I've reached out to the maintainer of a project using a GPLv3 license before, for example, and said "Any chance you could change to Apache 2?" and the maintainer has come back and said "Sure!" if it's been fairly trivial for them to do so. I will note that this tends to be more realistic if the project has only one or just a few contributors, but larger projects likely won't be as receptive.

Building the business case

Taking the general motivators from the previous section, you first need to work on building out a business case for why to open source a particular bit of code. There could be a multitude of reasons for it, including the following:

- The code isn't all that specific to the company, not mission-critical, and could benefit from the involvement of external people

- Developers are looking to scale up the code or have run into a challenging problem and could use the help of broader expertise

- The code is related to an open source project that the company is using, either building on the project or deriving code from it, and the use case is likely applicable to others, so upstreaming it would be good for the company and the project

Starting to build a business case around open source is fairly similar to building business cases in general, usually covering a few specific points:

- First is the problem statement. What is the challenge the company has today? Examples could be low bandwidth for the team to maintain the code or not having the expertise to continue development, or maybe it's more opportunistic, such as identifying a gap in the market or a challenge with a common integration framework between multiple solutions.

- Second is outlining the solution. This could be to start a new open source project or contribute to an existing open source project – which is a topic we will dig more into later in this chapter. What is key at this stage is ensuring you can connect the problem to the solution succinctly and showing how the solution provides a way to address the problems raised simply.

- Third is identifying the steps forward and what is needed to get there. Think in terms of the internal tactical pieces (legal reviews, engineering reviews, and marketing reviews – we will get into all of these things later in this chapter), but also budget needs, briefing and getting alignment with outside partners, and aligning the internal resource support that is needed.

Let's take a look now at how to build a business case more practically.

An example business case for open sourcing code from a company

Let's look at an example business case here. A project I worked on in the past was the COBOL Programming Course, which was launched by Open Mainframe Project in April 2020, and while this wasn't their exact business case, this is how I would imagine it:

- **Problem**: COBOL is a language heavily used in critical applications in finance, insurance, healthcare, government, and more. The new talent pool coming into COBOL is much smaller than the talent pool approaching retirement, and COBOL as a language is developed using tooling that is different from what a software developer uses today.

- **Solution**: Develop a programming course for COBOL, which teaches COBOL development using Microsoft Visual Studio Code and Zowe Explorer, and make it available as an open source project so that it can be broadly used by individuals to learn COBOL and by companies for internal training.

- **Next steps**: First, we will need to take the various learning materials around COBOL and fund building a course; this could be done in collaboration with an academic institution that might be interested in these materials for their classwork. Then, we will need to align a few industry partners to form a steering committee, set up a GitHub site, work with other organizations in the mainframe space, such as Open Mainframe Project, to provide a neutral home, make a public announcement, and launch the work. This will require two to three **Full-Time Employee (FTE)** resources at launch and ongoing fractional resources to support and drive the work.

The preceding outline is rather high-level both to keep this chapter from getting too long and also as a guide for thinking about the idea more succinctly. One thing to note in the early stages here is you want to leave some gaps open to have areas where others can fill in and provide support; in an open source project, the value of people outweighs that of funding, as people make the real difference in its success (or failure).

Here's another example more suited toward contribution to an open source project, where a company that will remain nameless was debating whether or not to continue to develop its own database interface layer, or leverage and contribute to another one:

- **Problem**: We've built our own database interface layer, which has served us well for many years, but is becoming hard to maintain. Additionally, we want to be able to support additional database backends and it's hard to implement them because of the design choices made.

- **Solution**: Review the existing database interface layers used and see which one most closely fits our needs. While we know it won't be a drop-in replacement, we do know that we can contribute some of our concepts to these projects and they will likely see value from that, along with more usage from embedding it in our product.

- **Next steps**: Pull together an architecture committee to review the open source database interface layers and make a recommendation on which one to move forward with. We then need to do a gap analysis on what functionality is missing and work with the upstream community to contribute these back to the project (this likely will require legal review for licensing compatibility). We will probably require two to three FTE resources at first, which is slightly more than the size of the team maintaining that piece, but we anticipate we'll be able to reduce to less than one FTE equivalent once the transition is complete.

What's good in this example is the disclosure that the investment upfront will be higher in terms of resources, but it will reduce to less than the present investment over time. Setting expectations appropriately is a real key at this stage, especially giving yourself space, as you will hit bumps along the way.

Getting allies

Now, it's time to start shopping around the business case within the organization. This is where each organization is a bit different, as there will be not only different personalities but also other key people who can help influence the decision. You know your organization best, so use this as a guide for the types of allies you will need:

- First, you need a **budget ally** who can help fund the time, effort, and expenses involved. There are a lot of pieces involved in open sourcing a project, including legal review, engineering work, marketing/PR, and community management, and these require personal time investment, as well as the funding to do the work. The budget ally will need to see how the investment will pay off in the long run.

  A well-crafted business case will go a long way and the budget ally will also be able to add perspective on things you might not see. For example, maybe they know that there are team members close to retirement, and there are concerns about re-staffing. Maybe there are some discussions around adjusting focus and goals, and the open sourcing discussion is timely. Perhaps this person shares some hunches you have, maybe even with past experience in open sourcing code, and can give you support and advice along the way. Organizations are largely driven by cost, so while the budget ally isn't the only key stakeholder, they need to be on board for you to have any success.

- The second will be **technical allies**. These can be software engineers, architects, or managers that are currently involved with the code and are expected to be involved in the future or impacted by the open source proposal. Often, these technical people are familiar with open source, and the idea of being part of the project will be exciting for them (or they may have had a bad experience and be put off from their experiences of open source as well). You may also have people with no familiarity with open source, or only *experience from a distance*, meaning they've heard of it and are skeptical, much like the example we discussed in *Chapter 1, The Whats and Whys of Open Source*.

  Either way, you need their support, as they will be doing the technical work at the end of the day. In addition, you will want to set the expectation of how to work in an open source community, meaning design and feature discussions should happen out in the open, releases should be planned within the community, and simple things such as the bug tracker should be open resources. Often, I see companies open source code and keep all the development meetings and scrums within the company itself; helping set a good pattern at the onset not only ensures success for the project but also sets the proper habits for the internal development teams. We will dig more into this in *Chapter 5, Governance and Hosting Models*.

- Finally, and this might not be needed in all scenarios, is an **executive sponsor**. This might be the same person as the budget ally, but the big distinction is that they will have sway in ensuring this effort stays as a strategic priority, which makes it easier to allocate more resources and budget in the future.

One other opportunity here is that this executive could be in the position over time to establish a more formal center of gravity around open source in the company. These groups are typically called **Open Source Program Offices (OSPOs)** and generally are cross-functional groups supporting open source efforts across a company. Getting an executive involved early on in the first open source effort for a company helps give them visibility of the work done, and allows them to become a great ally in providing advice and guidance in evolving the effort into a program.

Setting expectations

Once you have this alignment, you are often set to go. However, to be successful, I'd recommend one more step, and that's setting expectations.

With any effort, whether open sourcing code or any other business initiative, stakeholders such as those listed previously will have high hopes – and in some cases, they might be unrealistic. Maybe they think they will have 100 contributors in a month. Perhaps they think they will be the talk of Hacker News, or even that they will be able to scale back engineering efforts overnight. While sometimes you may get lucky with one of those, realistically, that's not always the case.

When setting expectations, consider these dimensions:

- **Time**, both in terms of how long the process to open source code will be and also building up a contributor base. The former will be longer than you will likely expect if it's the company's first time, as there will be a lot of legal review, in addition to the alignment of the stakeholders described in the previous section.

- **Internal impact**, as sometimes the code might not be as useful broadly as you think. Alternatively, the contributions won't be very substantial for a while. Very few open source projects ever reach the Linux kernel or Kubernetes level; a vast number are small-scale, low-velocity projects that have value in their own right but may not be massive.

- **Effort**, and this is a big one, as people often have a mental image of "*if we build it, they will come*" with open source. Building communities takes time and is hard; we will dig into that more in later chapters.

Make sure your company and stakeholders don't measure open source quarter by quarter, or else you will never see success. Do think of milestones along the way, but be careful of being too time-bound, as open source projects ebb and flow over time, and the company itself needs time to establish an internal culture. In future chapters, we will dig into project growth, scaling, and culture, and establish the base layer on which to build everything.

Hopefully, you now have the internal support for and alignment with open sourcing code for your company. Let's take a look at a checklist of items for getting the code into open source.

Checklist for open sourcing a project or code base

If you are at this point, you have your company's support for contributing to open source. Pat yourself on the back – what you have just done isn't easy, and many before you never got to this point.

To actually make this happen, there are several key things you need to cover – let's take a look.

Legal review

As the code that will be open sourced is effectively your company's intellectual property, you need your legal team to review it before contributing to a project or launching a new open source project within one. There are also additional considerations for that code base that will come to mind for legal teams, such as the following:

- Is there any code licensed from a third party in the code to be contributed? If so, what rights does the company have to relicense and redistribute it?

- Does the company have any software patents that are implemented in the code base? If so, how comfortable is the company in providing other companies and individuals a license to that patent in the context of how it's used in the project?

- What license is being used for the project, and will that enable the reuse of the project in the same way it's used today (for example, if it's part of a product, can the company redistribute the product with that code in it)?

- What contribution requirements are needed from a legal perspective? Do contributors need to provide a copyright license? Do contributors need to grant software patent licenses explicitly, or does the given license for the project cover this adequately?

- Are there other legal requirements the company will have to comply with for the license chosen? For example, if a company were to choose the GNU General Public License, there may be a case of needing to provide the source code for the parts of a product that could be considered derivative work.

With legal review, especially the first time a company is looking to contribute to open source or start a project, there is often a fair amount of education that needs to take place. Fortunately, there are some great minds in open source legal matters that will be helpful, which we shared in the previous chapter. Really, the main thing a company needs to decide from a legal perspective is how much risk is palatable given the opportunity. In other words, in open sourcing the code that a company owns, the company is in a sense giving its intellectual property to the world, but the question for a company is how valuable it is to them. Is it something that would bootstrap a competitor? Is it a big differentiator from other solutions? Is it a piece of code that isn't super-unique to the company, and having it out there can create more value than holding onto it internally? This last question is one we see more and more in open source, as companies are realizing that while the piece of code could very well enable a competitor to bring a product to market faster, it lets the company itself seed the market with that technology and gives them a head-start before competitors can catch up.

One of the projects I worked with in the past, Zowe, wrestled with this. The companies who came together, Broadcom (then CA Technologies), IBM, and Rocket Software, all knew they had some really interesting code that they had built for revolutionizing the way we interacted with z/OS applications and data. They also all realized the pieces each of them had could be products of their own – and thus had good intellectual property value – but they came together and realized there was more value in the combined solution being open source so that they could focus on investments further up the stack in integrations with DevOps tooling, application monitoring, and deployment. That is the type of trade-off that comes from legal review, but more broadly from aligning the legal strategy with the overall company strategy.

Technical review

Finally, before you put any code out there, you need your technical teams to review it. There are a couple of parts to this:

- For one, the team should review it to make sure the code works. A project with code that can't be used or is missing big pieces will wither from the get-go.

- Second, it should have documentation with it. It doesn't need to be 100% fully documented from end to end, but enough that you can get up and running with the code, understand how it's used, and navigate around the code base.

- Thirdly, scrub the code for any code or comments that might be tied to internal projects or tools that aren't being open sourced. The prominent examples I see are comments with vulgarities, calling out employees by name, or mentioning IP addresses and passwords for internal servers.

- Finally, the code should be tested to help validate that it is working. In open source, people will take the code and modify it, so tests ensure that what is expected to work keeps working. It also is helpful with code that is compiled, such as C code, to ensure the binaries built are as expected.

One trap technical teams can fall into at this stage is "perfect is the enemy of the good." I often talk with companies looking to open source code, and they tell me, "We need to build all our documentation, fix all the bugs, get 100% unit test coverage, and address any feature needs before we release it as open source." I applaud that nobility, but at the same time, it can give a community the impression that the project is more of a *product* than a *project*, meaning comes off as finished work that doesn't need any help or code contributions. Having a few loose ends in there – not any that would make the code non-functional but instead give space for someone to add to the code base or build it out – is a great opportunity to cultivate a contributor base. We will dig more into this topic in *Chapter 6* and *Chapter 9*.

At this point, you should have a project out there or have donated code to a project, but how can you determine whether this has been valuable to your company? Let's look more into measuring success for an organization.

Measuring success in open source to the organization

Success in open source is really hard to define. It's not as straightforward as when building a product – in building a product, the success comes from the number of users or customers and the revenue from that, while in open source, usage is one part but so are the other potential impacts on the organization. Since open source projects tend not to be tied directly to revenue (after all, you are giving away code for free!), it becomes hard to succinctly define the **Return on Investment (ROI)**.

But, there are some other ways to measure success. Let's look at a few.

Setting (reasonable) goals

We touched on this earlier, but the open source project being launched or the work of the team contributing to an open source project should have certain goals. We talked about open source being a long-term versus short-term play, so goal planning has to have that in mind. But knowing how to show incremental progress is key to continuing to get the company to invest in the project, as well as for your benefit to know whether your project is on track.

Specific, Measurable, Achievable, Relevant, and Time-Bound (SMART) goals are a good framework for goal setting. This both helps you be clear on the expectations of the company and keeps you focused.

Here's an example that could be used for the COBOL Programming Course example from earlier in the chapter:

- Within the first month, we will have our course fully uploaded to our GitHub repository, with all our governance and contribution guides in place.

- In 6 months, we will have 20 individuals who have completed the coursework.

- In 9 months, we will have 10 contributions not from the initial contributors to the course.

- By the end of the first year, we will have 5 regular contributors outside of our organization, and 40 individuals who have completed the coursework.

Two observations about these goals. First, they are focused on two metrics of success – contributions and usage. There isn't a desire to get into GitHub clones or stars, issues opened, or the number of comments on a Hacker News post. This is a good thing, as the organization was sold on the concept of industry impact (more people learning COBOL when using more modern tools) and industry cooperation and alignment (having people contribute to one curriculum versus a bunch of other ones).

Second, they are goals that aren't too much of a stretch; with enough awareness of the project, it won't be too hard to hit these goals. It gives the project some breathing room to work through the kinks of launching an open source project, such as how to handle contributions, getting people used to the workflow, and keeping internal teams aligned with the community work. Not per se something trivial, and this helps set up the project for a better chance of success.

Identifying and showcasing how your organization is contributing

A big challenge that companies run into is how to recognize the impact, as, again, it's not something that is tied to a tangible result such as revenue or customer counts as with commercial products and offerings. However, that doesn't mean it's impossible to get a sense of impact; in reality, an organization can use the motivations for open sourcing as a way to both measure progress and identify the wins and impact made.

Some things to consider for an organization here include the following:

- **Adopting measurement tools that track multiple areas of contribution**: For smaller projects, the GitHub community metrics might work well and integrate code commits, open issues, pull requests, and discussions. As a project grows, more complex tools such as Bitergia or LFX Insights will become useful; both will let you better associate contributions to an organization automatically and leverage a variety of data sources from different collaboration tools.

- **Motivating your teams by tying open source contributions to annual goals or KPIs**: This shifts contributing to open source from "*do it when you have some time*" to "*this is part of my job, and I'm measured on it*." Be careful not to position this as a negative but as an opportunity, as nobody likes to be measured on something that feels like a chore.

- **Developing internal recognition programs for open source contributions**: This could be something as simple as an email to the team recognizing new contributors or top contributors during a certain period. It could also be an award for the most or most significant contributions in a period. In the early days of open source, I heard of one company that would give spot bonuses to anyone who merged code into the Linux kernel project; this motivated many to do so, though, from my understanding, the legal reviews one had to go through were so arduous that it often made it not worth those contributors' time relative to the bonus (but hey, it was a good try!).

The main point to consider with all this is aligning recognition to the goals the project aims to achieve. Recognizing the *most issues closed* might be a fun metric, but does that help achieve the goals of obtaining more users and greater industry adoption? As mentioned, when you have measurable goals, it makes it much easier to set rewards.

Summary

This chapter focused on many of the basics of a company going down the open source road the first time. Every major company that has been involved in open source has gone through this, and there is a fair amount of learning an organization has to go through to be successful with open source. Fortunately, there are great groups out there, such as the TODO Group, which is a group of leaders from OSPOs along many different verticals and horizontals, who can be resources for seeing how to be successful.

Getting an open source project off the ground is one thing, and indeed a feat to be proud of. But running one...that's another fun challenge. In the next chapter, we will build from the launch of an open source project and learn about how to best govern it based on the community and industry you are working in.

Further reading

[1] *Lessons Learned: IT's Biggest Project Failures*: https://www.pcworld.com/article/537052/it_project_failures.html

Governance and Hosting Models

If you have 10,000 regulations, you destroy all respect for the law.

- Winston S. Churchill

It's always interesting to speak of governance alongside open source if we recall from *Chapter 1, The Whats and Whys of Open Source,* the ethos of open source coming from hacker communities that saw problems in the existing methods of producing and using software. You might call them a bit *counter-culture,* which is a characteristic that stuck with the free and open source software communities for several years of their existence.

But over time, you quickly realize that having models for getting things done is key to long-term success and sustainability. This has been part of our human history for centuries. The Code of Hammurabi in 1755 BC (`https://en.wikipedia.org/wiki/Code_of_Hammurabi`) focused on creating a standard set of laws and justice for the Babylonians. While mostly known for the principle of *"an eye for an eye and tooth for a tooth,"* it did accomplish the goal of codifying what was before a loose set of documents and writings in such a way as to set a basis for a society to function. Open source governance aims to provide similar clarity to the community and set a similar basis for projects to work.

This chapter will discuss how governance works in an open source project, looking at a few approaches that consider the different ways to run and organize your project. You will first learn about all the aspects of governance that a project should consider. Then, we will discuss the roles and relationships between maintainers and contributors, how to involve financial support, and how to best document a governance structure. The specific topics to cover will include the following:

- What is open source governance?
- Roles in an open source project
- Documenting your open source project's governance structure
- Financial support for open source projects

Let's start with digging into defining governance as we talk about open source projects.

What is open source governance?

Open source governance is simply the processes and policies an open source project needs to have to enable it to function. This can mean many things:

- How can a project accept code?

- How does a project create a *release* of its code?

- Who determines what code comes into a project and what code doesn't?

- What does someone need to do to contribute code to a project?

- How are issues handled?

- How are security vulnerabilities addressed and disclosed?

- Who can speak on behalf of the project?

- Who owns the name, artwork, and other assets of the project?

- *...and the list goes on.*

There are a few approaches to structuring governance in a project, each with different benefits and weaknesses to consider. One thing to know with open source governance is it's not *one-size-fits-all*, as there are unique qualities in each community to consider. Let's take a look at some of the more common options.

"Do-ocracy"

The most basic type of governance is the one that is driven by who does the work – most often called **do-ocracy**. In the past, this type of governance had been referred to as a *meritocracy*, but we've seen that term go awry, as often merit is tied to forms of discrimination and non-inclusivity. If you dissect the idea of this form of governance, it's much more aligned with the ethos of *those who do the work make the decisions*.

Do-ocracy, while being one form of governance, is effectively the basis for most of the forms we will describe in this section of this chapter. In *Chapter 1, The Whats and Whys of Open Source*, I mentioned Alan Clark calling open source *"the ultimate scratch-your-own-itch model."* Open source in general is driven by the motivations of its users and contributors; while many are paid to work on open source, they are paid by those who are motivated to see the given project become successful.

Where a do-ocracy type of governance starts to show its cracks is when there are too many doers. It's not out of ill intent, but it's more of a scaling issue. These doers coming to *scratch their own itch* can have conflicting agendas. Or you might see doers ebb and flow in their commitment over time, allowing some parts of a code base to develop more while others languish. Do-ocracys can often seem like *closed clubs* from the outside, which can make newcomers joining challenging. At this point is where you will start to see different forms of governance take prominence; one we will look at next is the **Benevolent Dictators for Life** (**BDFL**) form of governance.

BDFLs

When projects run into conflict or struggle, we often see them look back to the founder for guidance. This is similar to how start-ups often work, where even if a founder isn't a CEO, there is the perception that the company is *their baby*, and there is deference toward them in terms of critical decision-making. Other times, the culture of the project aligns with the vision of its founder from the onset. Both of these cases line up squarely with the BDFL style of governance.

BDFL can be a type of governance that is part of a project from the onset, or it can emerge from the *do-acracy* form described earlier. We most often see the former: Rasmus Lerdorf with PHP, Linus Torvalds with the Linux kernel, and Guido van Rossum with Python. You could argue Lerdorf and PHP started as a do-acracy, as Lerdorf worked on PHP/FI 2 based on the feedback of users as he released various scripts to the community, and other developers contributed code to the project. While there were numerous developers on the project, the community looked back at Lerdorf for the critical decisions, and he still is widely regarded and respected in the PHP community.

With BDFL, governance is a two-edged sword; many of the successful projects had humble, inclusive, and constructive founder-leaders that helped set a positive tone on how the community should function. Others were divisive, which led to forks in the projects.

Even with the best BDFL, you still have the bottleneck of all decisions flowing through one person. Even Torvalds saw this with the Linux kernel which had several other key maintainers who jump in to spread the load, as there are thousands of lines of code changed each day in the Linux kernel. In many cases, we see projects recognize that there needs to be some sort of formality to leading the direction of projects, which is where we see the next type of open source governance kick in – a technical council.

Technical councils

It's hard being a founder – just ask anyone who has created a company. It's also equally hard for a founder to know when it's time to delegate. Founders typically have a keen eye for how they want their company to run and look. However, at some point, founders do realize they need to bring others in to handle parts of the organization.

In open source projects that I've worked with, one of the first things I've done is help establish a **Technical Steering Committee** (TSC). The idea is this group can help lead the project as a group and not rely solely on one person. Here's the challenge – getting people to step up to be in a leadership role, as many of the technologists I work with simply love the technology and are less interested in the perceived bureaucracy of leadership. So, as a founder-leader needs to bring more people in, it's often those in the community that want to step up and lead – which is what self-appointing council governance is all about.

You could make the argument that a "technical council" is really a direct evolution of "do-acracy." After all, both are driven by the people who do the work and want to help lead the work. "Technical councils" are the formalization of the "do-acracy" ethos, put together to build a project that can be sustainable and not have a bottleneck of a single leader. Many of the projects in the Apache Software Foundation, Academy Software Foundation, LF AI and Data Foundation, and LF Energy Foundation are like this. Developers gain interest in a project, and then step up to lead it.

Where the "technical council" type of governance becomes a problem is when the leaders on the council or board start to lose interest, or when there's a disconnect between leaders and the community. Again, much of this is a natural part of the growing pains that an open source project goes through. When this happens, communities look to become more democratic in their approach, which brings us to the **elected** type of governance.

Elected

Elected governance is the evolution from a council or board in which those roles are elected rather than self-nominated. This tends to happen most often when competing interests among individuals and companies arise in a project, and a project needs to ensure that decision-making is fair and equitable. To solve that, they hold elections.

Elections can be used for a multitude of reasons. It could be to select leaders themselves, who will serve a term for a certain period. The **Cloud Native Computing Foundation** (CNCF) **Technical Oversight Committee** (TOC) does this and has put together a formal election procedure and schedule (see https://github.com/cncf/toc/blob/main/process/election-schedule. md). The idea here is to ensure leaders are rotated regularly, which is good not only for helping bring new ideas and perspectives to a project but also to ensure leaders avoid burnout because they feel they can't leave a project.

We also see elections used for decision-making within a project community. The Apache Way (https://www.apache.org/theapacheway/index.html) has one of its key tenets as Consensus Decision Making (https://www.apache.org/foundation/how-it-works. html#decision-making). Projects that use the Apache Way (along with many others) use what's called *a lazy consensus approach*. This is done by soliciting a vote on an issue of -1, 0, or +1, and if somebody does solicit a -1 vote, they need to either propose an alternative solution or explain in detail why they voted no. What's good about this is it provides space for constructive dissension and helps a proposal come together that is inclusive of feedback from all parties.

There is another style of governance we see from projects that tend to be more driven by corporate interest, which falls into either single-vendor or foundation-backed governance. Let's look at both approaches, starting with a single vendor.

Single vendors

Single-vendor governance was most often aligned with the **Open Core** development model described in *Chapter 2, What Makes a Good Open Source Project?*. This type of governance is rooted in a single organization creating an open source project, which might be rooted in an existing product the organization has, or could be some internal tool they use that they want to put out as open source.

We see single-vendor governance across three use cases:

- The first is often a pragmatic one; they have some code they want to put out in open source with as little fuss as possible. It's often code put out there just for the sake of it; if it gets contributions, the organization might just consider that a bonus. There usually isn't a significant desire to get a large contributor base; it's most often put out there as something to help users or other individuals that might have a similar use case. These tend to be smaller projects. An example is **dispatch**, which has been put out by Netflix. Looking at their top contributors that aren't bots at the time of writing (`https://github.com/Netflix/dispatch/graphs/contributors`), they're two Netflix employees, with the next closest contributor only having a small number of commits.

- The second use case is the aforementioned **Open Core** model, which was described in *Chapter 2, What Makes a Good Open Source Project?*. Here, the reason for open sourcing is the desire to have a freemium version of a product available, with the intention of users using the project in production and then looking for a commercially supported version. MySQL, Elastic, and MongoDB, among other companies, have used this approach, which, as I talked about previously, has drawn criticism from open source communities.

- The third use case is where a company uses the **single-vendor** model to seed interest and determine the viability of a project growing. Kubernetes was released by Google in the summer of 2014 (`https://cloudplatform.googleblog.com/2014/06/an-update-on-container-support-on-google-cloud-platform.html`), and after positive feedback, they used it to launch the CNCF (`https://techcrunch.com/2015/07/21/as-kubernetes-hits-1-0-google-donates-technology-to-newly-formed-cloud-native-computing-foundation-with-ibm-intel-twitter-and-others`). Let's look more at this style of governance in the next section.

Vendor-neutral foundations

We discussed in *Chapter 1, The Whats and Whys of Open Source*, how open source foundations came to be vendor-neutral homes for open source projects. It's often foretold that a successful open source project can often hit a glass ceiling, with many of the following attributes:

- It's not clear how a project is funded or how it operates, or there is a perception that it primarily benefits a single vendor

- There isn't a neutral owner of assets, such as the project name, logo, domain names, social accounts, and other assets

- The copyright holder of the project is a single entity, giving them unilateral control to change the license and intellectual property policies without the community's input

- Vendors leveraging the technology don't feel they have a space to fairly collaborate, especially if they are competitors

- The legal, fiduciary, and financial aspects of the project are managed by one organization without transparency or given processes

When any or all of these attributes appear, the solution is to look at vendor-neutral foundation governance.

Open source projects looking to go down the vendor-neutral foundation governance path have one of two options. The first is to start their own foundation. Examples here include the Rust Foundation, Python Language Foundation, PHP Foundation, Ruby Central, and GNOME Foundation. Each of these groups tends to be a non-profit entity, is backed either by donations or corporate sponsorship, and usually employs staff to manage and run it. There is a lot of work and cost in setting up a foundation for an open source project, but communities that decide on this usually have very unique needs and considerations.

If projects are less inclined to do the work of forming their own legal entity, existing foundations such as the Apache Software Foundation, Eclipse Foundation, Linux Foundation, or OASIS Open are often natural choices. Foundations such as these have the infrastructure and expertise to set up foundation-backed governance, with lower costs than an open source project trying to do it themselves. Each foundation I mentioned has different niches and strengths that might be of value depending on the needs of the open source project and its community.

With an understanding of the various types of open source governance, let's look at how the roles within an open source project factor into overall project governance.

Roles in an open source project

As I've said repeatedly in this book, every open source project is different. That being said, we generally see a few different classifications of roles in an open source project. Let's take a look at them now, starting with the user.

Users

Everyone in an open source project starts by using the project. It's the starting point of the *scratch-your-own-itch* model of open source; if a project is useful to you, you become invested in it.

As an aside, something we will dig more into in *Chapter 6, Making Your Project Feel Welcoming*, and to some extent in *Chapter 7, Growing Contributors to Maintainers*, is why keeping a focus on how users can use the project is so important. It's also important to recognize that not every user will be a contributor, and that's okay. However, with lots of users comes not only a higher likelihood of contributors but also a social aspect, which shows potential contributors the value and opportunity of being a contributor.

Nevertheless, having at least some users helping to form the community is the goal, and that comes via contribution. Let's look at the contributor role.

Contributors

You become a contributor when you do something for the benefit of a project. This can be quite simple. For example, a person puts out a tweet saying, "Just tried X project and it was so good!" It could be someone answering a question on a forum about the project. They might open a bug report, or maybe they have advocated for the project by recommending it to a friend or colleague. These kinds of contributions are often tough to track but are critical to growing a project's momentum.

Classically, open source projects consider contributors to be those directly providing code to a project. This usually is a high bar for casual users, and more rigorous than just telling someone, "Hey, check out project X!" When you have someone who provides code to a project, this means they not only care about the project but are serious about its usage. In *Chapter 2, What Makes a Good Open Source Project?*, I talked about my contribution to the `repolinter` project (`https://github.com/todogroup/repolinter`).

My motivation for this contribution was that I used this with several of the open source projects I worked with, and found the issue so annoying that I felt compelled to fix it. That's a high bar; it means that not only was I a user but I also was happy enough as a user to be recommend it in several other projects – and so happy that I saw something not working right and wanted to fix it. If you see contributors like that, be thankful. We will dig more into this in a future chapter.

When you have contributors who hit the high bar of providing a project with code, you can tell they are deeply invested. These are maintainers, so let's look more at what that means.

Maintainers

Being a maintainer, sometimes referred to as a committer, is one part commitment and another part trust. The commitment comes from that person's constant presence in the project and interest in driving it forward. This is a person who sees this project as valuable to them, scratching their itch, and helping them with the tasks they might have.

However, the trust aspect is a big part of being a maintainer. Maintainers can change code in a project – that's a huge amount of trust. You trust a maintainer to know a code base well, including what code is appropriate and what code isn't. A maintainer can help a contributor refine their code, giving them advice and guidance. And a maintainer knows all the nuances and details of the code base. The maintainers know where the code is good, where it's okay, and where it needs work. They know how to look out for maintainability problems and address security issues. Big responsibility!

In smaller projects, maintainers are your top role. I work with projects that have only three to four maintainers and several dozen contributors – and that's perfectly healthy. There is some management involved in keeping these projects sustainable, which we will dig more into in *Chapter 7, Growing Contributors to Maintainers*. However, for larger projects, we often see either a subset of maintainers or appointed community members that consists of leaders; let's look at that role now.

Leaders

Leaders in open source communities aren't dictators (well, except for the aforementioned BDFL, but note we used the term *benevolent* there ;-)). Yes, leaders in open source projects set the direction, resolve conflicts, and help balance priorities, but more importantly, they serve the community.

Across all of the governance types I outlined earlier in this chapter, leadership in open source means ensuring everyone in the project and community can be successful. This is often referred to as *servant leadership*, meaning being a leader who provides support, resources, and guidance for others to be successful. Yes, there are decisions to be made, but they aren't made in a vacuum; they are made with the consideration (and often consultation) of the larger community. After all, the leaders won't have anything to lead if they make decisions that the community doesn't like.

With a better sense of the roles involved in an open source project, let's dig into how to document governance.

Documenting your open source project's governance structure

As I grow older, I realize the importance of writing things down, mostly because I forget things easily. Yes, I'm that parent who has almost forgotten to pick a kid up from practice, sent them to school without their lunch, or had to run up a form I forgot to sign. That's part of being human, which is why documenting governance is so important.

It's also important because it's critical to understand past decisions in order to make better ones in the future. The whole concept of amendments to the US Constitution is based on that concept. The founding fathers knew that there would be changes in society and evolution in technology in decades to come, so when crafting the US Constitution, they ensured that while the ideals documented would stay intact, future leaders would have the ability to build on them as times changed. Open source projects are similar; the needs of a project with 10 contributors are a lot different from one with 1,000 contributors.

Rust as a project is a good example; while it was an open source project inside of Mozilla Research, it had *corporate-backed governance*, which made alignment on features and directions easier for the maintainers. However, as it grew to a project with contributors from multiple organizations and formed its own foundation, that simple governance gave way to the need for more structure; thus, the Rust RFC process (`https://rust-lang.github.io/rfcs/`) was born.

There are a few key attributes to think about when documenting open source governance. Let's look at the first one – discoverability.

Discoverability

Put simply, make it easy to find the source of governance. Starting with a good README file is usually the best way to get off the ground. A good README file answers the following questions:

- What is the project and what does it do?
- How can you install and use the project?
- If you have issues or questions, where should you go?
- If you want to contribute to the project, how do you do so?
- Where is the project going (also known as a roadmap)?

Resources such as Make a README (`https://www.makeareadme.com/`) and Awesome README (`https://github.com/matiassingers/awesome-readme`) are great guides for getting started.

Eventually, a README file can get long, so it's recommended to break out the content into several files. Typically files you see include the following:

- `LICENSE`, which details the open source license for the project
- `CONTRIBUTING`, which helps people know how to contribute code to a project
- `RELEASE`, letting people know how releases happen
- `SUPPORT`, where users can go for support

The key part again here is making sure people can find the project's governance, so sticking to conventional names such as the preceding ones is really important.

Let's look now at the next key attribute of documenting governance – simplicity.

Simplicity

I sometimes work on projects that feel like they need to make a lot of rules. When you deconstruct the thinking, it usually comes down to fear (which aligns with picking a license, as we chatted about in *Chapter 3, Open Source License and IP Management*). The feedback I always give is that lots of rules can make it more difficult to get things done, and as we spoke about earlier in this chapter, it's hard to anticipate every situation.

Some core bits need to be in every open source project's governance:

- How do you contribute code to the project?

- What is the license for a project?

- How do releases (or the equivalent thereof) happen?

- How are decisions made?

- What are the roles, and how does somebody attain a role?

- Who can you talk to if you have issues or questions?

If an open source project has answers to those points, they tend to be pretty good to go from the start.

I joke with projects sometimes that *we don't get tattoos of the project's governance on our arms*, not just because it would be a really boring tattoo but also because good governance evolves. Let's talk about that attribute – flexibility.

Flexibility

We've talked a lot in this chapter about how open source projects evolve. To do so effectively, they need to be able to easily adjust over time. This is where flexibility in governance comes in.

A good example here is the Zowe project I mentioned earlier. In the early days of the project, their predominant leadership was driven by product managers rather than developers. This was for both pragmatic as well as cultural reasons; pragmatically, code from three companies came together, which was complex, and culturally, product managers in that industry tended to be the primary drivers of software development.

As time went on, a disconnect between the developers on the ground and product management was recognized. Additionally, things such as releases being driven by a single organization were more natural for product management; this becomes a lot harder in open source with multiple organizations contributing. As they assessed the situation, they found that having stronger technical leadership would help them execute better, and thus they transitioned processes to give maintainers more control and leadership, putting the product managers in a supporting and advisory role. This has helped the project become immensely more stable, but also more open to contributions. It was all made possible by including flexibility in the governance model.

One important thing to note about flexibility comes back to the point in the Apache Way on driving consensus. Being flexible means understanding the community and working with them to find a solution. Most importantly, when there is dissension, understand the concerns and try to accommodate them.

One last thing to look at with governance is how to support it financially.

Financial support for open source projects

You may have heard the saying that open source is *"free as in speech, not free as in beer."* The *free* part of open source is the freedom of what you can do with the code, more than the cost of development or ownership being free. There is an economic cost to developing software, open source or proprietary, and that cost has to be borne by someone.

Too often that cost in open source is borne by the maintainer, as they give their time and energy to running an open source project that is used broadly. An **xkcd** comic (https://xkcd.com/2347/) provides a great illustration of this problem; modern applications stacks have so many dependencies, and a dependency quickly can become a critical one without people realizing how taxing it is on the maintainer.

We will explore more in *Chapter 7, Growing Contributors to Maintainers, Chapter 9, Handling Growth,* and *Chapter 10, Commercialization of Open Source,* including the nuances and tensions you see between users and maintainers and why burnout is so prevalent.

There are a few general classifications for open source funding – let's look at the first one, the **tip jar**.

Tip jars

The tip jar funding model is quite similar to the person playing an instrument in the street, having their instrument case open and hoping that passers-by drop a few dollars in the case. The mentality that goes into this model is, "Hey, here's some code I've written. Please donate whatever you can if it's valuable to you." Some project maintainers will link a PayPal or Venmo account for donations. Others might point to an Amazon Wish List, direct people to add funds to their Starbucks gift card, or maybe ask for donations to a cause that is important to them. Some open source projects that have taken this approach include Transmission (https://transmissionbt.com/donate.html), Conversations (https://github.com/sponsors/iNPUTmice), and Armory (https://armory3d.org/).

The biggest challenge with the *tip jar* funding model is that it's not sustainable, meaning that the revenue ebbs and flows. Another major challenge is that if you look at the cost of supporting a user, it often might outweigh any *tip* given by them. For example, a user opens three issues that collectively require 5 hours of development work. Let's say optimistically, the user *tips* the equivalent of USD $5. Assuming an hour of a developer's work is worth $20 (which is a low estimate), the cost for that user who gave $5 now is $95.

Additionally, the tip jar approach gives users the sense that *contributing* is putting money in that tip jar, where that user might be able to provide a more beneficial contribution. Expanding on that line of thinking from the example in the previous paragraph, would you as a maintainer rather have $5 or have that person help update the documentation around the three issues reported, which collectively is likely 1 hour of work? The math is pretty clear; while putting money in the *tip jar* is contributing, there are paths that the user could likely take to contribute that would be more valuable to the maintainer, while at the same time, bringing in the contributor as a participant in the project. This is a concept we will expand more on in *Chapter 7, Growing Contributors to Maintainers*.

There is another form of the *tip jar* that is a bit more formal, and we will explore it next – **crowdfunding**.

Crowdfunding

Crowdfunding is likely a concept many of you are familiar with, as it has become a part of our society through sites such as Kickstarter, Patreon, and GoFundMe. In open source, crowdfunding transitions from the informality of the tip jar to having something a bit more structured.

One key difference with crowdfunding is the ability to use it to raise funding for targeted development. This can go one of two ways; one model is that a maintainer puts out funding requests for a specific issue or feature, and once the required amount of funding comes in, the maintainer pursues development. This is not only a way for the maintainer to help fund themselves to do the work but it also helps that maintainer assess the value of work to the community.

With crowdfunding, you will also see a degree of formality or recognition toward donors, similar to how you might see various levels of donors to a theater or arts program. Blender is a great example of this (`https://fund.blender.org/`), where multiple tiers offer the donor a badge based on the monthly donation amount, and at higher levels, donors are recognized on the Blender website itself.

One thing about crowdfunding is that there often is a need for a legal organization to accept the donations. Many donors expect some tax benefits depending upon their location, and if the project doesn't have non-profit status, this could add to the overhead costs of accepting donations. For this reason, we often see projects look at a *foundation* funding model, which we will explore in a bit. First, let's look at one alternative path – **single-organization funding**.

Single-organization funding

If an organization sees an open source project as valuable to their business, they will often look to fund it either through donations, providing funds for developers to travel or the project to participate in events, or hiring all the key developers to be on their staff.

Note that this funding type, as worded, might make it seem like the governance is a single vendor as well, and that is not necessarily the case. Many projects around Apache Hadoop, such as Apache BigTop, Apache Ambari, and Apache Spark, were bootstrapped around single-organization funding even though the *foundation* governance model was used. Many of these projects with rapid user adoption quickly grew to have multiple vendors providing developer resources, but also had other needs, such as outreach, specialty built infrastructure, or events, funded by a primary organization.

The challenge with single-organization funding is similar to that of single-organization governance; that organization becomes the fulcrum for ensuring the project continues to move forward. For example, when Mozilla laid off many employees that were the core parts of Rust in 2020 (`https://blog.mozilla.org/en/mozilla/changing-world-changing-mozilla/`), this was seen as a potential blow to that community. Luckily, because of the heavy use of Rust in other organizations, talent was quickly snapped up, but it did cause friction in the community.

From the Mozilla layoffs, a foundation to ensure sustainable funding was born – let's look at the **foundation funding model**.

Foundations

The main idea behind the foundation funding model is to have all the funding go into a single, vendor-neutral entity that is overseen by multiple stakeholders and has an independent organization managing the day-to-day finances. For large, critical projects, this has been the trend over the past decade or two; it helps show a natural separation between corporate interests and community interests, and it helps bring together a diverse number of organizations to help fund a project.

There are both funding models for a single project and an *umbrella* of related projects. How the funding works can be different as well. Let's look at two examples:

- First is the **Python Software Foundation** (**PSF**), which is a US 501(c)(3) non-profit corporation that is an example of a foundation for a single project. The PSF serves three roles for the community; one is to run and manage the annual PyCon event in North America and support other regional Python events globally. Secondly, it manages the legal aspects of the Python project, including licensing and trademark defense. Thirdly, the PSF funds Python development grants.

  The PSF is centered around the Python project but also helps manage other related projects, such as the **PyPi** packaging service. There is some staff to help manage backend operations, as well as help with fundraising. There is also a governing board to provide oversight. Still, neither the board nor the staff gets involved in the technical direction or priorities for the project itself.

- Another great example of an umbrella foundation project is **LF Energy Foundation** (**LFE**), a home for open source projects specific to the energy industry and hosted by the Linux Foundation. There are many similarities between the PSF and LFE; both have staff and boards to manage day-to-day work and oversight, and neither the staff nor the board gets involved in the technical direction or priorities of the project itself. Both also fund events, infrastructure, legal aspects, and outreach, as well as providing funding for specific development needs.

- One difference between LFE and the PSF is the legal entity type. While the PSF is a US 501(c)(3) entity, LFE is a US 501(c)(6) entity. The difference in legal entity types in the US comes down to two distinctions; one being that a 501(c)(6) is considered a "trade organization" by the **Internal Revenue Service** (**IRS**), which means it is driven by member funding. The second is that contributions made to a 501(c)(6) are not tax-deductible in the US, while donations to a 501(c)(3) entity generally are.

The main differentiator is that with multiple projects hosted, there is a need to have some oversight and coordination between the efforts while at the same time ensuring each hosted project has autonomy. This means that there isn't an outside group involved in release planning, appointing maintainers, approving code submissions, and setting the direction. This coordination is handled by a **Technical Advisory Council** (**TAC**), which sets a life cycle for the project maturity (`https://wiki.lfenergy.org/display/HOME/Technical+Project+Lifecycle`), as well as a liaison into each project to help support its growth and connect it with other industry initiatives and hosted projects. The TAC has guidelines to help them determine which projects are a fit and which aren't through their guiding principles (`https://wiki.lfenergy.org/display/HOME/LF+Energy+Guiding+Principles`).

Summary

When writing this chapter, I came across its opening quote from Sir Winston Churchill – it really is great advice for open source projects.

If there is one piece of advice I could give any open source project, it would be to create the governance you need for today and not create governance for a hypothetical situation in the future. The needs of a project and the culture of its community change over time and adjusting the governance to support those needs ensures buy-in and engagement.

With this chapter, we've covered much of the groundwork for building an open source project. As we get into *Chapter 6, Making Your Project Feel Welcoming*, we will now look at more soft skills and community development to help grow and diversify your community, which is a key part of a successful open source project.

Part 2:
Running an
Open Source Project

In this part, we will focus on topics that will help you understand how to run a successful open source project. You will first learn about strategies for creating a welcoming open source project. Then, you will learn the best way to grow contributors in your project to become the maintainers of your project's future. Finally, you will learn about strategies and experiences in dealing with conflict in open source projects and the best way to manage growth.

This part contains the following chapters:

- *Chapter 6, Making Your Project Feel Welcoming*
- *Chapter 7, Growing Contributors to Maintainers*
- *Chapter 8, Dealing with Conflict*
- *Chapter 9, Handling Growth*

6
Making Your Project Feel Welcoming

In the United States, often, when a family moves into a new neighborhood, there is what's called a *"welcome wagon"* to help welcome people to the area. It's not a literal wagon (at least not here in Doylestown, Ohio). Instead, it's a group in a community that gets together and provides welcome gifts to someone moving into the area to help them get to know their new neighbors, and vice versa.

The idea of the *"welcome wagon"* is to help a new neighbor get past the awkwardness of getting to know a new group of people. As adults, it can be challenging to meet and make new friends, so local customs such as the *"welcome wagon"* help break the ice, so to speak, with the hope of integrating newcomers to the neighborhood into its activities and social circles.

Too often, open source projects look at themselves and say, "why isn't anyone contributing to my project?" There can be multiple aspects to this, whether being unable to find out how to contribute, feeling intimidated by donating, or thinking they have anything of value to contribute. As with the *"welcome wagon"* in neighborhoods, good open source projects look to bring in and make the community feel welcome. It might not be a basket of cookies or a casserole as with the *"welcome wagon,"* but it can be as simple as a thank-you in a pull request, a mention in a release note, or dropping a sticker in the mail to them.

With burnout as the number one challenge faced by open source projects, this chapter will focus on ensuring your project is welcoming to new contributors. We will cover some of the basic things a project should have, how to best support end users, and embracing community-driven collaboration. Specific topics we will focus on include the following:

- Getting your project set up for newcomers
- Supporting end users effectively
- Being where the conversation is

Let's start with the basics – getting the project set up for newcomers.

Getting your project set up for newcomers

The first part of having a welcoming project is to give the appearance that maintainers want newcomers. That might sound flippant, but too often, it doesn't appear that way. First impressions are everything in an open source project, and how your project is perceived is gauged by that first impression. Individuals and organizations use, participate, and invest in projects that they perceive to be run well.

Let's kick things off by looking at the basics of the infrastructure.

Setting up your project infrastructure

When you first come to an open source project, you likely have several expectations.

First, you want to find the code itself. We see most projects these days leverage a service such as GitHub or GitLab, which offer free code hosting services to open source projects. Additionally, there's the advantage of being close to other open source projects, which can help your project be more naturally discoverable. When you come to a project, the first file you often look for is the README file. If you are looking for guidance on setting up a README file and other governance-related files, review *Chapter 6, Making Your Project Feel Welcoming*.

However, a good open source project has much more than just a README file; it has different channels for communication. Things to consider include the following:

- **Mailing list**: Email is always the lowest-common-denominator medium anyone can easily engage with. Mailing lists are ways to hold conversations with other people in a project asynchronously, which lets people who might be in different areas of the world collaborate without having to worry about whether someone is available. Mailing lists also save past messages in archives, which are great ways to track past decisions and conversations and reference them in future discussions. Open source projects generally use services such as Google Groups, groups.io, or GNU Mailman.

- **Discussion forums**: Many communities will evolve from using mailing lists to using forums, which tend to be more discoverable and have better search capabilities than mailing lists do. They also, at the same time, have more overhead, as community members might have to moderate discussion threads and channels or help coordinate discussions. However, the way that multiple threads can be discussed simultaneously is one nice advantage forums have. Some communities leverage self-hosted or managed-hosting solutions, such as phpBB, Discourse, or vBulletin, which give a high level of control to the project, but can inadvertently create a *"walled garden."* Some projects try to get greater visibility using tools such as Reddit or Stack Overflow, where multiple communities converge but do have a degree of separation. The nice part here is the discoverability, but the downside can be the lack of control over the content and service of the project. Each project will have trade-offs to consider.

- **Instant communication channels**: In the early days of open source, you'd often see project members hang out on IRC channels, which was a great way to not only get quick help on a problem but also meet others in the community and get a sense of the culture and communication style. Over time, we've seen open source projects look at other tools such as Slack, Discord, Rocket.Chat, and Mattermost, each providing similar forms of instant communication and community interaction using different platforms and clients.

- **Meetings**: Whether this is a virtual web conference call or an in-person get-together, these are opportunities for project participants to speak live with one another. I tend to see meetings as the first point of engagement, especially for those contributing on behalf of a larger corporation. Just like with instant communication channels, these meetings are a good way to gauge the culture and communication style of a project.

Not all projects use all of these mediums. Good projects though tend to use a few of them. Here are some good rules of thumb:

- Always look to have at least one asynchronous method of communication that is easily discoverable, such as mailing lists or forums. This not only makes it easier to have people from different time zones collaborate but also those that might contribute during the evenings in a project that collaborates throughout the day. It also builds up a knowledge library, which while in a raw discussion forum, might not be easily discoverable, but at least gets things written down and makes it easier to build documentation or guides later on.

- Set a regular cadence for meetings and try to make sure that there is an option to join virtually. The regular cadence part is key, as on the one hand, this makes it easier for scheduling (that is, everyone knows that we meet on the first Thursday of the month at 12:00 pm GMT), and on the other, keeps touchpoints on the project more regular to help move work forward. We all get busy, but if we know we have a standing meeting to provide an update in, this at least consciously makes us plan for discussions to happen at the meeting (or lets you consciously say, "nothing new to report, let's skip today's meeting").

- Keep any meetings structured while still keeping them casual. Having a formal meeting might give the impression that the meeting is professional, but it can also be viewed as rigid and hard to participate in. However, a meeting with no structure or agenda will suffer low attendance, as people won't know why to attend. Good meeting practices apply to community meetings – send out agendas ahead of time, adhere to the agenda topics, keep time for open discussion, and share notes and action items afterward.

- Make it clear where to go for what kind of communication. Driving consensus is hard over an instant communication channel while immediate help is hard to come by on a mailing list.

Now that you have a good project infrastructure setup, let's put out that "*welcome mat*" and look at how to build a great getting started guide.

Creating a getting started guide

There's a general ethos amongst those in user experience design circles on the importance of the "*first 5 minutes*" that a user uses an application. If a user is successful in those first 5 minutes, it's usually a good sign that they will become a long-term user. On the flip side, if a user isn't able to be successful in the first 5 minutes, you've often lost them. Open source projects are much the same, even with a more developer- and hacker-oriented crowd; if someone can't figure out how to use the code quickly, they will move on to the next project.

Getting started guides can vary depending on the project and technology. For a command-line tool, using the --help command-line switch or using man should trigger a usage guide. Here's an example for the asana-cli project (https://github.com/AlJohri/asana-cli):

```
$ asana --help
Usage: asana [OPTIONS] COMMAND [ARGS]...

  Examples:

  asana list workspaces
  asana list projects --workspace="Personal Projects"
  asana list tasks --workspace="Personal Projects"
    --project="Test"
  asana list sections --workspace="Personal Projects"
    --project="Test"
  asana list tasks --workspace="Personal Projects"
    --project="Test" --section="Column 1"

  asana delete tasks --workspace="Personal Projects"
    --project="Test" --section="Column 1"

  asana mark tasks --workspace="Personal Projects"
    --project="Test" --section="Column 1" --completed
  asana mark tasks --workspace="Personal Projects"
    --project="Test" --section="Column 1" --not-completed

  asana move tasks --workspace="Personal Projects" --from-
    project="Test" --from-section="Column 1"
    --to-section="Column 2"Commands:

Options:
  --help  Show this message and exit.
```

In this case, the guide connects a few common use cases to the commands used and then the full set of command options available. This is the appropriate level of detail for people used to working with a command-line interface and Asana. It also does a good thing by putting the getting started guide in the flow of working with the tool, meaning that the user has to go nowhere else but the command shell to understand how to use it.

For more complex projects with different use cases, a deeper guide tends to be a better approach. Let's look at the **GET STARTED** page for **ONNX** as an example:

Figure 6.1 – ONNX Get Started page (https://onnx.ai/get-started.html)

This page presumes the user already understands machine learning models and has a model t this tool. So, the first task the user sees is getting that model into the right format for the option they choose, because otherwise, the tool isn't very useful. This is a perfect ap audience and is a big part of making sure the user is successful in the first 5 minute

We've seen from these examples two common themes to have in mind when started guide:

- Knowing your users and giving them the right level of education for where they are at. For the `asana-cli` project, trying to explain project management isn't very useful, as the user is already well educated on the topic, or else they wouldn't be seeking out a companion tool.

- Focusing on showing user success in the first 5 minutes. From the ONNX example, if the user can get a machine learning model in the ONNX format, they are set up for success.

A getting started guide serves as the digital presence for welcoming people to your project. Still, as people look to engage more profoundly, they will start to connect with maintainers and contributors. How that experience goes is key to someone wanting to continue being involved. Let's look at some strategies around being welcoming to new contributors.

Being welcoming to new contributors

As we learned in *Chapter 1, The Whats and Whys of Open Source*, in the early days of free software, generally, software was developed *"behind the scenes"* with limited end user involvement. There was a multitude of reasons for that, but one was that end users were generally considered not to have the right level of knowledge of the domain or project design to be helpful. We see this carried over to open source projects today occasionally, which can be a deterrent and hurt the later growth of a contributor into a maintainer. We will see more on this in *Chapter 7, Growing Contributors to Maintainers*.

Contributors are quite often intimidated by a project; a project has people they may not know, people from a different race, culture, gender, or region, or even people that might be high-level experts in a particular domain. Many software engineers have trouble bridging those social dynamics, so being on top of things is a good way to ease that worry.

hyper project does a great job of this with their contributor's guide:

~tributor's Guide

...'re probably interested in contributing to hyper . First, I'd like to say:

'ive-and-die based on the support they receive from others, and the

'ing hyper is incredibly generous of you.

~adthedocs.io/en/latest/contributing.html)

.les and processes – it starts with appreciation.

.nother key to success. Let's look at another example , the first pull request from a user (that user being me):

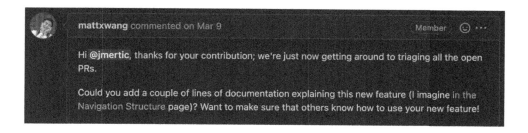

Figure 6.3 – Pull request response (https://github.com/just-the-docs/
just-the-docs/pull/726#issuecomment-1063254623)

Here, the project representative is humble at first; the maintainer realizes I contributed nearly 5 months prior and acknowledges that as part of the thank-you. As a contributor, this tells me that they weren't ignoring me on purpose, just that life got in the way, and they still appreciate my contribution. Secondly, the maintainer replies by asking me to add documentation, but not in the form of, "You obviously didn't read our contribution guide because otherwise you would have known to do this." Instead, the maintainer positions it in terms of value (wanting to make sure others know about the new feature) and offers guidance on where to add the documentation. If you read the entire pull request, you'll see the maintainer continues to help me to make sure the placement and form of the documentation are correct.

You see the themes of "*helpfulness*" and "*humbleness*" as attributes of both examples. When I talk with project leaders, I share that leadership in open source is "*servant leadership*," meaning the project leaders are there to ensure the community of contributors and users have what they need to be successful. Keeping that mindset toward all contributions, even challenging ones, helps set the right tone on how a project looks at its contributors. More on this in *Chapter 8, Dealing with Conflict*.

Welcoming is the first step in making a newcomer want to stay around, but to keep someone around, the project must show how they value a newcomer's contributions. Let's look at ways to quickly and meaningfully recognize newcomers when they make an impact.

Recognizing newcomers when they make an impact

Newcomers often see contributing to open source as a way to establish their portfolio of work for potential employers, as these code contributions help showcase the skill a developer has. We will dig deeper into this in *Chapter 11, Open Source and the Talent Ecosystem*, but knowing this, it's important to recognize contributors for their own career growth in addition to showcasing your project as a welcoming one for newcomers.

Every project has a way to recognize newcomers, even if they have no funds. A simple way is a thank-you in the release notes; here is an example from the just-the-docs project recognizing not only the new feature but also the contributor:

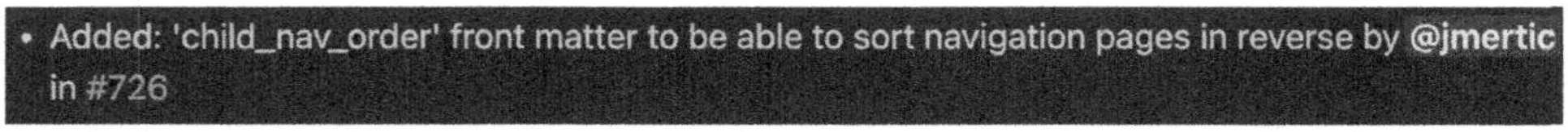

> • Added: 'child_nav_order' front matter to be able to sort navigation pages in reverse by **@jmertic** in #726

Figure 6.4 – Recognition of contribution in the release notes

What's nice here is that this becomes searchable within GitHub as me being a contributor and something that I could link back to.

If you have a budget, then there are a few other options you can choose from:

- Sometimes, contributors have a wish list from a site such as Amazon; go find something on there and buy it for them.

- Send them a t-shirt or sticker. If you don't have any handy, there are many print-on-demand services, such as Spreadshirt, that can create one quickly. More on this in *Chapter 12, Marketing for Open Source - Advocacy and Outreach.*

- Digital badge services such as Credly are increasingly popular, and setting parameters to recognize contributors with a badge helps give them something to put right on their resume.

We've looked at several key pieces and practices in the project setup for newcomers to the project. One big reason people come to a project is to get help, so let's look at ways to support end users effectively.

Supporting end-users effectively

Open source projects generally aren't set up to provide the level of support you need for a commercial product and for good reason. First is that just from a staffing point of view, there's rarely the capacity to dedicate the same level of support. And second, in open source, we see a community model, meaning we users help other users, and sometimes bugs and workarounds are worked out together in the open rather than behind closed doors.

While a project can learn from commercial products on strategies for supporting end users, there are some nuances in doing so in an open source project. Let's begin by looking at what effective support looks like with one of the first touchpoints an end user has with the project – submitting a new issue.

Managing issues

We talked earlier in this chapter about project infrastructure and in *Chapter 5, Governance and Hosting Models*, about the importance of a README file to guide newcomers on the governance of a project. One piece of that governance is how to raise issues, and it is also one of the key questions someone will look for an answer to in a project.

Some key attributes of good issue management include the following:

- **Making it easy to find out how to submit an issue**: Many projects that use GitHub or GitLab will use the default issue tracker for that issue, as users generally know of that part of the tool and there is little friction in getting somebody to submit an issue. If a project goes down the path of using an external issue-tracking tool, the project will want to call that out explicitly in the README, CONTRIBUTING, or SUPPORT file in the project.

- **Helping guide a user on how to submit an effective issue**: The best way to do this is in the flow of submission; if a project uses GitHub, you can use an issue template (https://docs.github.com/en/communities/using-templates-to-encourage-useful-issues-and-pull-requests/configuring-issue-templates-for-your-repository) to both help users self-triage issues into the right bucket (that is, feature request, bug report, and security issue) and make sure the user provides the relevant information for the project to debug (that is, the version used, the operating system or browser used, the exact error message, and the reproducibility steps).

- **Having a regular cadence of reviewing issues and communicating that with users**: If you use GitHub, there are various GitHub Actions you can use to automate a friendly message that lets a user know this. The key part of this is cadence – even if you aren't able to provide a resolution to the issue – is simply saying something such as, *"Thank you for the issue. We are a bit backlogged at the moment, but will get back soon."* This sets expectations for the user and lets them know that you are listening.

- **On the flip side, leaving an issue out there with no new comments or activity for a long period of time sends the message that a project ignores issues**: Making sure to be proactive in reviewing stale issues from time to time not only shows the project is actively paying attention but also helps the project prioritize better (a project might even want to look at automation with something such as the Stale Issue GitHub Action at https://github.com/marketplace/actions/close-stale-issues. Even something as simple as marking an issue for a future release makes a difference – the key here is letting the user know the issue has been acknowledged, is considered valuable, and that there is a plan for a resolution.

Having a good issue management process shows end users that you value their feedback and appreciate them as users, but submitting an issue isn't the only way that end users engage, so let's look at broader community and developer management strategies.

Community and developer management

As a project grows and many users use the project in various ways, you will see a natural community form around it. This happening is a great thing – and these communities can take on a life of their own (more on that in the next section of this chapter), but it also requires work for the project to manage.

When I use the word "*manage*," this isn't about control but more about support and guidance. Think of the reason people use an open source project in the first place; it solves a problem they have. When the user comes to a project, they are looking to solve that problem, and the role of community and developer management is to be a guide. Good community and developer management has these attributes:

- It recognizes the needs of a user, meaning that it can see the comments and feedback and help roll them back into the project or showcase how to resolve them.

- It's proactive, meaning it looks to share content and insights as early as possible so that other users don't have the same struggles.

- It's embedded into the community by engaging other community members directly, speaking at events, doing meetups, posting videos, and other engagement activities.

- It's empathic and positive, as good community and developer management takes into account that the users often come to the community out of frustration, and the role of community and developer management is to be understanding, help resolve concerns, and have the user walk away with a positive experience. More on this in *Chapter 8, Dealing with Conflict*.

A great example of the value of good community and developer management is looking at when Apache Cloudstack and OpenStack were the two predominant open source projects for **Infrastructure as a Service (IaaS)**. Both technologies were fundamentally sound, and each had something that the other didn't. However, in the end, OpenStack came to be the market leader. Why was that? OpenStack heavily invested in community and developer management, which helped users and developers be more successful quickly, and helped the project itself grow to solve the problems the users had.

While a vibrant community can provide an immense amount of support for an end user, it's never going to be at the level that commercial support would be. Let's look at how to best have commercial permission to support end users effectively.

Commercial support

We spoke at the beginning of this section about how open source projects are not set up to offer commercial support, but that doesn't mean that other companies can't step in and offer it.

A great example is in the Linux distribution space, where among a vast number of Linux distributions are several that offer commercial support (examples include Canonical, Red Hat, and SUSE). Each of these distributions is offered for free or has a free offering, but at the same time, they can provide the level of commercial support that a larger company would require. After all, not many open source project maintainers want to be fixing bugs at 11:00 P.M. on Christmas Eve.

We see more formal models of this in other projects. The **Kubernetes Certified Support Provider (KCSP)** program (`https://www.cncf.io/certification/kcsp/`) provides a mechanism for vendors to indicate that they offer commercial support for Kubernetes. What's nice about this program is it's not run by any one vendor, but by the Kubernetes community itself, so end users have an unbiased and objective view of the service providers, knowing that the community standards around training, business models, experience, and upstream support. This particular requires vendors to be members of the **Cloud Native Computing Foundation** which means some of the revenue they take in from support is funneled right back into the for infrastructure, events, and community support.

A key takeaway is that commercial organizations getting involved in an open source project is a good thing, just as we discussed in *Chapter 4, Aligning the Business Value of Open Source for Your Employer*. As described in *Chapter 5, Governance and Hosting Models*, good governance helps ensure vendor neutrality for a more collaborative project.

We've looked at some strategies for supporting end users in your project's community. What we often see in vibrant communities is that the community starts to form new spaces for collaboration, which can be helpful for the project but also does require some degree of management from the project. Let's look at this now.

Being where the conversation is

Nearly all the best things that came to me in life have been unexpected, unplanned by me.

– Carl Sandburg

Open source communities are not something you can completely design. Indeed, you can provide infrastructure, support, and guidance, as we've spoken about in this chapter, but the magic of them is when they take on a life of their own. When I was a community manager at SugarCRM, I remember always being amazed and delighted at the interesting extensions that the community members built and the motivations behind them. Linus Torvalds did an interview a few years back, and when asked about what was surprising about Linux development, he said the following:

"What I find interesting is code that I thought was stable continually gets improved. There are things we haven't touched for many years, then someone comes along and improves them or makes bug reports in something I thought no one used. We have new hardware, new features that are developed, but after 25 years, we still have old, very basic things that people care about and still improve."

(Source: `https://www.linux.com/news/linus-torvalds-explains-how-linux-still-surprises-and-motivates-him/`)

We often see virtual collaboration as the first channel to take off for communities, so let's look at how to best manage online forums and social media.

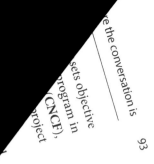

cial channels

pen source enthusiasts grow in their careers, you tend to see them
munities. Back in the early days of open source, we saw platforms
ity, and over time, newer platforms such as Reddit, Stack Overflow,
enter point for these discussions. Add to that the growth of social
an be talked about all over, but it might be hard to stay on top

ut conversations regarding their project for so many reasons, but
mmunities in which collaboration only happens through specific forums
can become an unintended *"walled garden."* But it's not easy – here are some tips and
practices:

- First is to use the subscription features in Reddit, Stack Overflow, and other platforms to be alerted when your project is mentioned. Other services can track the web more generally, such as Google Alerts. These are great ways to use automation to alert a project about a conversation happening.

- When you find these conversations, promote them! Sharing that someone on Hacker News used your project in an interesting way not only shows appreciation for that person sharing their story but also showcases the project as mainstream.

- Comment in those conversations to connect the author of the comment and the other commenters to areas of your documentation or other blog posts. This helps connect someone who might have stumbled onto that conversation to the right resource. If something isn't written up, write it up and link it back to that conversation. This helps drive people back into the project but ensures there aren't loose ends of discussion out there at the same time.

- Post about the project on those online forums and social channels where the discussion is happening. This comes back to what we talked about with good community and developer management – it's proactive.

One thing I will say from personal experience as a community manager is that managing all these online forums and social channels can be taxing. It's easy to get caught up in discussions, and before you know it, a full day has gone by. Think about smart engagement and management; one tip I would share is to limit how much time you spend on this in a given day/week and try to stick to that. It's okay if you miss a post out there; what I have found out is that on the online forums and social channels, you see the participants starting to do the work for you.

Community members often start with virtual engagement and then move to more direct engagement with peers in the community. Let's look at the role of regional meetups and events.

Regional meetups and events

Meetups and events are a large part of the open source culture. They are also crucial for sparking collaboration. If there is one thing I've seen as we've emerged out of the COVID-19 pandemic and started to be a part of in-person events again is that face-to-face interactions spark innovation and collaboration. Online collaboration can provide some of this, but it's so much more natural and organic in person.

Having your project be part of events such as these is an easy way to increase its visibility:

- First of all, give talks at conferences. Larger conferences can be harder to break into as a new speaker, but smaller regional events or meetups always look for new topics and speakers. Some of these events also provide travel funding or stipends to offset costs, which can be helpful if the project isn't sponsored or supported by your employer.

- When you are at a conference, don't sit in the corner with your computer hacking away at your project. Go up to people and meet them. Attend sessions of interest, speak with the speaker afterward to learn about the work they are doing, and see whether there are ways to work together or maybe get some advice. This organic conversation is better known as the "*hallway track*", and is where so many interesting ideas start.

- If your session is recorded, share it in your community or via your social channels. If not, share the slide deck and write up the event. This shows a connection to both the event, its community, and your project's community as well. Plus, it also gets that content to a wider audience.

Communities from digital and in-person collaboration start to gravitate around natural leaders and influencers and having a project recognize them helps motivate the person and guide the society toward them.

Being supportive of the community taking on a life of its own is a validation of the value of the open source project. That doesn't mean it's always easy, and we will dig more into this in *Chapter 8, Dealing with Conflict*.

Summary

This chapter covered several aspects of making your project feel welcoming, including having a good project infrastructure, a positive and inclusive culture in bringing in end users, and enabling the larger community to showcase the project in new areas and drive collaboration in different arenas. We scratched the surface of community management, and there are entire books out there that go deeper into the topic, which would be great reads if you have more interest in this area.

A key aspect of making newcomers feel welcome is supporting them in becoming contributors and maintainers over time. Let's look at this in more detail in our next chapter, *Chapter 7, Growing Contributors to Maintainers*, and see how to help contributors make that transition.

7

Growing Contributors to Maintainers

When I talk about open source projects, a huge point of emphasis for me is sustainability. It's also a point that is quite challenging to wrap your head around; after all, it's really hard to think about the future with so much going on in the present. Open source projects often model the same pattern that start-up companies have, and for a start-up, thinking about the long term before the short term is hard because, without some degree of revenue and success, there is no long term. Open source projects tend to not be so heavily dependent on the short term, but at the same time, they can't ignore it. A good project, just like a good company, focuses the appropriate attention on both and considers both in decision-making.

A piece of the sustainability puzzle is bringing more people into the project in various roles. The natural pool of these individuals is people already invested in the project; within a community of end users, contributors will naturally emerge that help drive new ideas and fixes into a project. This chapter will talk about how to grow those contributors so that they become the maintainers of the future.

We'll cover the following topics in this chapter:

- The importance of growing contributors into maintainers
- Finding contributors and being a mentor
- When is a contributor ready to become a maintainer?

Growing contributors into maintainers is a piece of the larger conversation we will get into in *Chapter 9, Handling Growth*, but with this chapter, I want to take a deep look at this topic, as it tends to be one of the most dominant struggles for project maintainers. Part of this is likely due to some of the social dynamics we talked about in the last chapter, but also it comes down to having an intentional focus on identifying talent within your community and helping find a place for them in the project.

Before we get into identifying potential maintainers, let's first chat about why this is so important.

The importance of growing contributors into maintainers

When someone is a new maintainer and sees their personal involvement in a project increase, they are often ignorant to the larger needs a project might have as it grows. It's easy for them to say, "this is an easy bug fix; I can do it" or "I can spend a weekend writing documentation," which is appealing when they are so heavily emotionally invested in the project. But what happens when that one bug becomes five, or a weekend that needs to be invested in writing documentation also has to compete with spending time with friends and family or being able to rest and recharge? Having more maintainers lessens that load and helps all maintainers focus on where their energy is best spent.

Let's look more specifically at some of the main reasons why growing contributors into maintainers is so important to a project, starting with the need to alleviate the stress on current maintainers.

Alleviating the stress on the current maintainers

Coming out of the COVID-19 pandemic, one of the greatest challenges is maintainer burnout. Maintainer burnout has in some sense always been a problem in open source, but like many things, has been exacerbated by sudden cultural and lifestyle changes. It also hit hard with the Apache Log4j vulnerability that was big toward the end of 2021, just like the OpenSSL Heartbleed vulnerability many years before was critical for maintainers whose projects did not have good security practices.

With open source software being so ubiquitously used, the pressure on maintainers is at an all-time high. One article in *Business Insider* (https://www.businessinsider.com/open-source-developers-burnout-low-pay-internet-2022-3) talks about how some maintainers have gotten to the point where they are sabotaging their own projects. This sabotaging is not because of a lack of love for the project but because of the pressure put on them by end users and other downstream constituents, treating maintainers as though they are a full software development shop and not somebody maintaining all the aspects of a project in between different activities.

I've worked on a few projects that had great potential but suffered from this. Each one had maintainers with interesting code and a valuable use case, but they struggled to get others involved in the project. These maintainers had the stereotypical "if you build it, they will come" philosophy, but it never panned out. Here's what tended to happen instead:

- The maintainer would switch jobs, and during that switch, the maintainer had to spend considerable time getting up to speed on their new job. Otherwise, that job switch involved new technological areas of expertise for the maintainer, whereas before, the previous project aligned well with the "scratch-your-own itch" motivation, but in the new role, it became something less aligned and useful for them.

- Health problems, with themselves or loved ones, took away their time and attention. Some maintainers see the work in open source as something of an outlet for them to escape the present challenges they might have, but the reality is that they don't have the energy they need to continue driving the project at the same pace as before.

- The allure of running a project becomes less and less strong as it doesn't grow how the maintainer or creator thought it would. One maintainer I worked with particularly struggled with two projects they started and ultimately ended up shutting down; in each case, they did a fair amount of outreach, but couldn't ever get broader interest.

All of this adds to stress on the maintainer. Having contributors grow into maintainers can help offset the stress and keep maintainers engaged and excited.

But it's not all about continuity planning; new maintainers bring new ideas and perspectives as well. Let's look more at that now.

Bringing new ideas and energy into a project

We talked about the "benevolent dictators" model of governance back in *Chapter 5, Governance and Hosting Models*. One challenge we illustrated with that model is the fact that the hub of decision-making comes back to one person, and depending on the style of leadership, that can end up either helping drive consensus or stifling other opinions. Either way, it's hard on a maintainer to be in that role; imagine being that person and every single project decision having to come through you. It's overwhelming, for sure.

When you bring in new maintainers, you bring in new ideas and energy. In my current role at the Linux Foundation, I work on a team with a group of skilled program managers and directors, each with different levels of experience in stakeholder management, open source project guidance, and general organizational skills. One of the things I like the most is bringing in a new member to the team, as each person comes with different skills and experiences. Some of our team members are **Project Management Professional** (**PMP**)-certified. Others come from the non-profit sector. Some might have event or marketing experience. Even a few of us have extensive open source project backgrounds. Most of us have a combination of these skills, and our outcomes as a team give us two key things:

- We learn new ways of doing things from one another. Someone with more events experience can share tips for helping a project prepare for an event, while someone with deeper open source experience might have insights on the governance setup for a complex project.

- We strengthen each other, both from an experience perspective, as in the previous point, and from a mental and emotional support standpoint. Working with open source communities is very rewarding, but it also can be stressful due to various personalities and priorities. *Chapter 8, Dealing with Conflict*, and *Chapter 9, Handling Growth*, will dig deeper into these topics.

When you, as a maintainer, get comfortable with new maintainers coming into your project, you no longer have to be the fulcrum of everything in the project. Let's look at how bringing in new maintainers enables current maintainers to step back from the project.

Enabling current maintainers to step back

Coming back to the point raised earlier in this section, the "Benevolent Dictators" model of governance back in *Chapter 5, Governance and Hosting Models,* puts the single maintainer in the position of the sole person allowing the project to "sink or swim." However, I've seen this happen in projects with several maintainers as well, especially if that group of maintainers has been the maintainers since day one.

This becomes a big problem in projects with a perceived high barrier to entry to be a contributor, let alone a maintainer. Media and entertainment space projects I've worked with have struggled with this, as specific domain backgrounds in visual rendering and color science were often requirements, in addition to deep C/C++ experience. Because of this barrier, they immediately had the challenge of getting new contributors to the project – which, in turn, created the problem of too much work on the maintainers and lots of stress overall on the project.

What I have started to see as a trend in the case I just illustrated is new contributors emerging that do meet the requirements, from two general categories:

- Existing organizations add additional resources, though usually, this is pretty minimal (maybe an additional full-time engineer equivalent)

- New organizations grow in value or independent developers do, who have experience and are often known in the industry already

For a maintainer to step back, they must feel comfortable doing so. In industries such as the media and entertainment, there is a small community of people who tend to move from company to company rather than floating between multiple industries. I will note that long-term, the pattern of "tapping the same well again and again" is not sustainable. Still, as a starting point, it creates the right culture of bringing in new maintainers and transitioning leadership, which can often be hard for the initial leaders of a project.

Another part of enabling maintainers to step back is thinking about how to best optimize the time of a maintainer. As open source projects I've worked with start to hit maturity, one of the best ways to help scale growth is building out documentation, training, and certification resources that enable mass education on the project itself. Building these out is a lot of work, and something we'll discuss in more detail in future chapters, but it also requires someone with deep project knowledge to direct and lead for it to be successful. If the maintainers spend tons of time doing singular enablement, meaning responding to forum posts and bug reports, they are caught in a never-ending cycle. Having new maintainers who can lead those activities effectively lets those other maintainers take on "higher-level activities" such as this, which helps the project grow and scale.

Stepping back as a maintainer can result in shifting roles and responsibilities, letting the maintainer focus on specific areas with their available time, but it can also be a path for succession, meaning a maintainer leaves a project entirely. As a maintainer, there is no requirement to be part of a project for life, just as in our careers; we aren't wedded to a single employer or job for life. We might even want to retire someday; Guido van Rossum, the founder of Python, has been able to step away from the project and retire, with Python continuing to grow and evolve as a key programming language. Having this foresight as a project leader helps you set a course for how to get there while ensuring the community and its work can continue.

Hopefully, this has given you enough perspective on why this is such an important focus for a project. Let's now jump into our next topic of how to find contributors with the potential to grow and mentor them to success.

Finding contributors and being a mentor

Identifying who among the current contributors will be a great future maintainer is the hardest part of getting new maintainers. In the early days of a project, or for a less experienced maintainer, everyone showing up looks like a possible maintainer. That's not only overly optimistic but can also deter people from becoming a contributor. Remember that often contributors and end users come to a project with the "scratch-your-own item" mentality and doing work in a project for a maintainer likely isn't that itch.

At the same time, as we will learn more about in *Chapter 11, Open Source and the Talent Ecosystem*, contributors may also have the motivation to gain development experience or even be part of the project leadership in time to open up their future employment opportunities. As a maintainer, know that you don't have the responsibility of career development for a contributor looking to become a maintainer, but if interests align, then it could be a good opportunity for the project and you as a maintainer

Let's start on the journey of identifying future maintainers by looking at what qualities you should look for.

Qualities of a future maintainer

Early in open source, when it was viewed as more "counter-culture," we had the idea that open source leaders resisted the concept of leadership. Leading an open source project is much harder than leading a team of employees. For one, contributors can bail out at a much lower threshold than an employee can, as there is rarely any economic impact on the contributor. Secondly, these contributors don't come with any vetting process ahead of time; they see your project, like it, use it, and contribute to it as it fits their needs. This requires a maintainer to look at both the technical and soft skills of the individual to see how they could evolve into being a maintainer.

Let's break down the skills into two categories – technical skills and soft skills. Here are some of the typical ones I see:

Technical skills	Soft skills
Knows the code base well	Organized
Understands the technology	Good communicator and writer
Can debug issues	Problem solver
Good software development skills	Curious thinker

Table 7.1 – Technical skills versus soft skills

Being a maintainer is one part technical management and another part people management, which requires soft skills. The technical side is usually fairly trivial to evaluate; look at the code contributions made and you can quickly see whether the person is a good software developer or not. However, for the soft skills side, there isn't one place to look and evaluate; you'll want to review a number of different places:

- Do they post in mailing lists/chat channels/forums? What is their tone like? Is it respectful and humble, or arrogant and confrontational?

- Do they answer questions from others or help debug issues and problems people are having? Are those interactions patient and understanding, or frustrating and demoralizing?

- When this person is involved in a conflict, how do they respond? Do they engage directly and point fingers? Do they run the other way? Do they try to understand others' points (a topic that we will dig more into in *Chapter 8, Dealing with Conflict*).

- Is the person a regular in the project, or does their participation ebb and flow? If they are needed for something, can you count on them to come through?

- What are the long-term career goals of this person? Are they someone who jumps from thing to thing, or sticks with jobs and works for a longer period?

Knowing what qualities a good future maintainer has is a good indicator of which contributors could be future maintainers, but know that many of the preceding questions can't fully be answered upfront. As you build a relationship with the person, you learn more about their style, personality, work ethic, technical skills, and more. Additionally, the project might have some excellent documentation and governance written down, but there is still a fair amount of "cultural knowledge" in the project, so the person will learn about the current maintainers' style, personality, work ethic, technical skills, and so on over time, which will determine whether this is the right fit for them or not.

Mentorship is a great tool here, as it gives both the prospective maintainer and current maintainer that space to determine whether the fit is there; let's learn more about that now.

Using mentorship to bring in a new contributor

One of the biggest challenges talked about with organizations is hiring great talent. As I spoke about in the previous section, both the organization and the employee need to see whether there is a mutual fit. Open source projects are no different; each has a different style and culture, which aren't right or wrong, but not everyone is a great fit for each one. A great way to discover this for both maintainers and prospective maintainers is through mentorship.

One of the groups I work with, Open Mainframe Project, holds a summer mentorship program. The goal of this program is to bring in students and those in career transition to work on one of the open source projects in the mainframe space, with the anticipated end goal of both good contributions to the project and involving the mentee in the industry and the project going forward. The project has seen this work out great for bringing in new persons to the mainframe industry, with many taking jobs in the mainframe ecosystem post-mentorship. For projects, we've had three great examples of a mentee getting involved and taking leadership roles in the community:

- **Alpine Linux** (`https://www.alpinelinux.org/`) was ported to s390x (the architecture for the mainframe) in 2017 thanks to a mentee doing the initial porting work during their mentorship and then sticking with the project to complete the porting work. This person as of the time of writing is a maintainer for Alpine Linux and both the s390x and POWER ports.

- **Software Discovery Tool** (`https://www.openmainframeproject.org/projects/software-discovery-tool`) is a project that builds a tool for discovering open source project compatibility with the mainframe, as well as working with various Linux distributions and other groups to maintain a database of compatibility. After doing a mentorship to help build out parts of the infrastructure, a mentee stayed involved in the project and became a maintainer after they had a great experience working with the community.

- **COBOL Programming Course** (`https://www.openmainframeproject.org/projects/cobolprogrammingcourse`) provides an open source course for learning COBOL. This project also did a mentorship and had a few mentees participating in building parts of the coursework. One mentee in particular really enjoyed both the project community and the mainframe ecosystem itself and stayed involved in the project by becoming a maintainer, and the next year became a mentor to the next group of mentees.

These examples illustrate formal mentorships, but informal mentorships work just as well. Early in my open source career, I built the PHP Windows Installer with support from the current maintainer of the Windows support project for PHP. This person provided me with some advice and guidance on how PHP is best installed and configured on Windows, helped validate my approach, and then worked with me to get the code into the project itself. You could use this same pattern for getting people engaged in other aspects; I've seen projects that might not have a strong **Continuous Integration/ Continuous Deployment (CI/CD)** environment have someone step up to help, and this person has become a maintainer of that work with the support of other maintainers. The main idea here is that there is an interest for the person, a need in the open source project itself, and the opportunity to work together on something that gives each party a good sense of what working together is like.

As mentoring and shadowing continue between a current maintainer and a potential future maintainer, you get a better feel for whether this contributor will serve well as a maintainer. Let's now look at those conditions.

When is a contributor ready to be a maintainer?

Mentorship can be a slow path. You don't want to overwhelm yourself or the contributor too much, as it will become frustrating to you both. On the other end, if the contributor isn't getting involved in the maintainer group much, they will become disinterested and drift away. Mentorship done well is an intentional process, with both the contributor and the maintainer setting clear goals and timelines to ensure the expectations are clear while having good communication to know how things are going and address concerns early on.

Sensing the moment at which a contributor is ready to become a maintainer tends to be more of an "art" rather than a "science." There are some signals to look for to best gauge how things are going – let's look at some of them now.

Signs that mentorship is going well

Each mentorship and project is a bit different, but you can generally look for a few signs to tell whether things are going well; here are some:

- The contributor proactively engages. This could mean the person asks and answers questions regularly on mailing lists or forums. It could be they do timely reviews of bugs and issues. You may see them speak publicly about the project in meetups, events, or blog posts. The key is "proactive" – meaning you as a maintainer are not specifically asked to do something, but you are out there doing it. They might ask whether something is okay first – and that's fine – but the point is they are taking the initiative.

- The contributor understands the project and the community. You can tell this by the engagement; does it have the same tone as others in the project leadership? If a maintainer has given feedback on something, has the contributor taken this feedback and incorporated it into future work (and hopefully not repeated their mistakes)? This doesn't mean the person doesn't have their own personality and approach – in fact, it's good if it is a bit different. What you are looking for is someone that does things in a way that allows other maintainers not to worry about what they've done.

- The contributor is recognized in the project community as a leader. Being a leader isn't something the person can accomplish alone; it's based on the work they do and the interactions they have. If the project community doesn't recognize this person as a leader, that could mean there is friction between this person and others, or maybe the person isn't being vocal and presenting themselves as a leader.

- There is a good personality fit between the contributor and the other maintainers. This doesn't mean everyone is best friends, nor is it a "personality contest"; the contribution should be via good, professional interactions and communication.

- The contributor has the aptitude to grow from any shortcomings they have in terms of the previous points. We are all humans, and sometimes we struggle to see our weak points. What's most important is whether a person can learn and grow from those points. Note that a person might not be perfect on each of the preceding points; that doesn't rule them out from being a maintainer but gives them space to grow.

Building on that last point, a great example in a different domain is being a sports official. Recently, I got involved in being a certified volleyball official, and one thing that impressed me is all the good and great referees who constantly work on improving their skills. It might be that they are good at recognizing net faults but aren't good at recognizing alignment issues, or perhaps they understand how to properly assess sanctions but aren't as good at back-row awareness. Officiating has multiple aspects to it and can be demanding, but the way you improve is by recognizing what you've done well and not as well and setting a plan on how to improve on each skill. Becoming a great official requires humility, recognizing the skills you need to improve on and having the desire to improve.

The same is true of being a maintainer; great maintainers are made over time. The domain and scope of a maintainer stretch across deep technical knowledge, public speaking, and community management; you will rarely be good at all of these at first, but over time, you improve in each area. All maintainers go through the same struggles and learning experiences, but much like the examples with a volleyball official, the great maintainers go through those experiences, learning how to improve and grow.

We hope that mentoring a potential maintainer goes well and that they develop into the maintainer role and become an asset to the project, but it doesn't always end that way; how do you manage a situation where they may never be ready to be a maintainer? Let's look at this situation and see how to handle it gracefully.

What if the contributor is never ready?

Sometimes, even with the best of mentors, the contributor isn't a great fit for being a maintainer. It could be the person is a poor communicator, or perhaps disorganized. Maybe the person's personality isn't a great fit for the project community. This doesn't mean they are wrong for the project, just not right for the role. And that's not a permanent status; over time, people grow and change (as the project does as well) and the fit might be better at a different stage.

Some tips for managing when it might be good to end a mentorship include the following:

- Talk to the person directly and privately about the concerns.

- Be receptive to the feedback they have. When there are issues, it's rarely one-sided, so they may have critical feedback for the maintainers themselves. It could be resolvable feedback, or it might not be. There's more on this in *Chapter 8, Dealing with Conflict*.

- Ensure everything they were involved with has a new owner, which might be yourself ;-).

- Try to find other ways a contributor could participate. Maybe there is a feature that needs to be developed and the skills they have are a better fit there. Perhaps there is documentation or other writing needed, or they could just help answer questions in mailing lists or forums.

- Try your best to end the mentorship amicably. Often, if you do not see the fit working, the other person likely sees the same thing as well. Walking away amicably ensures goodwill and sets a tone for how maintainers interact with others.

Remember – being a maintainer isn't for everyone. Even if someone has the aptitude to be a maintainer, it doesn't mean the interest is there. Another thing to remember is that moving from being an end user to a contributor and then to a maintainer isn't per se a career path, and not becoming a maintainer isn't a failure. There might be other roles the person might have within the project community; perhaps they will be out there answering questions or writing blog posts. Be appreciative of any contributions people make to a project because without them, it would fall on you.

Summary

If your goal is to have a successful, sustainable open source project, thinking about how you develop your project leadership over time is crucial. As we spoke about in *Chapter 2, What Makes a Good Open Source Project?*, and *Chapter 5, Governance and Hosting Models*, end users look at how a project is run as much as the code itself. A project might have an amazing code base, be technically innovative, and solve the exact problem an end user is looking to solve, but to use it as a critical part of their infrastructure, they will want to make sure this project is maintained for years to come. As a maintainer today, that might not seem like a big deal, but after years of maintaining a code base, answering questions, fixing issues, and doing releases, being a maintainer can lose its luster. The only way to make a project sustainable for the long term is by bringing new maintainers into the project regularly.

One of the main stressors on maintainers, as well as open source projects in general, is conflict. Conflict is a sign of a healthy project; it means you bring diverse opinions and perspectives to help a project have better outcomes, but conflict can be a stressor, especially when that conflict becomes negative. Let's look at strategies for dealing with conflict in our next chapter, *Chapter 8, Dealing with Conflict*.

8
Dealing with Conflict

It's natural to have conflict in open source projects, as a good project will bring together individuals from different backgrounds, cultures, and experiences. Those conflicts are quite often good, as they come from people expressing different opinions, approaches, and thoughts. Each person brings validity and merit to their area of focus.

That being said, coming together from different backgrounds, organizations, or locales can be challenging. I've similarly seen this with groups coming into a structure that is new to them, such as open source projects. The group might be used to how things work in their own companies but need help adjusting to a more open environment. Often, these changes are quite subtle, such as *"We like using Box or Google Docs, not a wiki"* or *"We use WebEx or GoToMeeting, not Zoom, as this project does."* It might also be related to something such as decision-making, such as *"I need to go and ask our company whether we can allow this code to be added."* These conflicts on tools and processes usually emanate from project participants who are new to a process and trying to understand how things work. However, there can still be underlying issues and frustrations that prevent people from coming out of their comfort zone. Addressing these issues at an early stage helps the issues not become larger concerns.

This chapter will dig into how to recognize when conflict can occur, how to best approach and manage it in a project, and how to remedy toxicity. The specific topics will include the following:

- Understanding people and their motivations
- Inclusive decision-making
- Remedying toxic behavior

When you see public conflict, such as explosive email discussion chains or people flaming each other in a chat channel, be aware that the antecedent for that conflict didn't start then and has likely been brewing for quite some time. To gain this awareness, you need to understand people better. Let's take a quick dive into that.

Understanding people and their motivations

In an interview, I was asked what the best and worst parts of open source are. In a somewhat knee-jerk and cheeky way, I responded, *"The people."* My response was in no way meant to be derogatory but more of a reflection of the central role of people in the success and failure of open source projects.

To understand people, you have to understand how they think. Let's take a quick dive into understanding the human brain.

The human brain

The human brain is a complex beast, controlling how we live, learn, react, and execute. What is most interesting is that different parts of the brain control different functionalities, as we can see in *Figure 8.1*:

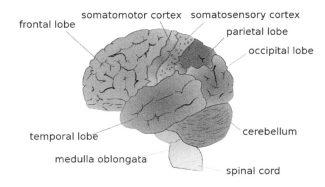

Figure 8.1: A breakdown of regions of the human brain (https://commons.wikimedia.org/wiki/File:Cerebrum_lobes.svg)

Each section of the brain is connected to the other in many ways, and these connections are grown and weakened over time. Some of this is age-related, as children will not have all areas of the brain developed, while those later in life might have some degeneration that happens with age. Sometimes, people have brain injuries that damage sections of the brain, such as in a car accident. But these connections are mainly developed or impacted through life experiences.

There are two parts of the brain we will focus on in this chapter:

- **Limbic system**: This is responsible for impulses, reactions, and pure emotion and is often thought of as controlling the *fight or flight response* a person might have. I'll refer to this as the *lower brain* in this chapter.

- **Prefrontal lobe**: This is responsible for executive functions such as decision-making, planning, and short-term memory. I'll refer to this as the *upper brain* in this chapter.

As we go through this chapter, we will look at interactions and responses from the perspective of which part of the brain is responding. Generally, *upper-brain* responses will be more thoughtful, rational, and strategic, while *lower-brain* responses will be more reactionary, impulsive, and can be considered rude or inconsiderate.

The other aspect of looking at the human brain is understanding neurodiversity, namely the effects of different neurological disorders and conditions that impact reactions. The most well-known neurological condition is called **Autism Spectrum Disorder** (**ASD**), a wide range of conditions and symptoms that impact how we approach social interaction and behave in social situations. There is quite a bit of variability in this area, and I would encourage you to check out the **US Centers of Disease Control's** (**CDC's**) information on ASD (`https://www.cdc.gov/ncbddd/autism/index.html`).

With a better understanding of the human brain, let's now look at the impact of culture and life experiences on how people act and respond.

Cultural and life experiences

Many life experiences are good. For example, getting a good grade in a class will build connections in the brain that good grades lead to positive outcomes. Winning a sports game builds the connection between hard work and the joy of winning. But some can be difficult. Being yelled at by a parent builds the connections between a behavior and a negative consequence. Losing money gambling can build a connection between taking chances and loss. All these experiences shape who we are, how we think about things, and how we react and absorb information.

With negative life experiences, the resulting impact on a person is called trauma. The trauma we often think of is related to serious threats to our physical safety, such as physical violence, loss of a parent during childhood, assault, or severe injury – you will see this called big-T trauma. But much more often, we see little-T trauma, which is negative things that happen in everyday life, such as losing an item, being treated poorly, or hearing disappointing news. Either way, these experiences will impact your response to situations and interactions with people.

Another element of life experiences is the culture we are in. This could be cultural as it relates to the region of the world or country we are from; for example, growing up in the United States is quite different than growing up in China, and someone living in France will have a different life experience than someone in Brazil. But it could also be living conditions; if you grow up in a lower-income household, you will certainly have different experiences, traumas, and life prospects than a higher-income household. Culture forms part of our identity, and understanding a person's culture makes it easier to understand them.

Each of us has different life experiences, so those connections in our brains will be built separately. With different connections, this might lead to different outcomes when interactions happen. Let's now look more at interactions within communities in this context.

Example interactions in an open source project

Let's now look at a few sample interactions between project participants, thinking about what we learned in the previous section about the human brain. For each, we will both detail the interaction and then break it down to look at it from several different perspectives. Let's look at the first from the perspective of a rude maintainer.

The rude maintainer

Let's look at this interaction. For reference, Sally is a maintainer, while Bill is a new contributor:

> Sally: I just saw your `pull` request; there are several issues.
>
> Bill: OK, what are the problems?
>
> Sally: Well, first, there is no documentation or tests. Did you read the `CONTRIBUTING` file?
>
> Bill: Sorry, I didn't.
>
> Sally: Go back and read that first, and then send in a new pull request. I'm closing this one.

On the surface, you might look at Sally as a bit of a rude maintainer, whereas Bill is the victim of that attack. That is accurate; as we talked about in *Chapter 6, Making Your Project Feel Welcoming*, this sort of interaction isn't a good way to make a contributor feel welcome.

But there is likely more to the story. After all, Sally likely didn't wake up that morning and say, "I want to be a jerk to a new contributor today." Consider the following:

- In some cultures, people are just naturally direct. Sally could be from such a culture, and her reaction is the norm.

- Sally might have ASD, and one thing we often see from those with such a diagnosis is a tendency to have a more "matter-of-fact" reaction and a high adherence to rules and policies.

- Sally could have been through the fiftieth pull request in a row with no documentation or tests and has become frustrated with contributors and chosen to air that frustration with Bill.

- Bill might not be that new a contributor, and he has made a bunch of pull requests over time and continuously doesn't add documentation or tests, despite many times being asked to.

Note that Bill didn't react much to Sally, which is a good *upper-brain* response. Bill might not even think of this interaction as rude or confrontational because of past traumas or from having similar direct feedback from previous managers, teachers, parents, and/or authoritative persons. This could also be because Bill is non-confrontational. Maybe Bill has seen a pattern of these reactions from Sally and/or other maintainers and has decided it's not worth reacting to.

Let's flip this around and look at the inverse example of a too-direct contributor.

The angry contributor

Consider the following interaction. Alice is the maintainer and Greg is the contributor:

> Alice: Hi Greg, just reviewing your pull request and have a few questions.

> Greg: OK, fine, what is it?

> Alice: Yes, so I'm not sure whether you have looked through our CONTRIBUTING guide, but one important thing is adding tests and documentation...

> Greg: Ugh, it's too hard for me to write tests, and I don't have the time to write the documentation.

> Alice: Yes, but that is required.

> Greg: Well, that sucks.

If you have experience in conflict resolution or management, you can see that Alice handled the situation quite well (and better than Sally did in the previous section). As we observed, Greg has a *lower-brain* response, while Alice kept her composure for the most part with an *upper-brain* response.

However, as we discussed in the previous interaction example, there is likely more to the story. Consider the following:

- Like Sally, Greg might have various cognitive conditions that impact interactions, resulting in him being more direct than socially appropriate

- Greg could have had several different projects or maintainers push back in the same way, which resulted in Greg showing his emotions and taking his frustrations from previous interactions out on Alice

- Greg might have been conditioned through past interactions to complain and push back on policies, and he has been successful in getting those policies ignored

- Sally might be a bit too much of a *rule follower*, and Greg's contribution could be a few lines of code that another maintainer/project might see as not such a big deal

Sally, while responding well, could be perceived as being a bit "*cold*" toward Greg. This could be because she is anticipating Greg's reaction, and/or she is a bit new to being a maintainer and is uncomfortable in these interactions. Sally could also be preemptively aware that Greg will likely have a *lower-brain* response and is intentionally responding with an *upper-brain* response to avoid negativity.

Observations from these examples

Both interactions focus on the same topic, but with different individuals interacting, we see vastly different conversations occurring. These interactions wouldn't be ones considered to be entirely positive. They can either lead to further negative conflict (for example, Greg posting on Twitter on how frustrating it is to contribute to that project), the contribution never arriving as the contributor walks away, or possibly the contribution arriving. Still, that type of interaction is established as appropriate in the project. All three of these outcomes are only sometimes the best ones.

Here are a few other observations to consider:

- If this is the same project, having vastly different reactions from the two different maintainers gives mixed signals about the culture of the project. Is Sally the outlier, or is Alice? If it's Alice, is she a dominant force in the project that everyone tolerates? If it's Sally, is she new in the role, or is the project generally a bit uncomfortable for contributors?

- Various cultural, social, and cognitive conditions are at play in every interaction. Alice may be viewed by some as completely appropriate in her interaction, while others might look at Sally's interaction as avoidant or disengaged. Be aware that each person looks at situations differently because of their background.

- With minimal context, it's easier to say one person is right while the other is wrong. And as we looked at other possible dynamics at play, both persons could be right or wrong in how it was handled. Knowing the full story is key – but in the eyes of outside people, that story is not always evident.

A better understanding of people makes it much easier to navigate decision-making. Let's build upon what we've discussed in this section as we examine how to achieve consensus inclusively in our next section.

Inclusive decision-making

A good open source project functions well by having the community largely aligned. I say *largely* because it's nearly impossible to get everyone to agree on anything, both in life and in open source projects, but good projects have a degree of alignment in purpose and focus. Even minor disagreements create fractures and bring out many negative emotions when a project isn't aligned. When the project is aligned, it has the resiliency to get past minor disagreements and drive forward.

You often hear a term in open source community management called "*herding cats.*" If you have a cat, you know that cats are often independent and difficult-to-control animals, and in the same way, trying to pull together large groups of people from different and diverse backgrounds can be equally challenging. So, how can we be successful at "*herding cats*"? Let's consider some key things, starting with good communication.

Open communication and collaboration

In any group, big or small, communication is key. This is even more true with open source, as you have people from all over the world contributing predominately in an asynchronous way. Keeping communication open and inclusive is an intentional action. Best practices include the following:

- Have dedicated, open communication tools. Most open source projects will leverage an email mailing list, and email is a good lowest common denominator. It's also great because it's asynchronous, and mailing lists save archives, so you can easily track past conversations and discussions. I also see forum tools such as Discourse or chat clients such as Slack, Discord, or Matrix used.

- Also, be sure your collaboration tools are open as well. Most open source communities use their GitHub or GitLab organizations as a unified collaboration tool, but some also use wikis, which work well. Internal company collaboration tools such as Box or Google Drive tend to be poor choices, as collaboration is gated by default, and it's challenging to get access or discover the collaboration without proper access.

- Some communities I've worked with have tried to drive decision-making over a chat client such as Slack, Discord, or Matrix. Because chat clients are synchronous, it's not inclusive (not everyone can always be available simultaneously).

- With all that said, from time to time, you need to get people together to participate in a live conversation. If you need to do that, use meeting best practices such as providing a fair amount of notice (if it's an online meeting, at least a week; for in-person, it should be several weeks), distributing the agenda well ahead of the meeting, and making sure any web conference tools used are accessible on several different platforms.

The key here is to ensure the project's mediums for communication and collaboration are open and easy to access. Additionally, you want to ensure that communication and collaboration are fully driven using these platforms; if a project has too much conversation happening in closed channels, it creates unintentional divides.

Now that we have the right tools to communicate and collaborate, let's see how to best make these decisions.

Methodology for making decisions

Transforming the *herding cats* into orderly, inclusive decision-making requires a good structure. This should be well defined in a project's governance, as we discussed in *Chapter 5, Governance and Hosting Models*. Good decision-making has a few elements:

- **Having a period for discussion and a period for voting**: This keeps the focus separate and ensures alignment before going to a vote. It also helps solve the problem of someone in the middle of a vote throwing a wrinkle into a process (for example, someone saying, "*Hey, we should chat about this aspect more*" when you are partway through a vote).

- **Give options for both a "for" vote and an "against" vote, as well as an "abstain" vote**: Also known as "lazy consensus," this provides space for someone who might have a conflict of interest to not submit a vote, or someone who doesn't feel they have either the right context or a strong feeling either way to express their preference.

- **Clear timelines to avoid a never-ending vote**: Many projects I work on will keep a period for discussion open for a week, and then, if there aren't major objections, the project will proceed with a vote that is open for a week. Depending upon your project size or the type of decision, you should consider adjusting this; the Community Specification process (`https://github.com/CommunitySpecification`) sets different thresholds of decision-making and the mechanisms for each.

- **Who can vote/discuss, and how**: This should also be outlined in the project's governance, as we discussed in *Chapter 5, Governance and Hosting Models*. The key point is that voting and discussion on the issue being considered should be centralized so that all feedback can be gathered.

> **Important note**
>
> The Apache voting process (see `https://www.apache.org/foundation/voting`) is a commonly used approach that Apache Software Foundation-hosted projects and other projects adopt, as it's well known and clear.

GitHub/GitLab-centric projects might choose to do this in the context of an issue or pull request, and both have nice features built in to require a certain amount of approvals before code can be merged in (`https://docs.github.com/en/pull-requests/collaborating-with-pull-requests/reviewing-changes-in-pull-requests/approving-a-pull-request-with-required-reviews` and `https://docs.gitlab.com/ee/user/project/merge_requests/approvals/`).

Sometimes in projects, even with a clear methodology and tools for voting and discussing in place, votes need help to move forward. Let's look at how you can unblock things.

Making decisions

Trivial decisions, such as merging simple pull requests, are usually easy to make, though they are not opinionated, as Parkinson's law of triviality tells us (see `https://en.wikipedia.org/wiki/Law_of_triviality`). Opinionated decisions can be the most complex to get through, which can be opinionated based on personal preference (project logo designs are quite notorious for this) or more foundational (such as expanding a project's scope or bringing in a major feature).

The tone of these discussions can lead to one of two possibilities having the effect of lots of conversation with little constructive outcomes, often referred to with the metaphor "*signal-to-noise ratio*," alluding to a high level of noise or irrelevant or unproductive conversation relative to the "signal" of a topic or productive conversations. Typically, this indicates conflicts in the project, which can be good for getting a discussion happening, but it can also be off-putting for those who tend to avoid conflict or, as discussed later in this chapter, turn toxic. Here are a few strategies to consider:

- Monitor the conversation, look for possible actions and outcomes, and try to suggest them. Consider the following interaction between David and Amy on adding internationalization to a project, with David being one of the decision-makers and Amy trying to drive a vote:

  David: I see a lot of projects just spin their wheels on internationalization, and it just doesn't seem like something we should get into.

  Amy: Thanks for the comment, David. Can you specifically outline why you believe they "spin their wheels"?

  David: There are just too many languages to consider, not enough people to maintain all of them, and lots of tools out there, and it needs to be clarified which one to pick.

  Amy: So it sounds like your concerns are related to (a) the scope of supported languages, (b) the ability to support internationalization for a given language, and (c) the tool to pick. Is that a fair summary?

  David: Yes, I think that captures it.

  Amy: Great! So I would suggest we augment the proposal to address these concerns, adding specific policies/plans for (a) determining which languages to support and what is required to support a language, and (b) a review of the tools and a decision on which ones to use. Would you agree with that, David?

  David: I like that! Happy to help!

  You can see here that Amy takes a broad comment, narrows it down to specific concerns, and outlines actions. Amy also does this collaboratively with David, validating his comment at each step in the process. David sees this willingness to work with him and offers to take part – exactly the outcome you want to see.

- Keep an eye out for people who can but aren't voting, especially if they commonly do vote. It could be that the person is on vacation, or for some reason, they don't have access to the accounts used before or are not getting the messages. I see a lot of situations where people get frustrated that a decision is made and they can't offer their opinion or vote, and it all comes down to a communication gap for the aforementioned reasons. Taking that extra step of reaching out avoids this.

- For those people who aren't voting, it could also be that they are uncomfortable raising their feedback with a group. Reach out and chat with them while trying to help them get that confidence; sometimes, they need to talk it out with someone. Alternatively, they might be concerned about negative or toxic feedback and need help navigating that. You want to be careful here not to take the full discussion offline and instead preferably help people to have the discussion openly.

- Know when to say when. This can be if a decision needs to be fully reconsidered, if there are a lot of problems with the decision to be made, or if there is a fair amount of misalignment. Stopping the voting process and going back to a design phase stops unproductive discussion. Consider this exchange with Bob, Sarah, and David, all involving pushback during a discussion after work was done on updating the proposal. Amy again came through to avoid an unproductive discussion:

David: I keep looking at this internationalization proposal, and I still don't get why we should prioritize this.

Bob: I agree, there is a big backlog of performance bugs that I think are more important to our community.

Sarah: I understand your points, David and Bob, but we are making it really difficult for those in other regions to use our project.

Amy: This is a good conversation, and it sounds like there is a concern about prioritization and what is most important to our community right now. Would you all agree?

David: I think that sounds right.

Bob: Agreed.

Sarah: + 1.

Amy: Okay, let's table this discussion and vote, and we can go back and look at doing a community poll to determine how to prioritize this versus other concerns.

David: I like it!

Bob: Sounds good! Happy to help!

Sarah: Me too!

- Similarly, if there is a fair amount of unproductive discussion blocking what appears to be a consensus vote, you need to curb that behavior as well. Let's assume the issues on prioritization for internationalization have been solved, and now we have Aaron chiming in and taking the discussion off course among David, Bob, and Sarah. Amy notices this and successfully pulls the conversation back:

Aaron: I've read the proposal and it's good, but it will be interesting to see what languages are supported.

Sarah: I agree. I wonder how many do we think there will be?

Bob: I could see three languages: French, German, and Japanese.

David: I'm not sure about Japanese; do we have a lot of Japanese users?

Aaron: That's a good question. I've not seen many on the mailing list.

Sarah: Have we thought about Spanish as well?

David: That's a good one too!

Amy: Hi, everyone! That's a good conversation on languages likely to be supported. Do we need to align on this before moving forward with a vote, or can we figure this out afterward?

Aaron: Oh, sorry, no, I don't see this as something blocking a vote.

Bob: Me neither.

David: + 1.

Sarah: Agreed.

Amy: Great! We will get the vote started at the end of the discussion period then, provided there are no further blocking issues.

As you can see, inclusive decision-making is a lot of work. But that work pays off in the end, as you avoid deeper conflicts by not only having decision-makers at the table early on but also seeing where conflicts start happening, and looking for constructive ways to bring them to resolution.

When not managed well, conflict can turn from constructive to toxic, which has a negative effect on your project. Let's look more at how to remedy this.

Remedying toxic behavior

Toxic behavior can take several forms. It can be what is called *flaming*, which refers to individuals going back and forth attacking one another with those *lower-brain* responses we spoke about earlier in this chapter. It can also showcase itself with people disconnecting or becoming disengaged, or just people having short or trite responses in conversations. Both are highly disruptive, holding a community back and causing stress and friction.

Often, this comes down to communication issues, where there need to be collaborative and constructive conversations, like what Amy achieved in the examples previously in this chapter. Let's look at another fictional example of such an exchange; here, we have Ray as the contributor and Sam as the maintainer:

Ray: I keep looking at this pull request to refactor some of the tests, and I'm not sure I understand it.

Sam: What's not to understand? It's simple tests.

Ray: Well, not all of us are as smart as Sam I guess.

Sam: At least I'm trying to make things better, unlike you.

Ray: YOU ARE CRAZY!

Sam: GET LOST, RAY!

I'll stop the interaction here, as we all know where this is likely headed. But you can see that Sam is offended and comes back with a *lower-brain* response, and then Ray goes into his *lower brain*, and the conversation implodes. Not all of these interactions are direct like this; some take the form of being more passive-aggressive in tone, but the result is the same.

I had an experience like this in one project I worked on, where the maintainer coming in had a lot of frustration with the recommendations I was making and the support we were providing. This person viewed my interactions as being like a *dictator*. I viewed their comments as not having the intention of building an open community, so I was being a bit too rigid in my responses. We both had a bit of this *cold war* between us; we would interact on calls, but it always felt like we were trying to prove the other wrong in some way. It was certainly toxic.

One day, in our regular one-to-one call, I said the following to the maintainer:

> Me: Hi! I think we are thrashing quite a bit, and I want to give you a chance to voice your concerns. To do that, I want to give you 10 minutes to share everything that is frustrating you. I'm going to put myself on mute so I can't interrupt you but will take notes. How does that sound?

> Maintainer: That would be great!

Note how I purposely used an *upper-brain* response as opposed to a *lower-brain* response. Certainly, I could have attacked him for the problems I saw in him, but if I did, I wouldn't have given space for him to help me see the problems he saw in me. Going down the route of the *upper-brain* response gave us both space for a dialog to solve our differences, instead of creating more conflict.

The maintainer shared a number of concerns and, as it turned out, didn't need the whole 10 minutes. I think it was therapeutic for both of us; that call and future calls discussed some of these concerns, but more importantly, it made us more conscious of how our actions and words were being perceived.

Looking at that experience and, to a degree, the fictional interaction below, here are some observations to consider:

- People want to be heard. When they aren't, they will either retreat or flame back. Giving someone a chance to be heard validates them, even if their opinion isn't one you agree with.

- Reviewing your own actions through the lenses of others helps you be more conscious of your actions. There's a term called *unconscious bias*, which refers to bias we don't see but is visible to others. This comes up largely in the context of creating inclusive communities where, because we come from different backgrounds, cultures, genders, races, or sexual orientations, we don't see how the words and actions we use have an impact on those not like us.

- Remedying toxicity isn't an overnight process, as there are feelings hurt on both sides that may take time to heal. In the example with the maintainer, it took several months for things to turn from toxic to positive; this doesn't mean it became more toxic, but we both needed to go through interactions and see how we both could do better.

- It requires intentionality to resolve toxicity. I often wonder if I didn't have that call with the maintainer how things would have turned out. Would the person have just left the project and things then improved? It's unlikely, as the maintainer wasn't the only person seeing that issue.

Toxicity is certainly something that can be avoided, both with good habits in communication, as we looked at earlier in this chapter, but also by recognizing when it happens and taking the time to resolve it. Additionally, projects should adopt a code of conduct to set the right expectations. Contributor Covenant (`https://www.contributor-covenant.org/`) is a popular one that is widely adopted.

Summary

This chapter scratched the surface of dealing with conflict, recognizing that it is good to have as long as it's constructive. Projects I've worked on that had conflicts coming from vendors who were competitors tended to actually have a higher velocity of code and innovation than those that didn't. The same is true for projects with more diversity from different backgrounds, nationalities, races, genders, sexual orientations, and so on. That seems a bit counterintuitive at first, but if you think about it, having people in the room who all have the same experiences produces relatively predictable results. But when there are differences, we see a variety of perspectives and needs flourish, and that diversity brings new ideas and novel solutions. But when the conflict turns toxic, it becomes a distraction to a project and takes a lot of work and time to fix.

Handling conflict well is a centerpiece to being able to grow and scale as a project. Let's look at the next chapter, where we will delve more into handling growth as a project.

Further reading

I encourage you to read more about diversity and trauma if you are interested in this topic, as there are professionals in this space that will help you be a more inclusive project. Here are a few:

- Karyn Purvis Institute of Child Development (`https://child.tcu.edu/`)

- Diversity, Equity, and Inclusion in Open Source report by LF Research (`https://www.linuxfoundation.org/research/the-2021-linux-foundation-report-on-diversity-equity-and-inclusion-in-open-source?hsLang=en`)

- CHAOSS Diversity, Equity, and Inclusion Working Group (`https://github.com/chaoss/wg-dei`)

- Software Developer Diversity and Inclusion initiative (`https://sddiproject.org/`)

9
Handling Growth

I was recently looking back at the recordings that the Kubernetes project has done of its community meetings since early 2016 (https://www.youtube.com/playlist?list=PL69nYSiGNLP1pkHsbPjzAewvMgGUpkCnJ). It's an interesting exercise to see how a community grows and progresses over time; some things change, but some don't. We spoke about open source being driven by "scratching one's own itch," and the way a community operates reflects exactly that. For Kubernetes, I look at the community meetings as driven by bringing together the large ecosystem for a few key purposes:

- Release, development, and **special interest group (SIG)** updates
- Demos of projects and work related to Kubernetes
- Shoutouts to specific community members who have made a noticeable impact

Such a simple structure – one that not only reflects the community as being development oriented but also highly appreciative of the work community members do to drive the project forward. It's also one that is highly scalable because of its simplicity; there is always development and updates going on that are interesting to the larger community, and recognizing great contributors shows the goodwill that brings in more contributors over time.

Open source projects typically start small with a single or maybe a few contributors. If a project is successful, you will quickly see interest from both users and contributors, which can be overwhelming. This chapter will dive into strategies for recognizing and managing that growth, as well as seeing when growth isn't happening and how to remedy that as well. Specific topics will include the following:

- Measuring growth
- Assessing and remedying low areas of growth
- Growing and scaling project leadership

Let's get started with the first task in being able to handle growth, which is being able to measure it.

Measuring growth

"You can't manage what you can't measure" is a quote you see thrown around quite a bit, and typically attributed to Peter Drucker, the Austrian-born American management consultant, educator, and author. Drucker's statement holds true, as when you say *"I want to improve X,"* you need a baseline to build your measurements and then a target to go toward. Let's say a project wants to get 1,000 commits a year; if that rate is 10 commits a month, there is a ton of work to do. But if it's 50 commits a month, it's a much more realistic growth.

On the flip side, Homer Simpson, the father in the long-running sitcom, The Simpsons, stated flippantly in an episode in which he was being interviewed, *"Oh Kent, you can use statistics to prove anything; 45% of all people know that!"* Simpson calls out a fair point, where you could find the numbers to make any assertion seem plausible. I see this from time to time in projects where they are on the hunt for the right numbers to measure. In open source, there are a ton of numbers to measure:

- Number of commits

- Number of committers

- Lines of code added/changed/removed

- Commits per week/month

- Commits by organization affiliation

- Project downloads

- Number of issues/pull requests created

- and the list goes on...

The CHAOSS project (`https://chaoss.community/`) is a community that focuses on open source metrics, with the intention of better understanding open source project health. They go quite deep into looking at metrics, focusing on topics such as **diversity, equity, and inclusion** (**DEI**) in open source, the impact of events and meetings on community growth, code base evolution over time, the social value of open source projects, and much more. Needless to say, there are numerous ways to measure the health and success of an open source community.

It's also important to note that not all metrics are created equal. For example, *"lines of code added/ changed/removed"* often isn't very useful as a metric if you apply code styling rules to a code base or have a large code donation, both of which create a skewed result that might indicate "high code velocity" versus the reality of a one-time touching of a lot of lines of code. *"Project downloads"* is also a metric I've seen skewed, as I've heard of cloud providers and sysadmins that, as part of a provisioning script, will pull the code right from the project to ensure its integrity. A project might boast *"We've had 1,000 downloads a week,"* but if 800 of those are from a single client using automated tooling, it's not the same story as 1,000 downloads from 1,000 different people.

Further, knowing the right metrics you can affect is important. An example project is OpenCore Legacy Patcher (`https://github.com/dortania/OpenCore-Legacy-Patcher`), which is a tool that enables you to install more recent versions of macOS on Macs that no longer receive OS updates. This project setting a metric around organizational diversity is likely something that they won't be able to affect; there likely isn't a vendor willing to support an unsupported macOS installation.

It's hard to focus on too many metrics at once, as it becomes hard to optimize for metrics that might be too different depending on how you get there. The **Rule of 3** is a great construct for goal setting for me, as it intentionally keeps the number of things to measure and manage low, but also helps me prioritize and focus on what is important at a given time. Open source projects adopting the same construct help them focus in the same way. But how do you pick which three metrics to focus on? Here are some suggestions depending on what your priorities are.

Growing awareness of the project

At the awareness stage, the goal is to get as many eyes on the project and see some sort of action being taken based on someone seeing the project for the first time. Here, you want to have a combination of both metrics that show someone coming in contact with the project, and also metrics that look at the next step they would take.

The challenge with this metric goes back to the "Rule of 3" constraint, as you can quickly find a bunch of metrics to go after. While challenging, this can help you focus on the initial journey a user goes through in your project. Let's look at a basic one that focuses on discovering a project and the steps where you might use it.

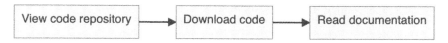

Figure 9.1: User flow from code repository to documentation

Here is a pretty basic flow that captures the steps a user would go through in downloading and using a piece of software. It makes the presumption that the validation of the step for the user is them going to the next step; namely, if a user views the code repository and likes what they see, they will download the code. If the user downloads the code and starts using it, they likely will start reading the documentation to understand how to best use it.

In this case, a project could set metrics like this:

1. 1,000 code repository unique visitors in a month

2. 100 code downloads in a month

3. 100 documentation unique visitors in a month.

I'll note that, often, this progression isn't completely linear as if there is some complexity to the software, the user might read more about it before actually downloading the code. In this case, the progression would be more like *Figure 9.2*.

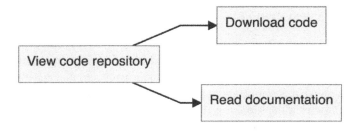

Figure 9.2: User flow to download code or read documentation

Awareness metrics are great starting metrics, but the ultimate goal is to have the project used actively. Let's look at some example project adoption metrics.

Project adoption

Once someone starts to use a project, the next step is looking at the adoption of the project in some way. In commercial projects, there often will be some sort of telemetry in use that is able to report the number of active users, but for open source projects, that invasiveness is often looked down on. Because of that, a project needs to look more at the actions a user would take once they've adopted the software itself. These might include the following:

- Reporting issues
- Asking questions on a mailing list/forum
- Blog posts or conference presentations on the use of the project
- Code contributions back to the project
- Testimonials or case studies about the project being used by someone
- Organization logos or names listed on the project website or in an ADOPTERS file in the code repository

> **Important note**
>
> Note that each of these actions reflects different levels of maturity by the user in their usage of the project. For example, someone using the project early on will likely be reporting issues and asking questions a fair amount. Once they have been using the project for a long period of time, they will be more inclined to be public about it, writing blog posts and testimonials, and indicating they are a user in public forums.

Looking at goal recommendations, if the project is focused on early-stage adopters, these goals might be appropriate:

1. 50 new mailing lists or forums topics per month

2. 20 new issues per month

3. 5 code contributions from new contributors per month

If a project is more focused on mature adopters, these goals might be a better focus:

1. Two blog posts a month from community members about the project's usage

2. Five testimonials a year made publicly about the project being used by them

3. Two organizations a year publicly saying they are using the project

The last two goals might seem too low, but in my experience, getting someone to identify as a user and advocate publicly for others to use it is a high bar to hit.

Some of the most important metrics to focus on are related to diversity; let's look at those now.

Project diversity

A diverse project is a sustainable one, as you have individuals from different areas who can help support the project and aren't reliant on one group of people, one organization, or one region to support your efforts. Diversity is something to think of at the onset of a project, as diversity is shaped by the culture of a project.

When you think about diversity, it has many angles. It could be around aspects of gender, race, age, economic status, or cognitive ability. It can also be more affiliation related, such as employer or nationality. Back to the "Rule of 3," a project needs to prioritize what is important for growth. Generally, for projects, I tend to recommend the following, as it relates to project diversity. When I use the term "maintainer" in this context, it refers to someone who has permission to allow code to be contributed to a given project:

*   No more than 40% of commits from any single organization

*   No more than 40% of maintainers from any single organization

*   30% of maintainers from an under-represented group

You'll note that for the first two organizational diversity metrics, intentionally, the metric is lower than 50%. This means that no single organization has dominance over a project. We saw in *Chapter 2, What Makes a Good Open Source Project?*, that there is value for multiple organizations – including competitors coming together – in driving an open source project. But just because an organization is invested in an open source project today doesn't mean they will be forever; I've seen organizations change direction, drop products, get acquired, and/or see the market conditions change, only to have them de-invest in the project. If a project can ensure that a company leaving doesn't mean the majority of people in the project leave as well, it avoids a catastrophic vacuum. That doesn't mean there won't be a noticeable impact on the project, but it does mean that the project can continue to function.

For the under-represented group metric, this is important to ensure your project is welcoming to all, as we talked about in *Chapter 6, Making Your Project Feel Welcoming*. People from under-represented groups will often feel intimidated in engaging in an open source project if they don't see people like themselves in the project, so having the project intentionally look to have diversity across race, gender, sexual orientation, cognitive ability, age, and more, makes those individuals from under-represented groups more comfortable in taking part in the project.

The metrics highlighted tend to capture the key areas where projects can measure growth: awareness, adoption, and diversity. These key areas are dimensions of how projects measure themselves, though often we see it as a progression – meaning early-stage projects focus on awareness, then projects with awareness begin to look at adoption, and then more established projects look at diversity as it looks to build a diverse and sustainable community. What does a project do when there are areas of growth that are low? Let's look at this in more depth.

Assessing and remedying low areas of growth

Before we dig into this more, I want to tell all maintainers that it's perfectly normal to have areas where growth doesn't hit the targets you are aiming for. Every open source project is a bit different, with different people, priorities, target audiences, industries, and paces of development, and it will tend to be discouraging if you look at your open source project in the same light as something like Node.js or Ruby. Setting goals and metrics is an iterative process, and it is important to re-assess as time progresses to ensure you have the right goals and/or metrics.

Fixing growth issues is quite unique to each specific growth metric. Let's look at a few metrics that I've commonly seen as ones that projects might struggle with and look at some strategies to fix them.

Commits/committers

Projects will often set a metric around the number of commits or committers in a project, which takes various forms, such as the following:

- Number of unique committers
- Number of new contributors in a time period
- Number of commits
- Lines of code added/changed

When these metrics are challenging to achieve, the strategies outlined in *Chapter 6, Making Your Project Feel Welcoming*, and *Chapter 7, Growing Contributors to Maintainers*, are typically ones to focus on improving, as the challenge is often related to contributor onboarding and management. Particular areas to focus on include the following:

- Review the contributor guide, ensuring that it's clear on the expectations and it's not too overbearing on the contributor where it might discourage simple contributions

- Ensure any contributions are regularly reviewed and responded to, and work with contributors to help bring their contributions in

- Recognize new contributors in release announcements to make them feel welcome and appreciated

Another challenge could be attrition happening among contributors. If a project looks at its contributor list and sees contributors "drifting away," meaning formerly active ones have stopped contributing, this could be a sign of burnout (a topic we will dig more into in the *Avoiding burnout* section later in this chapter) or perhaps contributors have changed roles in their organization and the project is no longer relevant to them. Project maintainers should try to reach out to contributors who have drifted away to see what the situation is. Natural attrition happens in open source projects where people ebb and flow as the relevance of the project to them changes over time.

Project usage

Usage metrics can be tricky to measure in open source, as using telemetry is typically discouraged. That all being said, there are metrics that are either leading or lagging indicators of project usage and can be used to help give a sense of project usage, such as the following:

- Downloads or repository clones/forks

- Posts or issues filed regarding using the project

- Blog posts or other social media using the project

Chapter 6, Making Your Project Feel Welcoming, has a number of great recommendations for improving project usage metrics by getting users started and successful quickly with the project. Additionally, a project might consider doing regular surveys of its user base to understand usage patterns and concerns a community might have. One important thing in surveys is to ensure data is collected anonymously, which will help the project get more candid feedback from users. Also, know that with surveys, the most likely people to respond are those with something of concern rather than someone who is perfectly happy with the project. Nonetheless, surveys are a great tool to identify troublesome areas of your project, along with areas where the project is making its users happy.

Diversity

Diversity tends to be one of the more challenging areas to grow in a project, for two reasons:

- It tends to push project maintainers to bring in people not like them

- People that aren't like the project maintainers will often find participating in the project intimidating

Growing diversity in a project doesn't typically happen by happenstance but is by intentional work of the project maintainers. Here are a few strategies to look at in improving diversity:

- Finding individuals already in your project community that come from under-represented backgrounds, and supporting and encouraging them. This can be as simple as sending them a note to thank them for their contributions, or perhaps bringing them to an event or meetup to speak about them using the project. Seeing you as an ally will help them feel confident, and then they will be able to bring others in based on their positive experience.

- Ensure your project has a Code of Conduct in place, as we discussed in *Chapter 8*, *Dealing with Conflict*. This is a great outward sign that the project cares about having an inclusive community.

- Look to grow diverse contributors into maintainers using the strategies outlined in *Chapter 7*, *Growing Contributors to Maintainers*. When people see project leadership as diverse, they will quickly tell that the project is diverse at its core and will be more likely to want to participate.

> **Tip**
>
> I encourage you to check out both the **All In initiative** (`https://allinopensource.org/`) as well as the **Software Developer Diversity Initiative** (`https://sddiproject.org`) for deeper insights and strategies to improve project diversity.

To be able to grow, the project itself needs to scale but project leadership also needs to have a plan for growth and succession. Scaling leadership is an important factor in growing a project and being able to support it long-term. Let's dig more into this topic.

Growing and scaling project leadership

Being a maintainer and a project leader is most often very rewarding, giving the person a chance to showcase their talents and skills while being able to make an impact on others globally. But at the same time, it can be quite stressful, as we saw in *Chapter 8*, *Dealing with Conflict*. I did a cursory search and came up with several stories about the stress a maintainer takes on:

- Being ridiculed for your open source project (`https://harthur.wordpress.com/2013/01/24/771/`)

- Maintainers hitting their breaking point and quitting or even sabotaging their own projects (`https://www.businessinsider.com/open-source-developers-burnout-low-pay-internet-2022-3`)

- Stress on how to say no to a feature request (`https://news.ycombinator.com/item?id=32366248`)

There is a similar pattern I've seen in early-stage start-ups, where you see founders taking on a number of roles from sales to marketing to product development, and roles such as "growth hacker," which, at scale, are completely unsustainable. Most often, this is unintentional, as the level of excitement and dedication grows to such a point where those founders are blind to the number of hours they are putting into their growing company and the impact it is having on them. Open source projects, as they are most often the "scratch-your-own-itch" for the maintainer, fall into the same trap.

We talked a fair amount about identifying potential maintainers and growing them into that role in *Chapter 7, Growing Contributors to Maintainers*, so I won't repeat much of what was discussed there. Instead, let's look at how to take an existing group of maintainers and how to scale them across a project.

From project generalists to project specialists

In the early days of a project, it can be a bit of "all hands on deck" as everyone tends to do a lot of everything. And in those early days, it tends to work out OK; many open source project maintainers tend to have skills that are more than just being a pure software developer. Many open source projects target software developers, which are the same persona as the maintainers, so it's easy for them to relate to their users. And having that tight connection between the maintainers and users helps push a tighter feedback loop from how users are using the project to the direction maintainers should guide the project toward. Thus, having a maintainer leading activities such as outreach, events, and support tends to make a fair amount of sense.

That being said, the project will often get to the point where you see the following situations occurring:

1. The demands of the project become so high that maintainers lack the time to properly devote themselves to a specific area

2. The skills needed to level up areas of the project aren't primary skills for the maintainers, and thus, while they *are* getting done, they aren't done well

It's a hard thing for a maintainer to recognize and acknowledge the preceding situations happening, especially the second one, where a maintainer needs to see the areas in which they aren't as strong. But even recognizing the demands can be challenging, and most of the time, it's in the area where a maintainer doesn't realize how much time they are spending on a task or duty that someone else could do better or more efficiently.

This came up in a project I've worked on (I'll leave the name of the project out). The maintainers were solid, taking the role seriously, and were doing a great job in managing the various processes, including the release cadence. But the problem they kept having was the barrier to entry to contribute to the project was quite high, and they were struggling to convert contributors to maintainers.

One part of the challenge was related to the missing mentorship and contributor development strategies we talked about in *Chapter 7, Growing Contributors to Maintainers*. But a larger issue was that the maintainers were so overwhelmed that they couldn't see how to make the time to develop contributors into maintainers. They saw the barrier to entry for being a contributor and realized they would have to spend too much time developing contributors, so much so that the other areas of the project, which were more important in their view, would suffer.

As I sat down with the project and broke down their challenges and opportunities, a few things emerged:

- There weren't great ways for new users and developers to "self-enable" themselves for the project, meaning there weren't great documentation or training materials. When materials like this were needed, they were largely re-created each time and not recorded or repurposed.

- Maintainers tended to hold similar leadership roles in related projects, which was leading to burnout for them.

- The maintainers would pragmatically tend to manage any participation at industry events, including running meetups, preparing presentations, doing social outreach, and coordinating with event managers. The number of events kept growing for the project, which again was taking away from the time the maintainers could spend in the code base.

- Maintainers were manually managing **contributor license agreements** (**CLAs**), sending out paperwork to each maintainer, and then having to manually cross-reference on the CLA signee list for each new contribution.

You could sum up this as the classic "*focusing on the short-term pains versus long-term opportunities*," meaning the maintainers saw the needs of today and focused on knocking them out, while not looking at larger ways to improve efficiencies and bring in new resources to help.

There were a few things we did quickly with the project that started to help out:

1. First, we implemented a tool similar to CLA Assistant (`https://cla-assistant.io/`) to handle CLA management. This was a quick win and even helped catch a few areas where there were contributions being made and the CLA wasn't in place correctly.

2. Then, we built out a list of the various events for the project, and what participation should look like for each (just a presentation, organizing a meetup, or actually sponsoring the event).

3. Next, I worked with each of the maintainers to understand their responsibilities outside of the project, both to other projects and their employers.

There were some immediate results, but the pain wasn't fully eliminated by a long shot. The next level was to bring in new resources to help in areas where the maintainers could use support but didn't need a maintainer's expertise to accomplish. Here's where we focused:

- We worked to find a technical documentation writer leveraging the **Write the Docs** community (`https://www.writethedocs.org/`). One of the maintainer's employers stepped up to fund this resource.

- One of the maintainers had a friend who was looking for some experience doing social media and blogging outreach for a university class requirement and got them connected to help do outreach for the project. They stepped in to maintain the event list we created, and then put together a simple plan on how to do promotion before and recaps after the event, leading much of the writing.

- We took one of the recent presentations on the project, cleaned it up some to make it more generic, and then recorded someone presenting the materials to make it an introductory training.

The results took a bit of time, as it required the maintainers to pause some of the project development to get these new resources involved, but after about 6 months, maintainers were already seeing how much less stress they had and the value these specialists brought to the project. It was also great for the technical writer and the intern on outreach, as both got jobs with the employers of one of the maintainers (and that employer ensured they had time to still contribute to the project). This is a great part about getting involved in open source, which can help get your work in front of potential employers; we will chat more about this in *Chapter 11, Open Source and the Talent Ecosystem.*

One of the things found in this story was a solution to help maintainers balance their time across other priorities. Let's dig more into that as we focus on maximizing time and managing expectations.

Managing time and expectations

Time management is also expectation management, meaning being able to set expectations of what can be done, by when, and what is needed to complete a task. This is where the phrase *"bite off more than you can chew"* comes into focus, because often, what seems simple becomes more complex as you dig into it. This could be a simple bug fix that highlights larger architectural problems in the code base or maybe responding to support requests and issues that become more time-consuming. For a maintainer, this could manifest itself as too many meetings, too many requests to present or speak about the project at events, or too many pull requests or code contributions to review.

Scaling is not just adding more resources but also working more effectively. Many in the software development field will reference Fred Brook's book *The Mythical Man-Month: Essays on Software Engineering*, in which the central tenet is the idea that adding manpower to a software project that is behind schedule delays it even longer. I've seen with projects that the problem isn't not having enough people involved but more with streamlining work and setting expectations.

Strategies for scaling and setting expectations include the following:

- Set boundaries for how much time you will dedicate to a task. For example, state that you will only dedicate an hour a day to triaging pull requests and issues.

- When the amount of time dedicated to a task appears to be not enough, assess why. It could be for several reasons:

  - What is needed is too tedious. For the example of the pull request and issue triaging, maybe the system being used isn't well set up and could be improved.

  - Are there better ways to accomplish the task? For issues requests, maybe if you are seeing the same issue over and over, there should be documentation added and the user directed towards that first. Or maybe common issues should be linked together. If the task is around preparing for a meetup, perhaps making a standard template for everything needing to be done would help streamline things.

- Do you just need more resources or a dedicated resource? Perhaps instead of a maintainer doing issue triaging, there should be a dedicated person doing the triaging who can bring in a maintainer when they have questions.

• Communicate the expected timeframe for when a task should be done. For issue triaging, this might be saying that all issues will be reviewed within 5 days.

Communication is key with open source projects – being as transparent and honest as possible can often build stronger bonds and trust between maintainers, contributors, and users. Looking at the aforementioned OpenCore Legacy Patcher project (`https://github.com/dortania/OpenCore-Legacy-Patcher`), the primary maintainer had a family based in Ukraine. This maintainer knew he couldn't support users for the time being as he needed to tend to his family due to the outbreak of war, so he opened an issue to explain the situation.

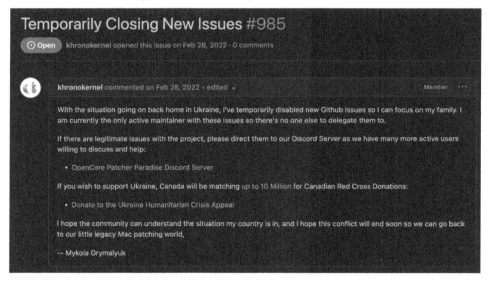

Figure 9.3: OpenCore Legacy Patcher maintainer indicating new issues will be temporarily closed (https://github.com/dortania/OpenCore-Legacy-Patcher/issues/985)

This maintainer did a great job of explaining his situation and setting expectations well. And as it turned out, the pause was fairly temporary as the project cadence continued a few months later once his family situation was settled.

The risk of not managing time well is burnout; let's look more at what burnout is and ways for a maintainer to avoid it.

Avoiding burnout

The articles I linked to at the beginning of this section point to a theme that, at the time of this writing, is one of the hot topics in open source: burnout. Burnout is often what we see, but in reality, it's the last step in a larger continuum of stress that isn't well managed by a project maintainer.

Figure 9.4: Burnout continuum

If you look at the continuum outlined in *Figure 9.4*, you can probably resonate with some of the stages/symptoms outlined. We've all been tired after a long stretch of work. Sometimes, the work we do becomes so much that we never think it's enough. Forcing yourself to sit down and concentrate can be a challenge when you have multiple other priorities to balance with both other work roles and also family and personal priorities.

There's a story from the great Pat Riley, who was a longtime NBA head coach and general manager, where he talks about a whitewater rafting trip he once went on. As part of the safety instructions they gave the group prior to getting in the raft, the instructor said,

"If you fall into the water, you can't just sit there in the water and hope someone comes to rescue you; you need to let the others know you fell out of the boat and try to swim back. You need to be an active participant in your own rescue."

That last statement rings true, as it's hard for other maintainers to often see the stress a maintainer is under and find ways to help.

So, what can a maintainer do to help themselves avoid burnout? Here are some suggestions:

- Use a task management system for capturing all the things you need to do. I'd suggest having one specific to the project itself, but also one for other areas of work and also for your personal/family to-dos. As we get older, it's hard to keep it all in our heads, but writing things down can also help us visualize what needs to be done.

- With a task management system, use some sort of system to help prioritize or schedule items. I like to put in dates for tasks to do, as this gives me a way to pace my work and know what needs to be focused on at a given time.

- Schedule downtime throughout the day, and stick to it. I try to block out 5:00 p.m. to 9:00 p.m. each day for family activities, limiting any work emails or meetings. Similarly, taking a midday break is important.

- Use weekends as much as possible for recouping, and not work. I try to keep work on projects to just a few hours in the morning before the rest of my family gets going for the day, and then step away from things for the day.

- Schedule holidays and vacations, and then actually use them for rest and recouping as well and not for working on that one project feature you've wanted to fix.

- Ensure you are eating well and getting proper sleep and exercise. Fatigue, illness, and anxiety, are all symptoms of not taking care of your health.

- Find activities outside of the project that brings enjoyment. This might be a sport (I ski, kayak, and bike), volunteering or other work (for me, this is volleyball officiating), spending time with friends and family, or hobbies. It's important that it's different from what you do daily, so taking on a new open source project isn't a really good hobby; doing something entirely different such as woodworking or cooking is.

- Get regular health checkups. For those of us in areas of the world with great healthcare systems available to us, we are often the worst about actually using them. Schedule at least a yearly physical checkup.

- When you hit a mental roadblock, walk away for a while and do something different. Maybe read a book, play a game, or go for a walk. Or even chat with someone about it. Changing mental perspectives helps get past mental roadblocks.

You'll probably note that most of this advice isn't specific to open source but to life in general. It's easy for any part of your life to be consuming, and when it becomes consuming, that is when the symptoms in the burnout continuum in *Figure 9.4* start to present themselves.

Summary

This chapter focused on how to handle growth in an open source project, both in the realm of setting good metrics to measure growth and also ensuring the project leadership can scale alongside this growth. Too often, projects that could become great projects are crushed under their own weight, and staying ahead of that ensures a project can become sustainable for the long term.

When a project is viewed as sustainable, organizations look to invest and adopt it for their own internal use as well as build it into their own products. Commercialization might be viewed as an anti-pattern to open source, but in reality, it's a validation that the project has value. In the next chapter, we will look at how projects can best manage commercialization.

Part 3:
Building and Scaling
Open Source Ecosystems

In this part, you will learn about some of the advanced concepts as your open source project grows to become an open source ecosystem and how to best build and scale that open source ecosystem. Topics you will learn about include commercialization strategies in open source, open source and the talent ecosystem, marketing for open source, and best practices for transitioning leadership. Finally, we will cover how to best sunset an open source project.

This part contains the following chapters:

- *Chapter 10, Commercialization of Open Source*
- *Chapter 11, Open Source and the Talent Ecosystem*
- *Chapter 12, Marketing for Open Source - Advocacy and Outreach*
- *Chapter 13, Transitioning Leadership*
- *Chapter 14, Sunsetting an Open Source Project*

10
Commercialization of Open Source

In *Chapter 1*, *The Whats and Whys of Open Source*, we talked about how open source was the realm of hackers and counter-culture movements and considered by many as the antithesis of commercial software. This is the case due to the actions of some prominent commercial software vendors in response to open source. Microsoft was known to be a primary opponent to open source back in the 1990s and early 2000s with the internal stance of "embrace and extend," which was a tactic used with other competitive software vendors to gain dominance over a market. Using that same strategy with open source generally isn't successful, as with its "scratch-your-own-itch" model, open source projects cover spaces that might not be profitable for a commercial product to exist in. Or many times, it's the ability to view and modify the source code itself that is valuable, and that's something commercial software generally can't provide.

I will say that corporate involvement in open source has come a long way, with these organizations taking a much more responsible and respective approach as they work with open source projects and communities. In my days maintaining the PHP Windows Installer, Microsoft approached me, asking me to fix a few issues to make the installer work better with Windows Server 2003 (yes, I'm dating myself). Microsoft set me up with a copy of Windows Server 2003 for testing and development, and as a token of gratitude not only recognized me publically for my contributions but also sent me a Microsoft Zune as a gift. This is something they surely didn't need to do, but they wanted to show goodwill for the work I did.

While open source software is free to use in compliance with the license it is released under, a successful project will see commercial usage. In this chapter, we will explore how a project could be used commercially, and how a project can be best set up for commercial use. We'll cover the following topics:

- The importance and value of an open source project being used commercially
- Commercialization models for open source
- Setting your project up for commercial usage

Let's start by addressing the concerns many in the open source community have when their project is brought into commercial software or delivered commercially.

The importance and value of an open source project being used commercially

As you may recall from both *Chapter 1*, and *Chapter 3* there have been generally two approaches to software licensing: permissive (meaning one that has minimal restrictions on reuse of the code) and copyleft (meaning that the code license has specific restrictions to ensure any derivative works also stay under the same open source license). Copyleft licenses are generally used by projects where taking the project and reselling it commercially is a large concern.

There are some use cases where that is a valid concern, namely in the area of open source software. which is more end user focused, such as a desktop application such as LibreOffice, Inkscape, GIMP, or Firefox. However, that doesn't mean the software can't be used commercially as over time, we've seen creative ways around this. Examples include offering services and support around the software itself, "open-core" models where commercial add-ons are licensed separately, or "Tivoization," where source code is made available but significant proprietary hardware and other software is required to leverage the source code modifications. We will dig more into those mechanisms of commercialization in the next few sections.

Is commercial usage ok?

In the introduction to this chapter, I talked about how open source was considered the "antithesis" of commercial software in its early days. Open source software is often lumped together with free and libre software under the term **FLOSS**, which stands for **Free Libre and Open Source Software**. If you are familiar with the term *libre*, you'll know it is an Italian word for *free*. There's a saying in the open source community that open source is "free as in freedom, not free as in beer," which ties to the root of the word *libre* being used more to describe freedom versus something of no cost.

If you create an open source project, you are effectively providing the software for no monetary cost (although in the early days of open source before the internet was prevalent, charging a nominal fee for a CD or disk with the software was acceptable; in fact, the GNU Public License specifically addresses and provides permission for this). Even though it is free, the license the code is under provides the terms and guidance to the user of the project on how to use it. While you cannot be discriminatory toward a particular class of users (that is, provide different terms for commercial versus personal usage), the maintainer can choose the degree of responsibilities the user of the project must adhere to. More on these license models was covered in *Chapter 3, Open Source License and IP Management*.

As shown in *Figure 10.1*, the sustainability of a project is dependent on its usage and market acceptance. Commercial usage is just like any usage, and whether a company is using it internally or making it part of a product, this validates the project's value on the market.

I often see sensitivities when companies use the project commercially without giving back in some form, whether this is by adding developers, funding, or other investments. Companies are looked upon as "taking advantage of open source" and "using projects as free labor for commercial gain," which you will find occurs in open source. While some companies might be predatory in this way, in my experience, many have good intentions and either are new to open source or have trouble knowing how to engage. We will dig more into this topic in the *Setting up your project for commercial usage* section.

In this section, we saw that commercial usage is OK, and just like any other usage of a project. Commercial usage, like any usage, contributes to a sustainable model for an open source project to exist in. Let's look at the sustainability cycle in more detail.

The sustainability cycle

There's a diagram I often use to illustrate how sustainability works in open source projects, which you can see in *Figure 10.1*:

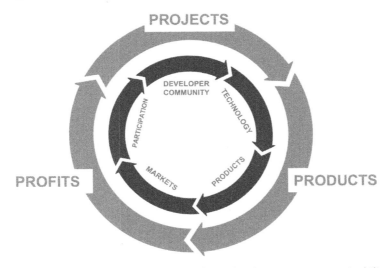

Figure 10.1 – Projects, Products, and Profits cycle of open source sustainability
(https://www.linuxfoundation.jp/blog/2017/09/new-initiatives-to-create-
sustainable-open-source-projects-at-the-linux-foundation/) – CC by 3.0

This diagram illustrates the continuous loop an open source project operates in concerning market viability. Let's look at each piece.

Projects

Projects are simply a collection of software code and also the community itself. Open source communities, as we've seen across this entire book, are successful when a strong, collaborative, and diverse group comes together to build technology that they all see as important to them and the work they do. This community can be a combination of corporate employees working on their employer's behalf, and/or simply individuals that have an interest and a passion for this space.

Products

As a project becomes more and more useful and valuable to the market, the project itself will become productized. Productization could mean several things, from taking the project and selling it as a commercial product, incorporating pieces of the project into a larger commercial product, or offering service and support. These are common areas where a software vendor sees an opportunity to use the project to aid in selling their software.

But another angle of productization is usage, meaning someone takes the project and uses it in one way or another. Perhaps this is a developer that leverages an open source library in something they are building. Or maybe it's a company using an open source project internally for doing reporting or integration. The very nature of the project being used by others is, in effect, productization, as the project is being consumed just like any other product would be.

Profits

Commercial software vendors release new software all the time to address what they see as the needs of a market. Sometimes, it ends up quite lucrative, where the software catches on and the vendor continues to support and update it over time. Sometimes, it ends up being a flop, and the vendor decides to no longer develop or support the software because it doesn't make economic sense to them. And over time, markets change and software that today is popular becomes less so due to economic, technological, or other conditions. All of these decisions are driven by economic value or profit.

For this sustainability cycle, profit is the key part that validates the productization of the open source project itself. That economic value can manifest itself in several different ways, such as these:

- Lower cost of research and software development, by not having to write and maintain code that an open source project could provide instead

- Larger addressable market, by adding features and functionality to a project that the current development team doesn't have the time or expertise for

- Faster time to market, where the development team can leverage one or more open source projects as building blocks for their commercial product rather than having to build them all out themselves

Each of these factors generates an economic value for the commercial software vendor. The same holds for a user of an open source project; the fact that they don't have to write the same code that exists in an open source project saves them time and money. Looking back on my example of the PiSCSI project in *Chapter 1, The Whats and Whys of Open Source,* (`https://github.com/PiSCSI/piscsi`), the existence of that project for me as I was restoring my Macintosh IIsi meant that I didn't need to track down expensive, slow, and hard-to-find SCSI hard drives and network cards, and instead could use an off-the-shelf Raspberry Pi Zero with an extra header board to emulate both. The savings to me was both time and money, with an additional value of the flexibility provided, all of which created economic value and represented profit.

What's important to complete the cycle is investing that profit back into the project. This could mean simply community participation and providing feedback. It could also be adding development support to the project by a company assigning developers to work on the project, sponsoring infrastructure, or marketing support, or in the case of an individual, that person helping maintain the project. It could also mean direct financial support to the project, a topic we will dig into as we discuss setting up your project for commercial usage. Either way, investing back into a project that has created economic value means it can continue to grow and function over time.

There are several ways for projects to be commercialized; let's look at those now.

Commercialization models for open source

As open source projects can have many forms, from code snippets to fully featured applications, the models of commercialization are different. Additionally, the license you choose impacts commercialization, as leveraging code under more copyleft licenses adds more complexities than code under permissive licenses.

The commercial model of open source has evolved over the years, but we generally see one of three models. Let's look at them now.

Dependency or component of a larger commercial software package

The first model involves using open source software as a dependency or component of a larger commercial software package. This is probably the most common example of open source software in commercial usage, and often the one most people don't see. *Figure 10.2* illustrates what the typical application stack looks like concerning open source:

Figure 10.2 – Breakdown of a typical application and where open source is used

Modern applications tend to be built on a framework of some sort, such as the **Linux, Apache, PHP, MySQL (LAMP)** stack, Bootstrap.js, or some other tool or development platform. The majority of these applications are built in open source, even ones developed by commercial vendors, as this aids in being able to handle broader use cases. At the top level, you see open source used in solving common problems, whether that would be using a SAML library to support authentication or perhaps a base theme for a WordPress or Jekyll website. If you look at the total lines of code, you generally see anywhere from 80-90% of the code base being open source, which most people don't realize. This especially comes to light when there are large security vulnerabilities in these base components, as companies are assessing how they are affected and how to upgrade those components to secure versions.

One consideration when a dependency or component is used as part of a larger commercial software package is to ensure that the proper attributions are kept in place in the open source code. This includes both license file headers in the source code, but also a more formal software bill of materials (also known as **SBOM**) that details the components and the licenses used in the product. If your commercial product uses a common tool for managing third-party dependencies such as PyPi for Python, this is usually easy to track down. If not, it can be a bit more manual. Further, using **Software Package Data Exchange**® (**SPDX**®) short-form license identifiers makes tools such as FOSSology that do license scanning produce more accurate results – learn more about this at https://spdx.org.

Let's look at the next example of how an open source project is commercialized: through service and support.

Service and support

Service and support was one of the earliest models in open source commercialization, popularized by Red Hat with its Red Hat Linux Enterprise support programs. The recognition was that open source software was essentially free to use, but as with all software, end users run into problems or have issues and need someone that can help. For companies, having problems with the software that their business relies on can be a huge problem, and having the proverbial "throat to choke" gives them a bit of peace of mind in using the software.

Service and support can mean a few different things:

- A traditional call center or support center where people can talk to someone about a problem they are having, get help on how to solve it, or a workaround

- Help with installing or implementing the open source software itself, such as setting up the server or building customizations

- Training and education, whether instructor-led or virtual training, or perhaps a book publisher such as Packt having a book on using a particular open source project

The biggest challenge in this model is also its greatest appeal – a low barrier to entry. This has been a space where many companies have set up businesses around supporting open source software. While this is often done with the best intentions, it also creates a bit of confusion. Think of this like when you might need a plumber to fix a drain or sink in your house; you can go through online resources to find several ones nearby, or perhaps chat with friends and family, but outside of rating systems, it's often hard to differentiate. For open source projects, you see the same model, where someone sets up a business saying "Provides commercial support for project X," but what that looks like can vary. The challenge here is that by using the brand of the project, it can provide a negative view of the project itself if that vendor isn't a good one, even though that vendor is likely not part of the project. We will talk about the use of vendor and conformance programs in the next section, where we will look at strategies to help.

Open Core

We talked about the Open Core model in *Chapter 2, What Makes a Good Open Source Project?*, along with the challenges of using this model. Nonetheless, it is still a common and valid commercialization strategy. I won't spend too much time on the model here as it was covered previously.

A somewhat analogous model to open core is where the open source might be a base framework, and there are several commercial extensions available that can connect or integrate with it. We've seen this in Linux with many specialty device drivers kept under a commercial license, but designed to work with Linux. We've also seen it in ecosystems such as Hadoop, where vendors would build integrations from data visualization tools to Hadoop to leverage data stored in those data lakes.

With an understanding of the various business models possible, let's look at how to best set up your project for commercial usage.

Setting your project up for commercial usage

Creating a way for commercial vendors to use and leverage your project invites more usage, often in ways you might not have imagined before. It also opens up the possibility of new contributors and maintainers to help support and drive your project, helping improve how things work and the quality of the code base itself.

There are some things we should consider for a project to ensure that commercial usage adds value versus creates confusion. Let's look at them now, starting with branding and IP management.

Branding and IP management

As we illustrated at the start of *Chapter 3, Open Source License and IP Management*, having solid management of your project's brand and IP is crucial. If you talk with a lawyer that specializes in intellectual property, they will likely stress how ensuring your project's brand is being used as intended is quite crucial to helping users understand the project.

We covered branding and IP management extensively in *Chapter 3, Open Source License and IP Management*, and encourage you to reference that chapter for more specific information on that topic. As it relates to commercial usage, there are two considerations to keep in mind:

- If you have a popular project, vendors will want to reference the name and/or brand of the project as part of their product name. This is an area where a project has to be careful, as it's very important to separate any commercial products from the project itself. I highly suggest building branding guidelines for your project to help describe the right and wrong way to reference the project or its brand in a commercial product; some examples are as follows:

    - **Open Mainframe Project Brand Guidelines** (`https://www.openmainframeproject.org/branding-guidelines`)

    - **HyperLedger Branding Guidelines** (`https://www.hyperledger.org/wp-content/uploads/2017/03/hyperledger_trademark_usage_guidelines_031417.pdf`)

    - **Eclipse Branding guidelines** (`https://www.eclipse.org/legal/documents/eclipse_foundation_branding_guidelines.pdf`)

- Depending on the license used, it's important that vendors properly attribute the use of the project to their product. This can be a hard one to police, but providing guidance on how to best do this usually will mean the vendor will comply.

Often, vendors are quite appreciative of the project community and want to work with them. Just like in *Chapter 6, Making Your Project Feel Welcoming*, creating ways to make your project welcoming and appreciative of vendors shows goodwill toward them too. Let's look at some ideas for this.

Recognition and conformance programs

Recognizing vendors being users of the project not only shows goodwill towards them but also shows validation of the open source project itself. If you have experience in commercial software product marketing, you know that one of the biggest sales aids for your product is the logo of a company or testimonial of a user that has used your software. Open source is no different, and many projects will leverage this to help them grow.

That being said, it's important to have mechanisms to make it easy for commercial users to both be recognized for using the project, as well as using the project in line with the way the maintainers and the larger community would expect. There are different ways to best do this, depending on how the project is intended to be used.

If the open source project is primarily meant to be consumed and used, a simple user recognition program is a great way to call out users of the project. This can take several different forms:

- The simplest way is for the project to have an ADOPTERS file in its code repository. Maintainers can add users of the project to this file (with their permission, of course), or better yet, end users can add themselves to the ADOPTERS file. The latter method is preferred, as the user doing a pull request to add themselves ensures explicit permission has been granted to reference the user.

- If you have users that are not only willing to state they are a user but are willing to provide an endorsement, then consider a user testimonial or case study program. If you are from a product marketing background, this might feel daunting or like overkill, but in reality, a good case study is pretty simple in form: what problem did the user have, why did they choose the project, how has the project solved their problem, and what plans do they have in the future? And if it's just a testimonial, it's a simple quote from the given user. If you use GitHub or GitLab for your project management, you can set up a pull request template or issue template to collect them, and again leverage an ADOPTERS file or something similar. If your project has a formal web page, then add them there.

If the project is designed to be a framework where users could build on the project or something that could be integrated into a larger software application to provide interoperability, then one possibility is to use a conformance program. We talked about the usage of conformance programs in *Chapter 1* and *Chapter 3*, but building on those chapters, conformance programs are simply a way for a project to create a neutral mechanism for recognizing vendor solutions related to an open source project.

Establishing a conformance program often takes the form of a legal contract between the project and the specific vendor. Here are the general steps for establishing such a program:

1. First, determine what conformance looks like. Often, this is API compatibility between different implementations, but could also be applications that integrate into a particular endpoint or part of the project in a standard way. Support and service vendors could also have a conformance program, where the project might want to determine if a vendor has the competence to properly support users of the project.

2. Once you have determined what conformance looks like, you can start to formally define the requirements. These should be driven by the project community itself openly and transparently, as conformance programs intend to be vendor-neutral. There are generally two parts to the requirements:

   - One is the technical part, where the community can define what the implementation or application needs to do to be conformant, or in the case of support or service conformance, what the vendor's capabilities must be. It's best to make these requirements both objective (meaning you can easily determine if it is fulfilled, and not left up to an opinion or personal preference) and preferably with some sort of battery of tests that can be run against the software. If there aren't tests, a simple checklist can suffice.

   - Second is the business requirements, which usually means some sort of funding for the project and obligations of the vendor to maintain the technical requirements for a given period.

3. Finally, a project needs to set up how to operationally process conformance applications. A project needs to be careful here, as competitors to the vendor submitting conformance might be part of the project leadership. Here, having an independent third-party (such as a project staff member) process applications is preferred, and these applications can be reviewed confidentially to avoid any concerns of vendor influence over accepting conformance applications. The project will also need to set up a place to list conformance applications and implementations, as well as logos and branding marks for the vendor to use to showcase their conformance.

Conformance programs are great ways to generate funding for the project, as we all know running an open source project has some costs involved with it. As we chatted about in *Chapter 5, Governance and Hosting Models*, using a conformance program is a great way to drive financial support for your open source project. This is because it ties back the support to a tangible value for the company, that being brand and market recognition for the application or implementation in line with the project itself. This makes it easier for companies to find the budget for funding from product marketing versus development, as the former tends to have more flexibility and be tied to profit centers in the business, whereas development costs are tied to cost centers.

Summary

In this chapter, we looked at how the commercialization of open source projects works while building on the concepts started in *Chapter 3*, as well as *Chapter 5*. We saw how sustainability in open source is tied to productization, whether that be by individual users or corporations/vendors. We then saw common models of commercialization for open source projects. Finally, we looked at some ways to best set your project up for commercial usage.

Commercialization of open source is still quite controversial, as it is sometimes viewed that companies take advantage of open source projects and open source developers for corporate gain. But I can first-hand say that this is an exception rather than the norm; look back to the story I led off with in this chapter in my work with Microsoft around the PHP Windows Installer. The work I did ended up being an opportunity for me to grow my career as an open source developer. While I didn't get a job at Microsoft, it did open up other opportunities for me. In the next chapter, I'll talk about my story more, and share some ideas on how open source can jumpstart your career as well.

11
Open Source and the Talent Ecosystem

As I've mentioned several times in this book, open source is a "scratch-your-own-itch" model, meaning individuals get involved with projects that interest them, solve problems they have, and contribute in beneficial ways. The benefit to the individual can be in several tangible ways and usually relates to an acute need, such as a framework for building a software application, tools for working with a device, or full applications to replace commercial software. But many also look at open source as an enabler for their career, where their contributions and peer recognition can be a way to showcase their skills to potential employers.

The investments we've seen by companies in open source in recent years are a testament to the importance of open source for them to better execute as a company, which we looked at in *Chapter 10, Commercialization of Open Source*. This chapter digs into one major aspect of that execution, which is attracting and retaining great talent. Developers today are keen to make sure they can contribute to open source as part of their job; for them, it's, in a way, an "insurance policy" in the sense that they are building a portfolio to make them more relevant in the job market. Employers naturally worry about this; if an employer's investment in an employee effectively makes it easier to leave, isn't that the wrong approach? It's not; we've seen in many research reports and surveys that employees value company culture and interesting work the most, so if a company continues to invest in that, they likely will better retain talent. Participating in open source fits into that value proposition for developers, so it's really important that employers recognize that versus trying to prevent it.

My passion for open source is because of not only the collaboration and innovation it drives, but because it has been an enabler in my career, which as of this writing, spans nearly 25 years of using, contributing to, and leading open source projects. I could trace it back even further, to the early 1990s, when, in computer magazines, they would have programs written in BASIC that you could type into your computer. BASIC interpreters weren't standardized, and the programs were often written in BASIC for Apple II or Commodore computers; my family had a TI/99-4A, so as I typed in the BASIC code, I would need to do the translation to the nuances of the BASIC dialect for the computer I had. If only we had a platform such as GitHub or GitLab back then; I probably would have published the code for others as sometimes it was quite tricky to get it all right.

In this chapter, you will see how you, as an open source project contributor or maintainer, could leverage your work to grow your career. Additionally, we will look at how organizations can find new talent among the contributors to open source projects that they use. Finally, we will build on *Chapter 4, Aligning the Business Value of Open Source for Your Employer* where we spoke about how organizations can recognize their own employees who contribute to open source, by seeing how organizations can support career growth for contributors. The topics we will cover include the following:

- Open source as your portfolio
- Finding talent through open source
- Recognizing employee contributions to open source

Let's start by looking at how open source can be a portfolio for a developer or open source enthusiast.

Open source as your portfolio

The concept of a "portfolio" is often associated with artists and photographers, where it is used as a tool to evaluate the skills and specialties of a person by seeing what they've done in the past. In software development, historically, there hasn't been this same tool. You most often see employers use coding challenges in addition to credentials from a candidate's resume or CV to determine the skills and capabilities of a software developer. Sometimes the strategy works, and sometimes it doesn't.

Back in the 1980s and 1990s, and into the early 2000s, most software developers were considered "full-stack developers," meaning they had competence in all areas of application development, from frontend design to backend coding, database management, and server installation and configuration. Software development became more specialized in the 2010s, with developers often more skilled in specific areas such as database management, frontend development, or specific technologies, such as Python, Java, or Node.js. This proliferation has made identifying talent more challenging, both from the perspective of finding developers with a particular skill as well as for potential employees to appropriately share their competence.

With open source, all the code a developer creates is made available under a license that allows it to be viewed by all, so potential employees can share links to code repositories they contribute to. Additionally, employers looking for specific skills can view the discussions and code collaboration of a community and find the developers who know the most – and then those employers can proactively reach out to them.

This shift has made an impact on software developer careers globally – even for me! Let me share my story.

My career story

I went to Kent State University and majored in computer science, learning several languages, including C, Perl, MATLAB, Lisp, Bash scripting, and PHP. PHP was especially interesting to me; we used it in a Capstone project where we built a website for a local county government. What impressed me the most about PHP at the time was how little code was required to do something useful. I even created a simple weblog site for my honeymoon.

My broad computer science education, and my growing PHP skills, were helpful in landing my first job as a software developer for a local financial services company back in 2001. If you were around in 2001, you know it was the high point of the first dot-com bubble bursting. Combined with the general economic downturn after the 9/11 attacks in the United States, jobs were difficult to come by.

At that first job, my primary role was development in FoxPro and Visual FoxPro as that was what the applications they used were developed in (a fairly common case for small businesses at that time). But they had an interest in improving how they engaged their customers and wanted to start offering access to accounts via the web. My PHP skills were immediately useful here, and in my 7 years, I built out numerous web frontends to the internal systems they had, which helped them better serve their customers and reduce internal costs.

Getting more involved in the PHP community

As I was getting more into PHP, I started getting more and more involved in the community. At first, I submitted a few bugs to the PHP project, which were fixed over time. Then I started attending PHP conferences, the first being php|works 2003 in Toronto; another PHP conference after in Vancouver; and the next summer, **O'Reilly's Open Source Convention (OSCON)**. It was quite an experience seeing the open source community up close and personal, hearing Rasmus Lerdorf himself speak, learning about new trends in PHP development, and meeting some amazing developers building applications, libraries, and tools in PHP. My biggest takeaway, outside of the technical skills and tips, was the strength of communities and how everyone had a way they could participate. I remember talking with a speaker about **AJAX** (which stands for **Asynchronous JavaScript and XML**) and at the time AJAX was an emerging technology topic. While I learned a lot from the speaker's experience, the speaker also valued what I had done with AJAX. It was quite cool that both of us were teachers and pupils in the same conversation.

I kept doing more and more with PHP, including using some of the newer features of PHP 5 and starting to refactor the web applications I was building to use the up-and-coming Zend Framework (which now is the Laminas project). One thing that stuck out to me was the experience of developing PHP on Windows. While it worked, it took a bit to get it all set up correctly. There were some efforts out there to build installer packages for PHP, but most were either clunky or included the Apache Web Server and MySQL. While that was helpful, the install wasn't very much like how Windows apps were installed.

I contacted the main developer for the current PHP Windows installer and shared that I was interested in rebuilding the installer using a new open source project from Microsoft called Wix. Wix was one of the first open source projects that came out of Microsoft and was designed to enable building native MSI-based installers for applications using XML. I was interested in playing with Wix, so this seemed like a great opportunity to do so!

It took a few months, as while doing this my wife and I were expecting our first child, but shortly after she was born, I put out the first beta release of the installer. *Figure 11.1* is my brave first post to the php.internals mailing list announcing the installer.

New Installer for PHP 5.2

From:	John Mertic	Date:	Mon, 24 Jul 2006 14:52:01 +0000
Subject:	New Installer for PHP 5.2		
Groups:	php.internals		

Hi there,

With the guidance of Phil Driscoll, I have put together a new installer for PHP on Windows. It replicates much of the same functionality of his installer, but also boasts the following features:

- Selective installation of all PHP components (CGI and CLI exes, server modules, standard and PECL extensions).
- Configures the php.ini for the installation, including enabling the extensions the user selected to install.
- Built as an MSI using Wix (http://wix.sourceforge.net) which is scriptable and open source so we can include the code to build the installer in cvs and automate building it. Also MSI Installers are very useful for Sys Admins since they integrate into Group Policies to allow unattended installation, and are better supported on Windows in general.

Thanks to Edin Kadribasic, the public test version (which installs a recent snapshot of PHP 5.2) is located at http://downloads.php.net/edink/php-5.2.0-win32-installer.msi.

I am looking for feedback on the installer, namely in the following areas:

- Default install options; what should the default install consist of?
- Lite Installer. The current install file weighs in at 18mb. Would we want a lite installer with fewer components and if so what would those be?

Figure 11.1 – Release announcement for the PHP Windows installer for PHP 5.2 (https://news-web.php.net/php.internals/24929)

I got tons of feedback from those on the php.internals mailing list over the next few weeks and released an updated version about a month later. It was an exhilarating experience – not just writing code with feedback from the community, but getting feedback from core developers of PHP at the time. Folks such as Ilia Alshanetsky, Wez Furlong, Steph Fox, and others chimed in to give feedback. It was like the moment you met a celebrity – it was surreal. But while they were amazing engineers with tons of experience, they were just normal software developers like me, which at the time I didn't expect, but looking back on, it aligns with many of the people I've met in open source.

What was a surreal moment was getting an email from Kanwaljeet Singla, who was a software engineer at Microsoft. Microsoft was wanting to improve its support for PHP on Windows, especially with Windows Server and their web server known as **Internet Information Services** (**IIS**). He had some feedback on how IIS worked and wanted to see if I could help improve the installer for a better experience on Windows. In my head, I thought "Microsoft wants me to write code to help them? Sign me up!" Again, probably one of those celebrity moments. We worked together for several weeks, and they provided a free copy of Windows Server 2003 for testing. We got everything sorted out and made part of a PHP 5.2 point release later that year. And as a token of gratitude, they sent me a Microsoft Zune MP3 player.

PHP community work opens new doors

As I was effectively a PHP maintainer at that point, I was getting more attention in the PHP community. I found out I made a card deck of key people in PHP that Zend put out in 2007, and had several job offers from employers looking for PHP talent. The open source as your portfolio concept was truly working for me.

In late 2007, I took a job as a software engineer at SugarCRM, then one of the biggest open source PHP applications in existence. What helped me land that opportunity was not only the work I did in the PHP community but the people I met. One in particular, Travis Swicegood, was working at SugarCRM at the time and got me connected to them. It was also my first time working as a remote employee, which was a big shift for me but one that, as of this writing, I've loved (going on 16 years!). I had a great opportunity to work with amazing engineers there: Majed Itani, Roger Smith, Collin Lee, Andy Wu, Jacob Taylor, and others.

Over time at SugarCRM, my interest in engaging the community grew, and I took the leap in late 2008 and applied to speak at conferences. I had several rejections, being a new speaker, but one took a chance on me: DC PHP Conference. It was a bit nerve-wracking as I was no longer as anonymous in the community, but now in front of people as an expert. I'll admit, the talk wasn't very good. But I got better over time, and today I have many keynotes under my belt and hundreds of talks done globally.

After a few years at SugarCRM, and being invited multiple times to speak at conferences throughout the United States, as well as Europe, I was promoted to community manager. This meant I was in charge of leading and growing the SugarCRM community, as well as being an ambassador for SugarCRM in the tech and open source world.

This opened many doors for me. I was invited to serve on the board of OW2 (`ow2.org`), as well as to be the secretary and eventually the president of the OpenSocial Foundation (now defunct). Speaking globally, I was invited to more conferences, meeting and learning from people big in open source – many I'm still connected to today.

One memory I have of that period was a dinner I was invited to by Larry Augustin, then CEO at SugarCRM, after his keynote at LinuxTag 2010 in Berlin. At that dinner was Chris Dibona and Dirk Hohndel. Chris, at that time, led open source at Google (and still does to this day) and Dirk, at the time, led open source at Intel and the Meebo project (later, he led open source at VMware and Verizon, as well as serving as an advisor to the Linux Foundation). Remember that celebrity moment I had when I first released the PHP Windows Installer? This was the same, times 100! Chris checked out my new Android phone, an HTC Incredible 2, as Android was quite new and he hadn't seen that phone yet. They all shared stories of their years in open source and I sat there almost completely frozen – half petrified and half taking in the moment. I look back and feel embarrassed about that dinner (Larry, Chris, and Dirk – if you read this and remember that dinner, apologies again!).

Community management grows into leadership

In my later time at SugarCRM, I helped jumpstart our software partners program, which gave me some great experience in connecting business value back to open source. I was able to do that again in my next role at Bitnami, where Daniel Lopez Ridruejo and Erica Brescia trusted me to launch a similar program with the growing cloud enablement business. Both experiences weren't perfect; I hit a number of bumps in the road but also has some nice successes in helping both companies drive more revenue. It was valuable for me as it made me realize what drives collaborative work – mutual benefit.

In 2015, Jim Zemlin connected with me about roles in the growing Linux Foundation. The opportunity for me was a dream come true – the opportunity to work in driving open source across multiple companies and industries, with the ability to focus on making open source projects successful. Late in 2015, an opportunity opened up to lead the newly launched ODPi project and the Open Mainframe Project. In my time at the Linux Foundation, I've been able to connect my experience working as a developer, maintainer, and community manager in open source with the business leadership I learned at SugarCRM and Bitnami to help multiple open source foundations and projects within flourish, including the Academy Software Foundation, LF Energy, LF AI & Data, and many more.

While I hope you have found my career story up to this point interesting, you might be thinking "so what does this all mean, John?". Well, let's look at how to apply what I've experienced to your career.

Growing your career in open source

Everyone's careers are winding roads, and rarely – if ever – predictable. My career certainly has been – going from being a computer scientist to an open source leader and expert certainly isn't a career path my high school's guidance counselor even knew existed. But what it says is that your career path is one part opportunistic and one part luck. For me, it was opportunistic that I was able to take over the PHP Windows installer, and pure luck that I met so many open source leaders. Both helped catapult me to the next phase of my career.

As I look back at my career journey, there are a few patterns that stick out that I think will be helpful to you as you grow your career in open source. Let's look at them now.

Showcase your work

We live in an age where our digital footprint is in effect our identity, and showcasing that broadly and accurately is crucial. I heard someone say once that "if you don't define yourself in the market, someone else will do it for you." Being successful means owning your work and accomplishments.

There are a few key platforms to pay attention to in relation to open source:

- **GitHub** or **GitLab**, both of which are presently looked at as the primary portfolios for open source work. Here, you want to make sure the open source projects you maintain look well put together: working code, solid README files, clean structure – all the best practices we outlined in earlier chapters. While employers look at competence with technologies as a key for hiring, they also highly value code that is readable, easy to understand, and documented, as code bases for companies are maintained by teams that need to work together. GitHub and GitLab are also both good at showing other projects you might have contributed to.

- **LinkedIn**, which again is a de facto platform in the technology world. Here, you want to focus on your employment history, giving details of the roles and responsibilities. Additionally, call out the open source work you've done; call out being a contributor or maintainer to a project and describe what you've done. Provide links to blog posts and conference presentations you've created, which show both expertise in the technology but also your ability to talk about technology such that others can understand it – a really important skill to employers.

- **Twitter**, **Mastodon**, and **Facebook**, all of which are currently popular social platforms that employers will look through to get a sense of who you are as a person. Companies look for cultural fits as much as they do technical skills. I personally am not a big user of those platforms, or any other social media, but if you are, ensure that you don't have embarrassing pictures or posts, or ones that are derogatory or attack others.

Many developers have personal websites if they aren't into using the platforms above, and if you go down that path the same general guidelines apply. You probably want to also search for your name in search engines and see what comes up. If you use the platforms outlined previously, likely those will get the job done, but if it's a personal website you probably will need to pay attention to the results and work to get your website toward the top through **Search Engine Optimization** (**SEO**) techniques.

For me, I focus on maintaining a LinkedIn profile for showcasing my professional career, as well as using my GitHub profile to showcase all the projects I've worked on over time. For me, as an open source expert, it showcases both my professional dimension as well as my experience working on open source projects by showcasing all the ones I've made some sort of contribution toward. Additionally, I maintain a few small open source projects around DCO signoffs and managing ecosystem landscapes, which show others good practices in presenting smaller projects appropriately.

With your portfolio in place, you now have a great resource that showcases your work. Even with a strong portfolio, it's hard to get that "in" or opportunity to showcase yourself. This is where, sometimes, you have to look to solve the problem others look past. Let's learn more about that now.

Look for opportunities people look past

The PHP Windows installer was an afterthought for the PHP community; most of the primary maintainers of PHP were Linux users and saw Linux as the best platform for deploying web applications. Combined with the disdain the general open source developer had for Microsoft at the time, it made the opportunity of the PHP Windows installer a great one.

The beauty of open source is the wide breadth of projects and problems to solve. And in those projects, every one of them needs help in one way or another. Finding your way into the project, perhaps by tackling one of those "good first issue" bugs that the primary developers have eschewed, is a great way to make inroads without the stress of needing to compete with others and getting lost in that mess.

With the PHP Windows installer, the opportunity was driven by the work I was able to do myself. But as I grew in my career, the opportunities became ones where I had to influence others. This is where I learned the next pattern – being an enabler to be a leader.

Be an enabler to be a leader

One big criticism of the career path for software developers is that it often leads to management – a skill no software engineer is at all prepared or trained to do along the way. Criticism aside, growing one's career means learning new things, and often you need to go outside of your immediate role to learn them. For me, the transition from software developer to community manager – effectively from being an individual contributor to being a leader – was a challenging one. I had to re-learn a bunch of things along the way to be successful, such as how to enable and support others to help me achieve my goals, how to prioritize and shift focus, and even how to see down the road of opportunities ahead. I had to stumble and fail – a lot – and I had to learn to be okay with that. As an individual contributor, you often see your value as the work you can do yourself. But as a leader, your value is the outcomes you can enable.

As you grow your career, keep up with trends and start to learn about them. Take on projects that are a bit out of your wheelhouse as a way to learn new skills and spaces. Rethink how you measure success. Early on in your career, you focus on your individual success as you are trying to stand out in the crowd. But later, you realize that your larger influence is what opens up opportunities. Additionally, communities such as the TODO Group (`https://todogroup.org`) are places to meet people in the same transition that can help guide you.

Additionally, as we talked about in *Chapter 6*, *Making Your Project Feel Welcoming*, *Chapter 7*, *Growing Contributors to Maintainers*, and *Chapter 8*, *Dealing with Conflict*, it's important to engage others in humility and kindness – which is the next pattern we will look at.

Treat others with humility and kindness

If there's one thing I've learned in my career, it's that when I do good by others, in time that goodness comes back. I look at my early days in the PHP community as I started work on the PHP Windows installer. What if when Microsoft approached me about some issues they wanted fixed, I reacted with "Oh Microsoft, you are so mean to open source. I'm not helping you." Maybe I'd get a high-five from the anti-Microsoft crowd, but would that have hurt opportunities down the road with SugarCRM, Bitnami, and the Linux Foundation – all of which have good relations with Microsoft?

As I talked about in *Chapter 8*, *Dealing with Conflict*, with open source participants across geographies, genders, races, sexual orientations, and beliefs, it is a space where being understanding of others goes a long way. For me, being able to be a leader in open source means I have to learn from these communities to best serve them, so reacting harshly and making hasty judgments doesn't get you anywhere.

Enjoy what you do

In *Chapter 8, Dealing with Conflict,* I mentioned that when asked about what are the best and worst parts of open source, I cheekily replied "the people." One of the skills that was the hardest for me to learn as I transitioned from being an individual contributor to a community manager was the people management aspect. One fellow community manager at the time told me "hacking code is trivial, hacking people is hard."

What has always kept me going in communities is the people and the technologies, and when those motivate me, the minor skirmishes from day-to-day activities are really minute. Once in a while, communities I've been a part of have become too overwhelming, and stepping away was a healthy choice, but the vast majority of the time, having humility and kindness has given me joy in the work I've done with open source communities.

You have to find that joy as well. Work in communities with people you enjoy working with, and on technology and using tools you enjoy using. Be careful about obsessing over a project, as it leads to burnout, as we talked about in *Chapter 9, Handling Growth.* Not every day will be the best day ever, but you should be able to look back and be proud of your work and happy about the interactions you've had with others.

Let's look at open source careers from the aspect of employers. First, let's see how organizations can use open source to find talent.

Finding talent through open source

We talked earlier in this chapter about how software development and technology jobs, in general, have become more specialized in many cases as the breadth of technology grows. Add this to the fact that technology jobs are shifting more and more to remote opportunities (meaning employees working from home rather than within a traditional office). This has made it tremendously difficult to find talent to fill the roles companies have, as well as to retain that talent. We'll talk more about the retention part in the next section, but first, let's look at ways that employers can leverage the open source communities they work with to find talent to fill open roles.

Participating in communities

The easiest way to find talent in open source communities is...show up in the communities. Isn't it obvious? Well, not always. As we talked about in *Chapter 6, Making Your Project Feel Welcoming,* sometimes these open source communities aren't the simplest to navigate if the project hasn't intentionally created a smooth on-ramp for new community participants.

If the community doesn't have a clear way to get involved, ask. Many open source projects don't see companies wanting to get involved, and when they do, it can be one of those star-struck moments like I had with Microsoft earlier in this chapter. You will occasionally run into a project that is hesitant or not interested in corporate involvement, and that's okay. You have to be respectful of the project and its culture. In these cases, actively trying to find talent will be hard, so taking an approach like the one outlined here might be better:

1. Have your staff software developers contribute to the project in the same way other developers contribute to the project.

2. Focus on building camaraderie with the other maintainers and growing respect for others. Ensure the developers follow all the contribution guidelines they have set forth. Have them be active in the project's communications channels.

3. As your developers are working on the project, have them get to know other contributors and maintainers. If those contributors and maintainers are seeking a job opportunity, then have your company's developers mention any open positions the company has available. Don't be pushy or overly public about it; only share when someone asks.

Point 3 is important – you don't want to look like you are trying to swoop in and hire all the developers. Position yourself as a helping hand. You will encounter communities who frown at this passive approach. If that's the case, it's best to avoid directly referring developers from the community and instead add knowledge about the project as a "desired skill" to your general job posting.

If the project does have more of a clear-cut way to get involved, they may have forums or job boards they maintain to direct hiring opportunities. The Zephyr Project provides such a job board on their website (`https://www.zephyrproject.org/careers/`), with defined guidelines on job posts, and they have additionally established a `#job-postings` channel in their Discord. Sometimes these channels are maintained outside of the project itself. For example, the Golangprojects site (`https://www.golangprojects.com/golang-remote-jobs.html`) is maintained independently of the project by a company that participates in the community.

When community members look at companies wanting to hire developers from the community, one key factor is how much the company is "giving back" to the community. While one part is certainly putting in developer resources, many projects have additional needs around infrastructure; let's look at how to best do this as a company now.

Sponsoring project-related infrastructure

The amount of high-quality tooling available freely to an open source project is immense compared to a decade or two ago. Tools such as GitHub, GitLab, SonarCloud, 1Password, Confluence, JIRA, Netlify, and others are made freely available to open source communities, often as those companies are huge users of open source and see making that infrastructure available open source broadly as a way to give back to those communities.

If you are part of a small company or one without developer tooling it could provide to an open source community, you might think that there isn't a way for you to help a project out in such a way. But there are often gaps in the project that frankly just need someone to foot the bill. These might include the following:

- Specialty hardware, such as GPU test runners, hardware for niche architectures (arm64, ppc64, and s390x are some I commonly see), or a specific data center or lab configuration. The project will often try to provide best-effort support in these cases, so stepping in to provide this missing infrastructure that can be part of their CI/CD processes can be a huge help.

- Web conference tooling. While many platforms, such as Zoom and Google Meet, are available for free, they can be limited in terms of meeting duration or the number of attendees. We have a local Big Data Meeting group in the Cleveland area (`https://www.meetup.com/cleveland-hadoop/`) that I started providing the use of my Zoom account for, which supports up to 500 users for their meetups during COVID, and they still use it, which has been very helpful as they now have a hybrid meetup that attracts people further outside the Cleveland area.

- **Swag** (an acronym for **Stuff We All Get** – think of things such as t-shirts and stickers with the project's logo) and funding sending out swag. You might not think of swag as project infrastructure, but as we saw in *Chapter 6, Making Your Project Feel Welcoming*, and will see in *Chapter 12, Marketing for Open Source - Advocacy and Outreach*, it builds the project's brand and notoriety as a tool to help recognize key developers. One thing I will note: unless the project is explicitly okay with it, don't put your company logo on the swag; it's generally in poor taste as it appears as free advertising for the company.

Open source community members rarely see each other in person. There are projects I've worked on for years and might have met the maintainers once or twice, but that is the exception. When people get together, great ideas emerge, and a closer community forms. This costs money; paying for a meeting space, travel costs, food, and so on. This is a great opportunity for a company to help. Let's look at that now.

Sponsoring or hosting a mentorship, hackathon, or another event

Events are important for an open source community. In addition to great ideas and community building, it gives the project visibility to the outside world. Whether it be a vast community such as Kubernetes or the Linux kernel, or even a more niche community such as OpenVDB – it's like a shot in the arm for community health.

We will talk a bit more about strategies for events for a project in *Chapter 12, Marketing for Open Source - Advocacy and Outreach*, but here specifically, I want to think about how a company can best support events for a community. Some ideas I've seen work well include the following:

- Giving the project an in-person event the company runs. This works especially well for projects specific to a vertical industry or specific application ecosystem. When I was community manager at SugarCRM, I started an "un-conference" as part of the event. These un-conferences were really just spaces for informal discussions and ad hoc talks, which were selected based on the attendees to the un-conference. This was great as we had several open source extensions to

SugarCRM, and those developers could get together in person and collaborate across projects – even pulling in SugarCRM staff developers. It typically is low-cost for a company to do this – and generally demonstrates a lot of goodwill to the project community.

- Pick up the tab for a speaking track or developer room at a broad open source or related technology conference. There are many open source and technology conferences that are broad, such as the Linux Foundation's Open Source Summit (`https://events.linuxfoundation.org/open-source-summit-north-america/`), FOSDEM (`https://fosdem.org/`), `Linux.conf.au` (`https://linux.org.au/linux-conf-au/`), and many more that target specific regions. Some events give space for open source projects at no cost, but there might be costs for food and beverages, audio/video equipment, or internet access. All these items make a big difference to the experience for an attendee.

- Include the open source project in talks your company might be giving. This one you want to be a bit careful with as you want to keep a separation between the project and any products your company might offer, but if you think more in the context of talking about how your company uses several open source projects together (for example, React, GraphQL, and Node.js), it raises awareness of the project, shows the project is ready for production usage, and gives others ideas on ways to use the project.

- Give the project your offices for a local meeting. Even pick up the bill for food for the group. Local meetups' biggest challenge is space, and your company providing that usually costs you nothing and makes your company name synonymous with giving back to and supporting the project community.

Thinking outside the box of traditional events, there are other gatherings that companies can help sponsor and support to gain the interest of the project and build the community. Two ideas I've seen are the following:

- Host a hackathon, which is an event that brings together developers to build interesting add-ons or tools for a project, or perhaps focuses on new features or bug fixing. This is something we will talk in more depth about in *Chapter 12, Marketing for Open Source - Advocacy and Outreach*, where we will talk about all the required components to make this work – many of which cost money and are opportunities for a company to sponsor.

- Fund or host an internship or mentorship where the intern or mentee contributes to the project. We talked about mentorships in *Chapter 7, Growing Contributors to Maintainers*. Funding stipends or gifts for mentees or providing mentors for a project help the project enable new contributors, but further, the company gets a great "try before you buy" experience working with individuals the company could offer a job to afterward.

There's one key thing I cannot stress enough: as a company, you are providing these contributions in stewardship, and not for commercial gain. If you have a bunch of HR recruiters at these events, the community will be suspicious of your company's intentions. Remember how I spoke about a "passive" approach in the previous chapter – taking that here shows the community you are investing in its success.

That talent you attract is most likely interested in your company because they know that working for you means they will still be able to participate in that open source community – and likely contribute to other open source projects as well. If your company doesn't provide that, it might lead to these new employees being "flight risks" to other companies that do allow and encourage open source community participation. Let's look at how to retain and recognize those employees that are active contributors to open source.

Retaining and recognizing talent coming from open source communities

We talked about recognition of a company's employees for their contributions to open source at the end of *Chapter 4, Aligning the Business Value of Open Source for Your Employer*, and when your talent comes from leaders in the open source community, it is critical to ensure those contributions are highlighted and celebrated. When it's not, not only does the company walk away with a poor reputation, but the project suffers as well.

Further, bringing in talent from open source communities often is a catalyst to improve a company's internal development processes. Open source community leaders and maintainers are of a culture that sees openness and collaboration as the way to build better software, faster and more efficiently. We've seen a trend known as **innersourcing** emerge in organizations, where the processes of open source development are applied to a company's internal, proprietary software development, which opens up collaboration and communication between different areas of a company. I won't dig much into innersourcing here but do encourage you to read more about it at the Innersource Commons (`https://innersourcecommons.org/`).

On the topic of recognition and retention of employees coming from open source communities, the place to start is measurement. It's usually fairly easy to track contributions and impact made internally on products the company develops or applications built internally. But contributing externally – that can be a bit more challenging, as it's more of an indirect benefit to the company rather than direct. Further, imagine a company with multiple divisions, and offices in multiple countries, all with separate development teams – being able to have a view of the open source engagement of that company is a lot of work to stay on top of (in fact, many companies are surprised to learn they are contributing to or even using open source). Let's start by looking at the measurement and management of open source engagement by a company.

Measurement and management of open source engagement

Let's look at the scenario I just illustrated – a company with multiple divisions, offices in multiple countries, and software development teams unique to each – and think first about risk management. How can a company know whether there was **intellectual property** (**IP**) contributed to a project that a company might not be comfortable with? Or whether the projects being used by a division are under a copyleft license (which we discussed in *Chapter 3, Open Source License and IP Management*), and mixing internal code with that open source project's code might require open sourcing a part of your product? This is usually the primary driver around the formation of an **Open Source Program Office** (or **OSPO** for short), cataloging open source use in a company, ensuring compliance with open source licenses, and overseeing contributions made to open source projects.

As an **OSPO** matures (check out the resources of the TODO Group for a maturity model for open source projects), the focus becomes more around capacity building rather than compliance. Mature OSPOs work across the organization to advocate for the use of open source. Part of the work they will do is to track that usage and see where they can improve participation. For example, maybe one software development team is doing a great job working with an open source project, proposing code fixes, answering questions, and generally working upstream (remember that means doing development on the open source project itself, not creating their own fork with their own changes). Another software development team is at the other end of the spectrum – uses the project, doesn't participate in the community, and doesn't share any code fixes back with the project. Here's an area where an OSPO can help by giving the developers in the latter example support and training, and even recognizing when they improve their participation to be more aligned with the guidelines the OSPO lays out. And for the former developer team, they could be ambassadors to other divisions.

We often see talent coming from open source communities as natural leaders within an OSPO. After all, these individuals have a great sense of how open source communities work, which makes them ideal persons to mentor and guide a company's software development teams in participation in open source communities.

One major challenge companies run into is seeing how the work done in open source weighs with the work they do directly impacting the company. This usually comes down to employee goal setting – let's look at that now.

Setting annual goals

In most companies, there is an annual review cycle, where the employee has a set of mutually agreed upon goals for the year. Success in achieving those goals often aligns with compensation increases, promotions, or bonuses. Good goals are considered **SMART** goals, which stands for **Specific, Measurable, Achievable, Relevant, and Time-Bound**. Often those goals are subsets of the management's goals, which most often are focused on revenue growth. As we spoke about in *Chapter 4, Aligning the Business Value of Open Source for Your Employer*, the impacts of open source on revenue are indirect, and further, aren't well time-bound as the timelines for work on an open source project are out of the company's control.

Let's go back to the chart I showed in *Chapter 10, Commercialization of Open Source*.

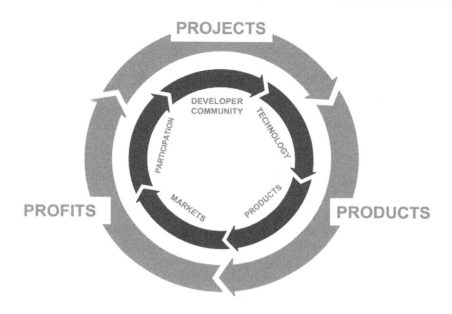

Figure 11.2 – Projects, Products, Profits cycle of open source sustainability
(`https://www.linuxfoundation.jp/wp-content/`
`uploads/2017/09/Virtuous-cycle.png` - CC by 3.0)

You can see there is a correlation with company bottom-line impact – does the open source project being invested in help the company reduce R&D costs, get to market faster, attract more customers, and/or add new features? If the answer to any of those is "yes," then the investment from the company in the project continues.

What does this mean for an individual developer? This means if a company is dependent on that project, a developer doing work on that project that is continuing to drive the value around cost, time to market, more customers, or more features works well. Some ideas for goals could include the following:

- Be a top 10 contributor to the project
- Upstream X new features or fixes to the project
- Improve the performance by x%
- Do a security audit of the project and resolve any known vulnerabilities

Another angle could be expanding the use of open source, perhaps bringing in a new open source project to replace a homegrown logging tool, or moving from a commercial developer framework to an open source one. These are impacts to the company by using code with more usage and, theoretically, better quality, security, and performance, as well as reducing risk by leveraging open source components versus proprietary ones that cause vendor lock-in.

A good OSPO will champion the use of open source in a company. One way to do that is public recognition. Let's look at ways to do that.

Create an internal awards or incentives program

Companies often have internal awards and recognitions for all sorts of things, such as top salesperson, best marketing campaign, or highest support ratings. Open source contributions and impact can be similarly rewarded.

This is an area that has evolved over the years. One large multinational technology company I know of used to pay out spot bonuses to developers who got code accepted into the Linux kernel. As it turns out, a lot of the reason for that was due to the high level of legal review and scrutiny that a contributor had to go through to even propose a code fix to the Linux kernel project; then comes the scrutiny of the project itself. Many saw the bonus as not commensurate to the work needed to actually get the contribution accepted. Over time, that was streamlined and contributions were much easier, but then the company removed that generous bonus.

There are some great ideas that come from welcoming newcomers to a project that we chatted about in *Chapter 6, Making Your Project Feel Welcoming*. Here are a few that I've seen work well:

- A special recognition the first time a developer gets a code contribution accepted. It could be as simple as a thank you note, maybe a gift card, or a callout during a company or division all-hands meeting. In bigger companies, the latter can be extremely valuable as that developer will be visible to the whole company.

- Annual awards for the most contributions made to a project, which could be a bonus or maybe funding them to attend a developer conference. Both help drive developers to look for ways to work on open source.

- An incentive or bonus for starting a new open source project, especially as, as we learned about in *Chapter 4, Aligning the Business Value of Open Source for Your Employer*, it's a lot of work.

- Adding open source contributions and work as part of the requirements for more senior levels in a career path for developers. More senior developers should be pragmatic by nature, and they should be able to see how open source helps them build applications better and faster, so ensuring they have experience in that space is a key skill in a well-rounded senior developer.

OSPOs generally serve the whole company, so any programs you create should have that same reach across the whole company. Keep that in mind as you develop your programs.

Summary

We saw in this chapter how open source community participation is a career enabler for maintainers and contributors. Learning from my career story how open source participation has opened doors for me, we recognized the patterns you can apply to your career journey. We then looked at companies using open source as a path for finding new talent, showcasing how participation gains goodwill, and investments in the community are effective strategies for positioning a company as a great place to work that cares about open source participation. Finally, we looked at how companies can recognize employee participation in open source, from ensuring there is a central way to manage open source participation to ensuring open source participation is in a technologist's annual goals, and using awards and incentives to showcase those contributing to open source.

The next chapter shifts to a topic that might be thought of as the antithesis of open source but, in reality, is a crucial part of project success – marketing. This chapter will build on the topics in *Chapter 6, Making Your Project Feel Welcoming*, focusing more on outbound marketing and ways to make your project more relevant in the market. Let's dig in.

12
Marketing for Open Source – Advocacy and Outreach

Back in the early days of free software, the concept of "marketing for open source" would likely be considered sacrilege. Free software was the opposite of commercial software; instead of being driven by sales and marketing strategies, the software that was written was opinionated and driven by the author's interests. All was well if what users were looking for aligned with what the author was building.

Generally, these users would not be into sales and marketing anyways, which in one sense was good as the focus was on the software itself. This early era gave birth to some of the most popular free software tools out there, such as emacs and vi, which are hugely popular and have active and vibrant communities. These tools might not have gained the popularity they have if they did have more traditional marketing. For the audience the authors targeted, this grassroots-focused approach was the right one.

When we think about marketing for open source, which tends to take the form of advocacy and outreach more than traditional marketing, it can be many different things. At a base level, the early free software community focused on this exact community building and user connection. But as an open source project matures over time, there begins to be a need to more broadly enable and support the communities, a major part of which is marketing. In the late 2000s, two major competing open source **Infrastructure-as-a-Service (IaaS)** projects were Apache CloudStack and OpenStack. Generally, people familiar with both projects at that time would cite Apache CloudStack as the better technology. However, the marketing and developer evangelism support was much stronger with OpenStack as it had a foundation around it to specifically focus on the platform's growth. What happened in the end? OpenStack became the dominant technology – with marketing being a driving factor, even though it wasn't considered the best technology of the two.

Marketing and open source are classically thought of as opposites, yet in reality, open source projects with the best outreach and community management tend to be the more successful ones. In this chapter, we will cover marketing 101 for projects that dig into assets, thinking about the journey a user goes through and ways to promote your project. We will cover the following topics:

- What is marketing for open source and why does it matter to your users?

- Open source project "marketing runway"

- Next-level outreach and driving engagement

The one thing we won't cover in this chapter is using open source as a marketing strategy. That approach can often align with the "open core" model of open source we discussed in *Chapter 2, What Makes a Good Open Source Project?*, and other times is used by companies new to the open source world trying to make an impact on the market. This is a touchy topic as it doesn't position your organization favorably with the open source community as a whole.

Let's start by digging deeper into what we mean by "marketing for open source."

What is marketing for open source and why does it matter to your users?

I once had a colleague who said, "marketing is making your product relevant to the market at, a given moment in time." I've always liked this definition as it is succinct, quantifiable, and speaks to results rather than pure action. It also includes multiple marketing strategies, from the grassroots approach of putting code out there under an open source license and seeing where the interests are to a more comprehensive campaign leveraging press, analysts, events, digital promotion, and more. Either way, the goal is to ensure that the product is relevant to the market at that moment in time.

Open source, being the "scratch-your-own-itch" model I've referred to it as several times in this book, ties perfectly to the relevance aspect of what my former colleague would say. In *Chapter 10, Commercialization of Open Source*, the sustainability cycle diagram spoke to the need for the project to have a product fit, and that product is one with an economic benefit to the product vendor by its relevance to the market, with the profits from that being invested back into the project. Without market awareness and education on the project, the sustainability cycle breaks down, much like the Apache CloudStack example in the introduction to this chapter.

While open source marketing is similar to product marketing in many ways, some key subtleties often trip up even the most seasoned marketer. It's hard to see these without an example, so let's look at an actual project transitioning from a new project to an established community.

A case study in open source marketing – Mautic

Mautic is an open source marketing automation tool (https://www.mautic.org/), and during my research for this book, I reviewed the transitions in marketing messaging over time. I picked Mautic as it's an interesting project in a space where the competing solutions are not open source. After all, what better project to review regarding its marketing than one that produces software for marketers?

Let's look at their first blog post in September 2014, where they announced the project:

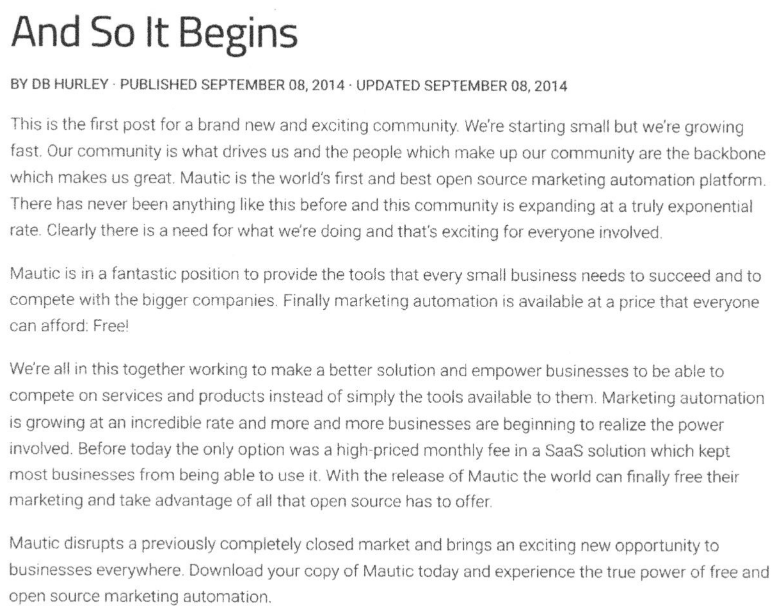

And So It Begins

BY DB HURLEY · PUBLISHED SEPTEMBER 08, 2014 · UPDATED SEPTEMBER 08, 2014

This is the first post for a brand new and exciting community. We're starting small but we're growing fast. Our community is what drives us and the people which make up our community are the backbone which makes us great. Mautic is the world's first and best open source marketing automation platform. There has never been anything like this before and this community is expanding at a truly exponential rate. Clearly there is a need for what we're doing and that's exciting for everyone involved.

Mautic is in a fantastic position to provide the tools that every small business needs to succeed and to compete with the bigger companies. Finally marketing automation is available at a price that everyone can afford: Free!

We're all in this together working to make a better solution and empower businesses to be able to compete on services and products instead of simply the tools available to them. Marketing automation is growing at an incredible rate and more and more businesses are beginning to realize the power involved. Before today the only option was a high-priced monthly fee in a SaaS solution which kept most businesses from being able to use it. With the release of Mautic the world can finally free their marketing and take advantage of all that open source has to offer.

Mautic disrupts a previously completely closed market and brings an exciting new opportunity to businesses everywhere. Download your copy of Mautic today and experience the true power of free and open source marketing automation.

Figure 12.1 – Mautic blog post "And So It Begins" (https://www.mautic.org/blog/and-so-it-begins)

This blog post was positioned for their initial goal of getting people to use the project. With open source that doesn't target a developer audience, it can be challenging to drive the concept of what building a solution in open source means as it's different than what the dynamic users are accustomed to in commercial software. Namely, these are the key messages they are trying to drive:

- The software is free (free is always a good motivator)

- The development is collaborative and open, which is different from the rest of the market (notice the use of the statements "We're all in this together" and "disrupts a previously completely closed market")

- Targets small businesses, who will immediately appreciate the price point and also tend to be more accommodating in using tools more early stage like this

- The **Call to Action** (**CTA**) is to simply download and use the software

If you've been involved in marketing in early-stage startups, you will see some parallels here; the focus is on building users at this stage rather than revenue. The key difference is that even though revenue isn't the focus for the early-stage start-up, it still is a focus; for open source projects, direct revenue is never a primary focus. Open source projects in a revenue aspect think more about economic opportunity, meaning what usage of the project will make an impact on the downstream users and vendors so that they invest back into the project with effort and funding.

Speaking of economic opportunity, one key challenge projects face in the early days is making the barrier to entry low, a topic we spoke about in *Chapter 6, Making Your Project Feel Welcoming*. For an application such as Mautic, which is keenly US and England-centric, it's a crowded field. If you are familiar with the Red Ocean, Blue Ocean strategy (`https://www.blueoceanstrategy.com/tools/red-ocean-vs-blue-ocean-strategy/`), you know that competing in an environment with tons of competition (Red Ocean) is hard, even for the largest companies. But finding the gaps (Blue Ocean) where competitors are weaker or aren't focusing on can be great opportunities. For Mautic, they saw international markets as this opportunity, as well as a way to start building out a contributor community. *Figure 12.2* shows the blog post where Mautic announced its translation initiative:

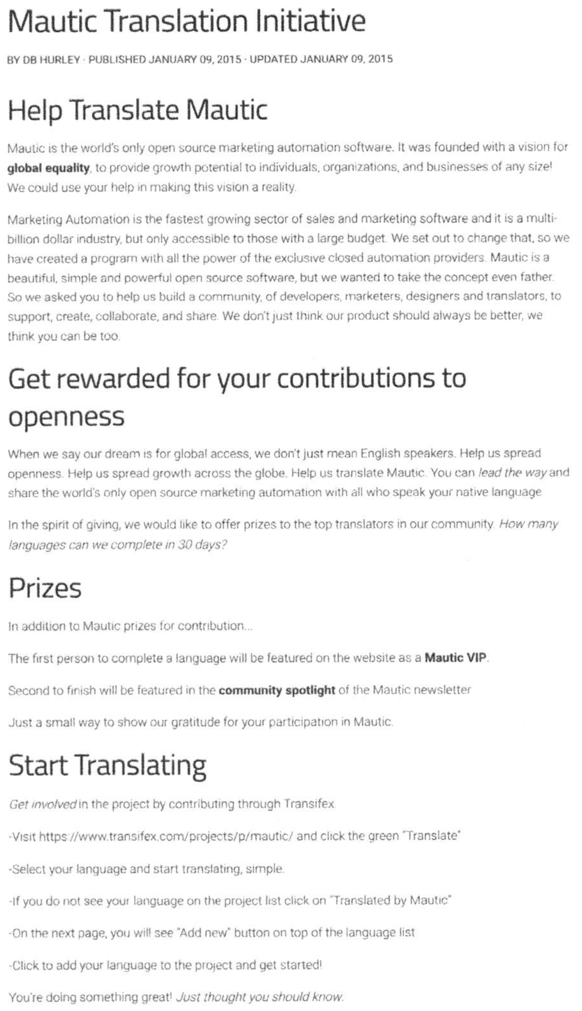

Mautic Translation Initiative

BY DB HURLEY · PUBLISHED JANUARY 09, 2015 · UPDATED JANUARY 09, 2015

Help Translate Mautic

Mautic is the world's only open source marketing automation software. It was founded with a vision for **global equality**, to provide growth potential to individuals, organizations, and businesses of any size! We could use your help in making this vision a reality.

Marketing Automation is the fastest growing sector of sales and marketing software and it is a multi-billion dollar industry, but only accessible to those with a large budget. We set out to change that, so we have created a program with all the power of the exclusive closed automation providers. Mautic is a beautiful, simple and powerful open source software, but we wanted to take the concept even father. So we asked you to help us build a community, of developers, marketers, designers and translators, to support, create, collaborate, and share. We don't just think our product should always be better, we think you can be too.

Get rewarded for your contributions to openness

When we say our dream is for global access, we don't just mean English speakers. Help us spread openness. Help us spread growth across the globe. Help us translate Mautic. You can *lead the way* and share the world's only open source marketing automation with all who speak your native language.

In the spirit of giving, we would like to offer prizes to the top translators in our community. *How many languages can we complete in 30 days?*

Prizes

In addition to Mautic prizes for contribution...

The first person to complete a language will be featured on the website as a **Mautic VIP**.

Second to finish will be featured in the **community spotlight** of the Mautic newsletter

Just a small way to show our gratitude for your participation in Mautic.

Start Translating

Get involved in the project by contributing through Transifex.

-Visit https://www.transifex.com/projects/p/mautic/ and click the green "Translate"

-Select your language and start translating, simple.

-If you do not see your language on the project list click on "Translated by Mautic"

-On the next page, you will see "Add new" button on top of the language list

-Click to add your language to the project and get started!

You're doing something great! *Just thought you should know.*

Figure 12.2 – Mautic blog post "Mautic Translation Initiative" (https://www.mautic.org/blog/community/mautic-translation-initiative)

If you talk to maintainers, they will tell you that documentation and language translations can be the most difficult type of contributions to get. This is mostly because they tend to be non-code, which isn't appealing as much to developers, and the tedious nature of those contributions (writing good documentation is a skill and can be quite a bit of work to research, author, edit, and so on, and translations require an understanding of how the language strings are used to do the correct translation). But in a community where there are likely more non-technical contributors than technical ones, combined with a marketing focus around different regions that have different primary languages than US English, it's a great target.

As community and momentum are being built, the next inflection point for a community is events. We mentioned events in *Chapter 6, Making Your Project Feel Welcoming,* at a very high level as a tool for making a project feel welcoming. The one challenge projects have is doing the right scale of events; we all envision grandiose events such as a KubeCon, but that takes a lot of effort and cost. Instead, since Mautic was early stage, they looked strategically and pragmatically at Detroit, Michigan to kick off their meeting program:

Figure 12.3 – Mautic blog post "Mautic Meetup: Detroit Michigan" (https://
www.mautic.org/blog/community/mautic-meetup-detroit)

We will talk more about events and meetups later in this chapter as we dig into next-level engagement, but for Mautic, this was an example of leveraging the existing energy in their community and enabling them to drive with the project message in places where the core maintainers might not have been able to reach directly (a theme you likely remember from *Chapter 6, Making Your Project Feel Welcoming*). What Mautic smartly did was harness that energy and give those community members a forum within the project itself to get more traction for those events, but also show community momentum and growth.

As communities grow, they begin to need structure to scale. Usually, in these communities, the structures have been informally coming together over time, as we spoke about in *Chapter 5, Governance and Hosting Models,* and more just need to be codified and documented. Mautic started seeing this after a few years of community growth and formalized this in a community structure that they continue to maintain and evolve (details on this can be found at `https://www.mautic.org/blog/community/call-for-volunteers-final-version-of-the-community-structure-released`):

Call for volunteers, final version of the Community Structure released!

BY NORMAN PRACHT · PUBLISHED NOVEMBER 12, 2019 · UPDATED SEPTEMBER 11, 2022

Photo by Juli Moreira on Unsplash

Figure 12.4 – Mautic blog post "Call for volunteers, final version of the Community Structure released!" (https://www.mautic.org/blog/community/call-for-volunteers-final-version-of-the-community-structure-released)

Note that not every project sees the scale where it needs to formalize a community structure like this, but those that do will see immense value as it clarifies roles and how to best engage. We spoke about the need for this back in *Chapter 7, Growing Contributors to Maintainers,* to illustrate how contributors can grow into maintainers, and we will continue that thread in *Chapter 13, Transitioning Leadership,* as we talk about leadership transition.

One other aspect of communities at scale is being able to report and communicate about progress and activities. Mautic did a great job of this by publishing a quarterly community report; you can see the one from Q4 2022 in *Figure 12.5*:

Q4 2022 Mautic Community Roundup

BY RUTH CHEESLEY · PUBLISHED JANUARY 10, 2023 · UPDATED FEBRUARY 03, 2023

Another quarter and another year has passed, and what a year it has been! Let's review what's happened over the last few months.

Read the previous reports here for Q3 2022, Q2 2022 and Q1 2022.

Figure 12.5 – Mautic blog post "Q4 2022 Mautic Community Roundup" (https://www.mautic.org/blog/community/q4-2022-mautic-community-roundup)

The focal points of the update included financial updates (new sponsors and overall budget available for funding community initiatives), along with the product team, marketing team, and community team readouts. It's a lot of data to present, and one where it is tempting to dump everything in there. Mautic took the approach of thinking about their audience and focusing the updates on exactly what is important to them and keeping each update as a few key points and supporting sentences for each. This is something every community needs to think about as its best approach, and something we will revisit later in this chapter.

Mautic's story – impact and purpose of open source marketing

Most marketers of software products are measured and compensated by their impact on sales; with that, the result of all the work they do ties right back to revenue. You see this in how companies measure their costs and profit structures as there are two key measurements product companies use to gauge their success: **Customer Acquisition Cost (CAC)** and **Customer Lifetime Value (CLV)**. Generally, companies look at both numbers in the aggregate, so a simple calculation for CAC would be to take all the costs involved in marketing, sales, product development, and other overheads, divided by the number of customers, and CLV would be the gross revenue from products divided by the number of customers. If CAC is less than CLV, then a company is doing well; if not, it needs to look at its cost structures and/or products and determine the problem.

With open source being free, CLV will always be zero, so using the measurements I just defined means open source projects will never be successful. Open source projects have a different element of what success is; eyeballs and interest. The Mautic story illustrates some of the key points a marketer for an open source project should be cognizant of. Let's look at them now.

The right message at the right stage of the project

In *Chapter 4* and *Chapter 9*, we talked about metrics for open source projects and that, depending on the stage of the project, technology space, and interests of the maintainers, they can be different. What is also true in marketing is that the message changes over time. Let's map the messages from Mautic on a typical product life cycle chart:

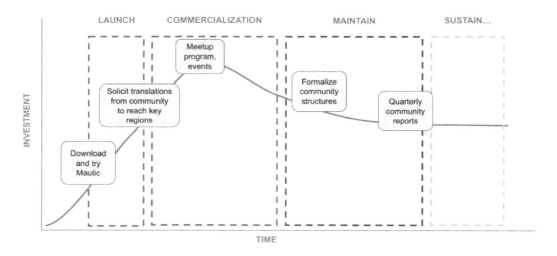

Figure 12.6 – Mapping Mautic messaging to the product life cycle

For a marketer, this points out the need to be focusing your messaging and what you're asking for as a project matures over time. Remember the quote I referenced earlier in this chapter from my colleague – "marketing is making your product relevant to the market at a given moment in time." It's key for a marketer to understand that to make the message clear and ask succinctly.

This calls out the need for marketing to not be one-way but a collaboration with the community. Let's look at that now.

Collaborative marketing with your community

We've seen a trend in the growth of social media that savvy marketers leverage their most prolific users as "brand ambassadors" or "influencers" to grow their brands and help connect users directly to their products through individuals who are their peers. Somewhat related are Amazon product reviews, sites such as IKEA Hackers, or even communities on Reddit or Facebook; these are all places where the community has a large presence, ideas, and feedback are shared openly. What do all of these have in common? It's marketing that is happening *with* users rather than just *to* users.

For Mautic, they knew from the beginning that getting users meant they had to not just educate them on open source, but help show them how open source works and the value it gives them. From the early days of getting translators to reach different regions and cultures, to meetups, and a formal community structure, the entire time, the focus was working with the community on the direction of the project. They take the sponsorship funding raised and invest back in the community to build out and develop new functionality.

Collaborative marketing helps form the ethos of a community, but to do so, it has to be intentional and honest. Let's look at the need to be authentic and inclusive as a part of not just effective collaborative marketing, but as a sustainable community.

Being authentic and inclusive

One lesson learned from the trend of social media influencers is that the relationship between an influencer and the user is built on trust. People look to identify with those they seek admiration and respect from. When this trust is broken, it is immensely hard to repair and causes ripples of damage to everything that the influencer stood for.

A unique challenge Mautic had was connecting with non-traditional open source users: marketers. While those familiar with open source might have a sense of how communities work and how these collaborations happen, marketers tend to be less collaborative than technologists. To help bring them along, in addition to just educating them on open source, they had to show them how to collaborate in open source.

Mautic was keen on using language such as "we are in this together" to show unity with users but would back it up by supporting community members looking to do meetups (like that first one in Detroit) and then later helping build a structure for the community to work and thrive. Doing those quarter community reports was important to show transparency, which educated the user community on how open source works and built trust.

Transparency leads to inclusivity. Every open source project maintainer knows that there are never enough hands to go around, but a really good one knows that being able to let the community see behind the curtain of projects builds trust while also opening up opportunities for others to get involved. Further, those maintainers also know that just because a project operates openly and transparently doesn't mean contributors and users will come flying in; the culture must be set that a project is inclusive and welcoming to others, as discussed in *Chapter 6, Making Your Project Feel Welcoming*. As a marketer, what you are selling isn't just the code itself but the community around the code, which gives the user confidence in being able to use the code.

As we've spent a good amount of this chapter looking at an example of a project's marketing strategy, let's shift to the practical, looking at what a project should have in place to be successful at marketing itself.

Open source project "marketing runway"

There's a phrase in marketing called "building your marketing runway," which refers to creating the set of materials you need to be able to execute any marketing strategy. Let's spend some time and highlight the needed marketing infrastructure an open source project should have as part of its "marketing runway."

Website and blog

The most basic need a project has is a home on the internet. For large projects, a visually appealing website that helps illustrate what the project is, predominant use cases, and who is using it are the basic things a project website should provide. Let's look at the Laminas project as a great example:

Figure 12.7 – Laminas project website (https://getlaminas.org)

Laminas has a simple, easy-to-navigate project website that ticks off the key boxes for open source project marketing; it makes it clear what the project is (enterprise-ready PHP framework), talks to the use cases (MVC components, middleware tools, and API tools), and showcases vendors who provide support. It also does a great job of connecting with users who might remember the project when it was the Zend Framework, which signals to those who might have been PHP developers for many years on the long lineage of the code base (this typically is a good thing, but for projects with a troubled past, this might not be something you want to mention).

While creating a website can be made quite simple thanks to static site generation tools that tie right into the code repository, platforms such as GitHub and GitLab can take content in **Markdown** format (which is a human-readable, lightweight text markup language for creating formatted documents) and produce a pleasant-reading web page inside those platforms. Let's look at the Open Shading Language GitHub repository as an example:

Figure 12.8 – Open Shading Language README.md file as viewed through the GitHub interface

(https://github.com/AcademySoftwareFoundation/OpenShadingLanguage#readme)

GitHub views tend to be quite developer-centric, as those viewing through GitHub will more than likely be technical-oriented and be looking for insights on the code itself. Being able to showcase the state of the CI builds, code license, and attributes such as the OpenSSF Best Practices badge status will be key questions out of the gate, and understanding how to build and use the project, use cases, who is using it, and how to contribute are aspects that need to be understood quickly. Much of this we chatted about in *Chapter 6, Making Your Project Feel Welcoming*.

One important aspect of any web property is having a tool for communicating with the community on the project's status. The best tool for this is a blog, which can be hosted as part of the project's website or using a third-party platform such as Medium. Looking at the Mautic project we dissected earlier in this chapter, we saw them use their blog to give the project a platform for announcing new initiatives, sharing use cases, providing project community updates, and showcasing events and meetups. Blogs are important in two aspects:

- They give us a sense of the current activities of the project, including focuses and investments being made and areas where the project could use help.

- They show those looking at the project that there is activity happening. As we chatted about in *Chapter 6, Making Your Project Feel Welcoming*, an active community in any form resonates with those looking to use the project.

The second predominant owned infrastructure for open source projects after their website is the channels for discussion. Let's look at this now from a marketing perspective.

Discussion channels

In *Chapter 6, Making Your Project Feel Welcoming*, we talked about the communications infrastructure for a project being crucial for a growing community. Just as a community needs to have effective and transparent tools for communication and collaboration with each other, these tools are also key parts of their marketing runway. Considerations a marketer should have include the following:

- Making it clear that you know where to engage and for what purpose. A marketer can help in this area. The Egeria project has a great community guide that helps us navigate the various channels (shown in *Figure 12.8*). Marketers can be valuable in helping people discover the project activities and how to get involved and should think about how this fits with the overall experience for users:

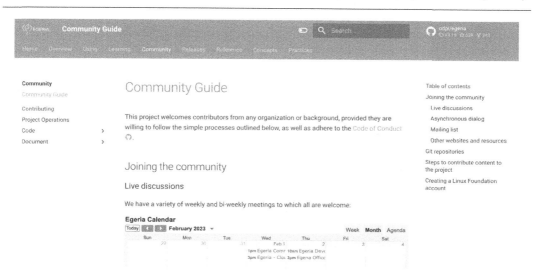

Figure 12.9 – Egeria Community Guide (https://egeria-project.org/guides/community/)

- Welcoming new community members and helping them find their way as they join the various channels. Just like in the community guide, these are the details a marketer can think about to avoid community members being frustrated with navigating the project. *Figure 12.10* showcases how the TODO Group project set up its Slack **#general** channel to direct people:

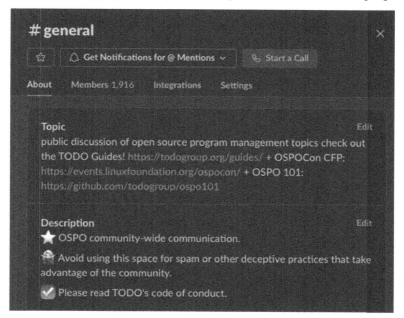

Figure 12.10 - #general channel guidelines for TODO Group Slack

- Use moderation not just for policing posters and organizing threads, but also as a tool for finding new content to uplift. This is a tactic I used as a Community Manager at SugarCRM many years ago; I would scour the discussion forums for key topics and then build a blog post that addressed the answer. Then, I would close those forum threads by pointing to the blog post as the accepted solution. You can do this for both technical and broad content; it ensures that the blog content you create is exactly what your users are looking for.

Projects should also consider their presence on social media; let's look at that more now.

Social media

Part of being relevant for an open source project is being part of the conversation. Product marketers that have leveraged social influencers know this well; if someone notable is using your product and that person broadly advertises that to others, your product will get attention by pure association. And when you post news and updates on your product, those social media posts are liked and shared by others, which garners more awareness of the project.

For open source projects, it's not much different. One key consideration is that you post on social media for the project, not yourself. This means the voice needs to be that of your community, reflective of its ethos and culture. Taking controversial or political stances has to be done with consideration of a project that is neutral and inclusive of the community. This doesn't mean that open source projects can't be outspoken on cultural and societal topics that have a shared viewpoint among project members, such as racism, violence, sexism, and other forms of discrimination; it means that the message shared should be inclusive, open, welcoming, supportive, and constructive, avoiding attacks, demeaning voice, or other toxic behavior.

Websites, communication platforms, and social media make up the marketing runway for an open source project. But that doesn't mean things stop there; let's look at next-level outreach tactics and how to use them to drive more project engagement.

Next-level outreach and driving engagement

In the previous section, where I described the marketing runway, you could characterize each of those tools in terms of "community management" or "inbound marketing," meaning tooling to help manage the engagement for those coming to your project. I see many projects stop there, as the social media effect, along with word of mouth gives the project the attention it feels it needs.

But sometimes, to be successful, that isn't enough; for a project that is useful broadly across many different industries and locales, it will be challenging to get the word out through social media and word of mouth alone. Further, a more complex project such as a framework or development tool might require the user to be more educated or the use cases on where and how to best use the tool to be outlined. This is where a project needs to take outreach to the next level; let's take a look at a few ways a project can successfully do this.

Events and meetups

In *Chapter 6, Making Your Project Feel Welcoming*, we saw that events and meetups are often ways the message and awareness of the project are grown organically, bringing the community together in ways that can help a project grow in a myriad of ways. Let's dig a layer deeper into event strategies for open source projects by looking at events as a marketing strategy instead of just a pure community-building activity.

The first consideration is which types of events to focus on. That depends a lot on the project and the audience you are after as events tend to fall into one of these categories:

- Events specific to a skillset or persona across industries. These include developer and open source conferences, but also might include conferences focusing on marketing technologies or perhaps events for university students.

- Industry events, such as those targeting a vertical such as financial services, healthcare, or the energy industry.

- Broad events focusing on technology that aren't narrow to a horizontal or vertical (the **Consumer Electronics Show** (**CES**) in Las Vegas is a prime example of such an event).

Thousands and thousands of events are held globally every year, and it's hard to prioritize which are important to attend. At the same time, an event might be the right one for a project one year, but the next it might not. How can we determine which events are important? Here are some questions to ask:

- Is the project relevant to the audience?

- Is the project at a state where it would be easily usable by the audience?

- Does the event have an audience that you see are highly likely to try out the project after they learn about it?

- Is it low cost in terms of time and investment for the project to participate in the event?

The first three questions are typical marketing questions to ask if you come from a product marketing background; very standard market and audience fit. The last one is important as open source projects – even those backed by large foundations – are limited in resources to participate in events. Not to mention that events are expensive; if you take into account someone traveling to an event, preparing a presentation, along with the lost productivity for that person in being at an event, ideally, the event should provide more value. However, many times, it doesn't.

In my experience, it's often hard to know ahead of time how much value you will gain from an event, but there are ways to maximize the event value opportunity, such as these:

- Delivering a talk during the event. If you cannot secure one, look for an opportunity at an ad hoc event such as a **Bird of a Feather** (**BoF**), unconference, or meetup. Use this talk to drive a clear presentation that lets people know what the project is, what the primary use cases are, who is using it and how it's being used, and how someone could get started using it.

- Attend other talks to find people who might be interested in your project based on the topics they are presenting on.

- Sit with others at lunch and attend attendee receptions to meet other attendees and learn more from them.

- Bring stickers and other swag about your project to advertise it to others.

Events are great as you have many people in one place that will hopefully have interest in your project. But the limiting factor of events is physical; even if the event is virtual, it only reaches those who are part of the event. Let's look at how to be broader in engagement by working with media and analysts.

Media and analysts

If you think of social influencers as driving awareness from the bottom up, media and analysts are driving awareness from the top down. Media and analysts specialize in topics and spaces and seek to become resources for those to consume the latest news across sectors of industry. Many are familiar with primary media outlets such as the BBC or CNN, and perhaps more vertically-focused ones such as Wall Street Journal and ZDNet. Within there are numerous niche and specialty publications that specialize in certain topics or go deeper into specific themes, such as Big Data, Security, Web Development, or FinTech, analysts take a slightly different approach to being experts in certain technology or industry spaces, driving deep research and analysis that aims to help a user become more educated to make better product and strategy decisions in the future.

Being effective in reaching press and analysts requires a **press and analyst relations (PR/AR)** skillset. It is often best to partner with a firm to do so. PR/AR firms have not only the skills but also relationships; they know reporters and analysts and can broker meetings and help projects build relationships through their credibility with various media outlets and analyst firms. That doesn't mean a project can try to do it alone, though – it can be challenging. If you do want to do it alone, or want to go into a meeting with a PR/AR firm in a better position to leverage their services, here are some tips:

- **Have a pitch deck for your project**, which outlines what the project is, what the primary use cases are, who and how it's being used, and how someone learns more and starts using it. The deck should be succinct and clear and use a minimal amount of slides to get those points across.

- **Know the audience your project will most resonate with**, and what media outlets and analyst firms cover those spaces. While larger publications such as WIRED or ZDNet can be challenging to get to cover your project, more niche ones looking at a specific audience might be more apt to take a call with a project if their volume is lower.

- **Approach paid media placements and paid analyst engagements with caution**. There are several credible firms and publications, and when the goals of the project and target audience align with the firm/media outlet, it can be a wise investment; this is especially true if your project targets a niche vertical industry with limited media/analyst coverage. However, many times, either the firm/media outlet has different priorities than the project on what success looks like, or they may fraudulent. Review opportunities carefully and do your homework on the track record of these firms/media outlets.

The big theme in being able to bring your project to events, meetups, media, and analysts is having the story of what your project is and where it's valuable. Articulating that well is done best by telling real-life stories versus hypothetical ones. Let's look at case studies and user stories as a way to help tell the project's stories.

Case studies and user stories

If you ask a product marketing professional what the most important marketing asset they have is, they will likely state it is an endorsement, case study, or user story. Why is this? Just like how social influencers connect with users in motivating them to use a product based on a recommendation from someone they admire and/or trust and media and analysts use their expertise and vantage point of space to help pick out the key things people should pay attention to, case studies and user stories are a tool for showcasing exactly how a product was used successfully. If you can see the problem they are trying to solve in the user or case being studied, you are highly likely to try out and potentially purchase the product.

Case studies and user stories need not be complicated; the more straightforward and consumable they are, the better. Many are written case studies and user stories, but I'm seeing more video recordings being used, which can be easier to consume. Whichever medium you use, these elements should be a part of the case study or user story:

- Who the user is (some people might not want to disclose this, so saying something such as "large financial services company" might be needed)

- What the challenge or problem the user was having

- How the user saw the project as a way to solve a challenge or problem they were having

- How the implementation or installation went

- What the immediate benefits were

- What further benefits or opportunities they see in the future

Products owners often ask me "how many case studies should my project try to get?," to which I answer "as many as you can." Case studies and user stories are the hardest marketing assets to earn for a project as it requires someone to be willing to put their name as an endorsement of the project itself. Show appreciation when someone is willing to put their name as an endorsement of a project and consider it one of the highest compliments.

Summary

In this chapter, we learned about marketing for open source projects, both stressing the importance of looking at examples of projects doing successful marketing versus those that didn't. We did a deep dive into Mautic, showcasing how the marketing messages changed over time as the project grew and matured, as well as when the needs of the projects and the role of the community evolved. Finally, we looked at the key elements in a project for establishing its marketing runway as well as ways it can up its outreach to the next level with events, meetups, media, and analysts, as well as by building a library of case studies and user stories.

As we near the end of this book, the last two chapters focus on key sustainability topics in open source projects; the first on how to best transition a project's leadership to ensure new people can come in and continue to drive the project forward, and then finally how to sunset an open source project. Both are key topics for projects and healthy parts of a project's overall life cycle. We'll start by looking at transitioning project leadership.

Further reading

To learn more about the topics that were covered in this chapter, take a look at the following resources:

- If you want to learn more about open source marketing, a great resource is the TODO Group's guide called *Marketing Open Source projects* (`https://todogroup.org/guides/marketing-open-source-projects/`), which focuses on the organizational benefit and engagement strategies as the primary audience toward **Open Source Program Offices (OSPOs)**

- Another personal favorite is Simon Sinek's *Start with the Why* (`https://simonsinek.com/books/start-with-why/`), which is a great construct for being able to home in on the value proposition for the project itself and put together an effective pitch deck and project presentation

13
Transitioning Leadership

"The greatest leader is not necessarily the one who does the greatest things. He is the one that gets the people to do the greatest things."

—Ronald Reagan

I once heard someone say that their goal as a parent was to raise kids that would be better parents than they were. And this was a really good parent saying this, one giving training and support to parents. What it speaks to is the intent to always know that your work can be improved upon and made better and that your humility will help it get there. Legacies aren't built from the work of your own hands, but by the impact and effect you have on others.

When I speak to projects about open source leadership, I emphasize the importance of servant leadership in open source communities. Contributors and users, unlike employees, don't have a financial binding to a project community; they participate because they want to be there. And the bigger part of the success and the work done in a project is because of those contributors and users; if they aren't there, there quickly becomes a lack of resources for development and, further, no audience for the projects. Being a great leader means ensuring those contributors and users can do great work in the project or with the code that comes from the project. Or better put, being a great leader means you are putting the needs of the project before your desires.

Leadership in open source projects is also a thankless job. In *Chapter 7, Growing Contributors to Maintainers*, we talked about the stress on open source project maintainers, as projects are used ubiquitously around the world, and typically a small percentage of users end up making any contributor back to a project outside of a support or bug fix request. It's a job that is certainly done out of passion and is usually hard to recruit. Often, when I work with projects in early formation, and the question comes up, "who should be the project chairperson?", everyone goes immediately silent. It's not all because of the workload either; most developers don't feel they have what it takes to lead a project, and often, they do but just don't realize it.

Open source projects, by the nature of having code put out under an open source license, are indefinite, but those contributors and maintainers aren't around forever. Projects must consider transitioning to the next set of leaders to be successful and sustainable. In this chapter, we will explore how to do that effectively:

- Why even think about transitioning leadership?
- Building a plan
- Stepping back comfortably

Let's start this chapter by answering an important question: why transition leadership at all?

Why even think about transitioning leadership?

Not all projects are forever, but once code is put out under an open source license, it is out there forever. While it's perfectly okay if a project sunsets (something we will discuss in *Chapter 14, Sunsetting an Open Source Project*), if the project is actively being used or has a vibrant community, bringing new leadership into a project is important for its sustainability.

There are many reasons why projects need to think about transitioning leadership, but there are three main patterns we tend to see that projects encounter: career change, project leaders nearing retirement, and a project stalling. Let's start with one of the most common: the leader has a career change.

Career change

In my post-university career up to this point, I've worked for four different organizations (which in tech is a really low number over 20 years). And my career focus changed over that time as well, as I spoke about when chronicling my career in *Chapter 11, Open Source and the Talent Ecosystem*. In generations before ours, it tended to be more common for someone to stay in the same profession for life; in our current world, that isn't a reality.

Going back to *Chapter 11, Open Source and the Talent Ecosystem*, open source projects are often used as a jumping-off point for a larger career. Someone might start a project to get on the radar of a larger company, and when they land that dream job, the open source project hits the back burner. This doesn't happen all the time; many developers like the open source project they are leading and work with their prospective employers to ensure they have the time to continue to maintain their project(s). Often, those employers are highly incentivized to allow this because typically, they are hired because the project is quite important to the employer.

Many who are skilled in software development do end up staying in that profession but might change focuses or domains. For example, someone who started as a full-stack developer (meaning they have no one area of an application stack they focus on but can be a software developer in multiple layers of an application stack) might look to specialize in frontend development (such as JavaScript coding or user interface design). If they have projects that are more focused on backend development (such as application logic or other backend libraries), they might not have the time to focus on those projects as it doesn't relate as much to their daily work. Additionally, as trends change over time and new technologies emerge, the developer likely would not be as current. Sometimes, that's a good thing; there's plenty of legacy code out there and a project supporting that isn't a bad thing. But largely, you will see the developer lose interest in the project and it gradually slows to a halt.

Career change is one aspect needed to transition leadership, but also is the biggest career change for all of us – retirement. Let's look at that now.

Project leaders near retirement

One thing that has come more to the forefront for me as my career progresses is the mortality of it all. You don't think about retirement as much as when you're in your 20s, but come your 40s and 50s, it's closer for you than the beginning of your career. All of us do retirement planning as part of our jobs in one form or another; in the United States, we have 401k and/or IRA plans that we contribute to, to ensure we have money at retirement. Our open source projects need that same planning since the code will live on without us.

Just as in the career change model, the pattern you typically see is the benevolent dictator model being the current leadership, and then either a transition to a new leader or a Technical Council, Elected, or Vendor-neutral foundation model of governance (see *Chapter 5, Governance and Hosting Models,* for more details on each of those models). It's often hard to find that same type of person that can step in with the same passion and broad skillsets as the current benevolent dictator, or the project has such mass adoption that a single leader cannot handle it all.

Projects such as Ruby, Python, and PHP transitioned from the benevolent dictator model to the Vendor-neutral foundation. PHP took the longest to get there as they went through the cycles of Technical Council and then Elected over two decades before launching the PHP Foundation in 2021. Ruby and Python moved to a Vendor-neutral foundation much faster; Ruby with Ruby Central in 2001 (5 years after Ruby 1.0) and Python with the Python Software Foundation also in 2001 (10 years after Python 0.9.0). Interestingly, the Python Software Foundation preceded the transition from Guido van Rossum as the benevolent dictator for life to a Technical Council in 2019; that isn't an uncommon problem as changing the governance for a project can be very disruptive, so focusing on succession and long-term asset management is the first and foremost concern. The Linux kernel is a good example here, with Linus Torvalds serving as the benevolent dictator here in 2023, and the CBT Tape project we spoke about in *Chapter 1, The Whats and Whys of Open Source,* being hosted by the Open Mainframe Project and Linux Foundation while having Sam Golob as the current sole leader.

With that, we have looked at two aspects of transitioning leadership where the leader is active but needs to move on. But what if the leader isn't all that active? Let's look at the case where the project might be stalling out.

The project is stalling

There is always lots of excitement when you start an open source project. Code begins to flow in, the repository is getting structured, and you see people downloading the code and trying it out. But over time, maintainers get busy in other areas of life, lose interest in the project, no longer have the same needs that the code addressed, or might just consider the work "done" and stop development. I did a quick search of GitHub and found that there were over 26 million GitHub repositories that haven't been updated since before 2021, with just over 12 million updated since, so projects stalling out is certainly prevalent.

For a leadership transition, I'd break down project stalling into two categories: projects that are "done/ no longer relevant" and projects that have been "abandoned," meaning the maintainer for whatever reason is no longer maintaining the project. It's hard to make the determination on which category a project is in, but there are some clues and tells that can help:

- Does the project address a technology that is current or not? For example, the project at `https://github.com/nudded/GoogleReaderAPI` is a Ruby wrapper for the Google Reader API. Google Reader was shut down on July 1, 2013, so this project is likely in the "done/ no longer relevant" category.

- Does the project have lots of pull requests/issues that were opened after the last commit to the main repository? This likely means there is some user base around the code and probably falls into the "abandoned" category.

- If the project has an automated CI/CD build system, did the last build succeed or fail? When was the last time there was a successful build? If it's been over a year since the last successful build, that probably means the project falls into the "abandoned" category.

One thing that is not a great indicator is when the last commit was; again, a project might be considered feature complete or done, so there won't be many (if any) changes. Or, some projects have a slow code velocity. OpenEXR (`https://github.com/AcademySoftwareFoundation/openexr/commits/main`) had only one commit to main in December 2022 and one commit to main in January 2023; knowing those maintainers, they certainly haven't abandoned the project, but considering that many projects will slow down in December and the maintainers tend to have other focuses after the holidays, this shows that velocity slowed down.

The big thing I want to emphasize is that before you declare a project as "abandoned," reach out to the maintainers and see if you can help. Some maintainers might take that as an invitation for you to take over the project; others might give you some sort of limited access to get things back moving as they still have interest but just lack the time currently. And sometimes, you hear nothing back; in those cases, it usually makes sense to create a fork so that you can continue with its development; if the maintainer emerges, they likely will appreciate all the work done and might bring you in as a maintainer. It's crucial to be respectful to the maintainer; they put their intellectual property out there under an open source license and it's helped you solve a problem, so working with them to make the code better versus forking without upstreaming the code back to them is generally the best approach.

Now that we understand the reasons why projects need to think about leadership transition, let's look at how a project can be proactive in building a succession plan.

Building a plan

Succession planning is something you see many organizations spend considerable time developing, especially large and long-running ones. These organizations build succession plans because they have people that depend on the organization in one way or another; they might be employees, customers, and/ or investors who have a vested interest in an organization continuing to operate successfully over time.

Open source projects similarly dependent on a large user community must also consider succession planning. Succession planning is not a single process, but it involves a few different pieces and can take some time to complete fully. But before you can start bringing in a new leader, you need to ensure the project's operations are well documented. Let's look at how to do that now.

Documenting your project's operation

In *Chapter 5, Governance and Hosting Models,* we talked about the importance of writing down your governance, not only for everyone to be clear on how things work but, more importantly, as it's easy to forget all the policies and processes a project has, especially when they are infrequent. As we consider succession planning, the documentation needs to go down another level to document how a project's operational aspects work.

Here are some key things to have documented:

- Credentials for any services the project uses (social media, build resources, code repositories, scanning tools, and any other collaboration tools). These credentials should be saved in a secure vault owned by the project; there are several services a project can use, such as Bitwarden or 1Password, that provide free accounts for open source projects.

- How the build and test infrastructure works, including the services and tools that are used and how they interact and work together.

- How to install or deploy the project's code.

- Release plans and roadmap.

- Code architecture and design.

Much of this seems trivial, but imagine if a maintainer is not around and it's all stuck in his or her's head; the project can certainly recover, but days and weeks must be spent trying to recreate this. And some of these items – such as credentials to various tools and services – are sometimes nearly impossible to access, and new resources must be built. I've seen it too many times where a maintainer of an open source project seemingly disappeared, and you see users scrambling to find out how to get access.

The curl project (`https://github.com/curl/curl`) has great project operations documentation. Some good reads they have are as follows:

- `RELEASE-PROCEDURE.md` (`https://github.com/curl/curl/blob/master/docs/RELEASE-PROCEDURE.md`), which documents step-by-step how to do a release of the project, including the release cycle down to how frequently a release should happen, even specifying to do releases on Wednesdays

- `VERSIONS.md` (`https://github.com/curl/curl/blob/master/docs/VERSIONS.md`) outlines the version syntax for the project

- `INTERNALS.md` (`https://github.com/curl/curl/blob/master/docs/INTERNALS.md`) documents the build toolchain and considerations to ensure maximum portability to multiple architectures

- `TODO` (`https://github.com/curl/curl/blob/master/docs/TODO`), which maintains a list of items the project would like to address in the future

The curl project goes into further details, which gets more into governance itself, down to etiquette and conduct standards, how security issues are managed, and even a history of the project. The history of the project is especially useful as it helps give a sense of the lineage of the project and gives future maintainers insight into its past.

Documentation is an ongoing process and something that a project should start early on and continue to maintain. While researching for this book, I came across a great article on open source project documentation (`https://opensource.com/article/20/3/documentation`) that recommended a project maintainer spend 10-20% of their time writing things down; I think that's a great measure for a project to align to. Speaking from experience of inheriting old code bases and transitioning projects to others, you never regret the time spent writing documentation.

With documentation in flight, the next phase is to start implementing a process for a leadership transition. Let's look at that now.

Timelines and enablement for new leaders

If an open source project were a public company, the Board of Directors would think about succession plans for key leaders such as the CEO from day 1. It seems odd at first glance; why would you plan for the new leader's successor when you just appointed them? For one, you never know when a CEO will look to leave the organization, die, or be underperforming, so having potential successors in the wings helps expedite any leadership transitions. But more importantly, it gives the organization a chance to mentor and groom future leaders using the wisdom and experience of the current leaders. As we discussed in *Chapter 7, Growing Contributors to Maintainers*, developing new maintainers is best done with mentorship from the current maintainers, using a gradual and intentional process along the way.

Now, open source projects typically don't have the same ability to have leaders-to-be in the wings waiting to be named a new project leader. Frankly, it's hard to find people willing to lead projects, let alone qualified. Open source projects don't have thousands of employees globally; most are single-maintainer projects, and only a small number of projects have more than a few dozen maintainers. And executive leaders in public companies typically have a generous compensation package, which is quite appropriate considering the responsibility and duties of the role. Open source project maintainers are rarely compensated, and when they are, it's very much below market rates.

But what open source projects can learn from public companies' succession plans is that planning ahead is better than scrambling when it's too late. The best way to set timelines is by working in reverse; when must the transition be done? This enables a project to set milestones along the way and realistically determine what degree of transition can occur.

Borrowing from the plans we would see in public companies, here's a good way for open source projects to make succession plans:

1. Assess how long the current maintainer/leader expects to be in their role. Are they only wanting to lead it for a year or two? Do they want to lead indefinitely?

2. Is it realistic to think one person could replace the current maintainer/leader, or should multiple people take on parts of the role? Ruby and Python were great examples where the benevolent dictators were truly unique individuals that a single person couldn't replace – and additionally, the needs of a growing project meant there would be additional needs over time that even the perfect replacement benevolent dictator couldn't fulfill. This might lead to moving governance structures as part of the leadership transition.

3. Identify potential leader(s) and have them take on some of the duties and shadow the current leaders. As we talked about in *Chapter 7, Growing Contributors to Maintainers*, this will also help determine if there is a mutual fit between the person, the role, and the project.

4. Get input on any leadership structure changes from key community members. See how they would react to a change and what things they see that should be considered as the project goes through the transition period. The key part is that you want to set up the new leaders and leadership structure for success.

5. Publically announce the new leaders and leadership structure. Ensure you give the community a chance to ask questions and engage the new and previous leaders. Transparency is key as you go public; you must provide the community with as much context and insight as possible so they can understand why the transition happened.

Not all projects will have the luxury of having other maintainers able to plan leader succession to this degree; smaller projects might have only two to three maintainers. But the same general process and structure apply; each maintainer should realistically think of how long they want to serve in their maintainer role, determine the best way for them to be replaced, and then find and mentor those replacements. What is key here is thinking intentionally and with a plan for the future; if people depend on your project, it's important to ensure there is a plan for how a project can be sustained over time.

Once a project has a transition plan, it's time to implement it. In my experience, the hardest part of that plan is for the previous leaders to step back. Let's look at how to do that comfortably for both the new and current leaders and the community as a whole.

Stepping back comfortably

Even with the best transition plan done, it's hard to "cold turkey" step back from a project. Stepping back is a gradual process, where the new maintainers and leaders can take over the activities while reducing their dependencies on the maintainers they plan to replace. Many maintainers tend to err on the side of caution when stepping back; after all, they put lots of energy and passion into the project and want to be certain that it will be in good hands (not always, of course; some maintainers might be so burnt out by the project that they are just thrilled to find someone to take it off their hands… hehe).

Presuming a maintainer wants to ensure a smooth transition, there are a few things they should do. We'll look at them in the upcoming subsections.

Being appropriately available

The most important thing is to ensure their previous maintainers don't completely disappear. But this has to be done with caution; you don't want to appear to be meddling or micromanaging the new leaders, but simultaneously you want to be a resource for those leaders as they run into challenges or need advice. Being an open source project leader is a lonely job, and having someone who has been in that role can provide great support and encouragement to those new leaders.

I've worked with a few communities that have undergone leadership changes and having previous leaders available as a resource was of immense value. In one project, the transition happened in the first year as the leader had to step away due to a job change and family illnesses. The previous leader would try to attend meetings and respond to emails occasionally after stepping down, but that leadership group would reach out to the person for questions they had or to understand past decisions made. It went quite well, and the new leaders have done a solid job of growing and maturing the project.

In another project, the project leader stepped down as they became absent from the project frequently, and other maintainers would need to step in and review pull requests and address issues in their absence. The project leader stepping down was not something they truly wanted to do; they saw much of their identity in the project, and they struggled to step back truly. This caused a lot of friction with other developers; the previous leader would start conversations in the community on directions for the project that wasn't representative of the other maintainers (in fact, much of the time, the other maintainers never even heard of the ideas proposed). This hit a breaking point after some time, requiring the past project leader and the current maintainers to meet to discuss the issues. In this case, the past project leader saw the project as an outlet for them; when the project leader had to step back, they had several family and personal issues ongoing. Participating in the project brought them a sense of belonging, but they struggled to find the best way to get involved again. In the end, the maintainers brought back the previous project leader in a limited role to focus on getting feedback from users and helping triage issues; something they truly enjoyed doing.

Being available is one thing, but previous maintainers don't always have all the answers. Let's look at helping those new maintainers with a broader support network.

Endorsing the new leaders

I sometimes get organizations that bring an open source project into a vendor-neutral foundation and become worried; what if the community takes over the whole project and pushes them out? I can understand the fear; it's a loss of control from a legislative perspective, and the decision-makers will no longer be dominated by one company. In reality, once it's in a vendor-neutral foundation, newcomers to the project tend to defer to the contributing organization around most key decisions. From those newcomers' perspectives, the vision and work the contributing organization put into the project, not to mention the gratitude the newcomers have for the contributing organization for contributing its intellectual property under an open source license, positions the contributing organization as "elders" in the project community.

This means that when new leaders emerge, those leaders, while they might have the "legislative" powers, might not have the "effective" powers. Open source is a scratch-your-own-itch model, and any project can be forked at any time, so if community members don't like the new leaders, they could either move on from the project or take it somewhere else to change its direction. Forks are very distracting for an open source project and generally result in either the fork or the main project winning out. When friction like this happens in the community when new leaders come in, this is where the previous maintainers can step in and help with endorsing the new leaders.

This is something previous maintainers have to be careful with; the new leaders might have made decisions or actions that aren't something the previous maintainers would be supportive of. Generally, previous maintainers have built up a fair amount of social equity with the community for their contributions, but that social equity can vanish quickly. At the same time, previous maintainers don't want to undercut the new leaders. It's a tricky balance. Good previous maintainers try to point the direction of the project to look toward the future and then continue to support the current maintainers to help them through rough patches.

Setting the right support network for new maintainers

I remember when I first became a community manager at SugarCRM and quickly realized "there aren't a lot of us community managers around." I ran into the same challenge when I started leading OpenSocial and, later, ODPi; it's a small circle of people with experience in open source, so it's best to leverage that collective wisdom.

Just as new leaders need to embrace their elders, it is just as important for them to embrace and learn from their contemporaries. There are lots of patterns you see that are successful in open source projects, and being able to share them is important for not only the project to succeed, but the entire discipline of open source project leadership to thrive (which is exactly the motivation for writing this book).

Here are some tips to get started:

- Attend open source conferences, as that's where open source leaders will be. Introduce yourself, buy them a coffee or other beverage, and learn more about them. The hallway track at these conferences is full of amazing expertise, and these people are generally passionate about helping other open source projects thrive.

- Keep the dialog going when you find a few project leaders you admire and find easy to chat with. Set up regular check-in meetings, offering to be a listening ear to them as much as you would like them to be for you.

- Consider starting a blog to talk about your experiences as a maintainer. Mike McQuaid is one of the project leaders for Homebrew (`brew.sh`) and has a great blog where he shares his insights on being a maintainer (`https://mikemcquaid.com/`); I'm sure writing all this down has helped broker great conversations with other project maintainers, and at the same time has likely been quite therapeutic... hehe.

With the right support, new leaders are set up for success. But sometimes, the community also needs that nudge to see the new leaders as the true project leaders. Let's look at the role of previous maintainers in endorsing the new leaders in the next chapter.

Summary

In this chapter, we addressed transitioning open source project leadership, looking first at why projects should consider succession planning as maintainers might be looking to change careers, getting ready to retire, or perhaps disappearing from the project itself. We then looked at building a plan for transitioning a project, including ensuring the project's documentation is in order and building a full transition plan. Finally, we looked at how previous maintainers could step back comfortably and be supportive of the new maintainers.

Succession planning is hard for projects, not just because of the work required but because of the reality of our mortality. We never want to think of the day we step back from our work and hand it to the next person to take it forward. We might think the next person won't do as good a job as we will. The reality is, that feeling is because we won't know what to do once the work is on to the next person. But there's always a new adventure ahead of us.

While transitioning to new leadership is one exit for a maintainer and their open source project, sometimes, the project has run its course, and it's time to shut it down. This is known as sunsetting and is what we'll look at in the next chapter.

14

Sunsetting an Open Source Project

Open source projects start with good intentions: a problem to solve, an eager and motivated maintainer, and users and contributors flocking to the project and providing feedback. If everything goes right, a vibrant community and a great solution will emerge.

While putting code out under an open source license is a permanent action, having an open source project isn't. In *Chapter 12, Marketing for Open Source – Advocacy and Outreach*, we looked at a chart that describes the life cycle of an open source project; *Figure 14.1* illustrates that chart:

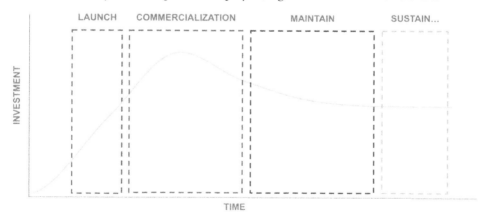

Figure 14.1 – Life cycle of an open source project

The backend of the life cycle is **Sustain…**, which sometimes means the project is just maintained over time. In those cases, there is still usage, but it's overall considered feature-complete, with any changes or additions solely focused on bug fixes and security issues. One example of an open source project in maintenance mode is the Apache Struts web framework. Struts was widely used to build Java web applications, but it has been in maintenance mode since the **version 2.5** release in November 2016.

While the project no longer adds new features or enhancements to the framework, patches and bug fixes continue to be released to maintain its stability and security, keep the documentation updated, and support the existing user base who continue to use Struts in their applications.

But sometimes, we see the community around a project, as it is in the **Sustain…** stage and starts waning, going to other solutions that are being actively developed or are better suited for their needs. This has a ripple effect; as users leave, so do contributors, and then maintainers leave the project with no one actively maintaining it over time. This is when a community starts considering the next and final step in an open source project's life cycle – **sunsetting**.

Do note that sunsetting isn't necessarily a bad thing either. In this chapter, we will see that for some sunsetted projects, other similar projects or successor projects allow the code and technology to continue. Open source communities tend to be lacking resources, so bringing project communities together helps grow a stronger project and avoid redundancies.

Sunsetting an open source project means winding down or discontinuing the development and maintenance of a project. This can happen for various reasons, including lack of funding, developer interest, or achieving the project's goals. Sunsetting a project can be difficult, especially if the project has a significant user base, but it can also be necessary to ensure that resources are used effectively. In this chapter, we will walk through how to sunset a project while touching on these topics:

- How to know when a project is slowing down
- The sunsetting process
- What comes after sunsetting?

Let's start by investigating the signs that sunsetting is in an open source project's imminent future.

How to know when a project is slowing down

There is often a nuance between a project hitting maintenance mode versus one truly sunsetting, and it usually connects directly to support for the project. As we've learned throughout this book, open source projects are multidimensional and require not only a strong community but a strong use case and strong investment back into the project. Let's bring back the sustainability cycle from *Chapter 10, Commercialization of Open Source,* to better illustrate this:

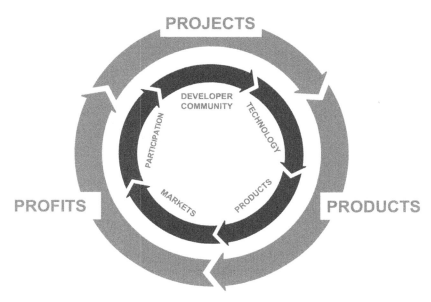

Figure 14.2 – The Projects, Products, Profits cycle of open source sustainability (`https://www.linuxfoundation.jp/wp-content/uploads/2017/09/Virtuous-cycle.png`)

A continuous cycle like this naturally means each part of the cycle must be working to keep the entire cycle moving. If one part goes off the tracks, the whole cycle grinds to a halt.

This is a great rubric on how to help identify when a project is slowing down and approaching sunset. Let's look at each of the **Projects**, **Products**, and **Profits** sections and see some examples and things to look for.

Projects – code velocity and community participation slow down

One of the most visible ways to see a project in decline and trending toward sunsetting is the code velocity (meaning the amount and frequency of code contributions over a certain period), and community participation slowing down significantly. If the project's user and contributor community declines to a point where there are few active participants, sustaining the project's development and maintenance may become difficult. If the developers who started the project lose interest or move on to other projects, finding new maintainers willing and able to carry on the work can become difficult. If the project has achieved its goals or completed its intended scope, there may no longer be a need to continue its development. For a project in maintenance mode, such as Apache Struts, which we mentioned previously, that might still be sustainable if the workload for maintenance is low, but often, that isn't the case.

The **OpenOffice** project is a good example of an open source project that has been sunsetted due to a declining community. OpenOffice was an open source office productivity suite developed by Sun Microsystems in the late 1990s. The suite included applications such as a word processor, spreadsheet program, and presentation software.

OpenOffice was very popular in its early years and was seen as a major competitor to Microsoft Office. However, in the late 2000s and early 2010s, the development of OpenOffice slowed down, and the project faced challenges such as a lack of funding and a decline in developer interest. In 2011, Oracle, which had acquired Sun Microsystems, decided to discontinue the development of OpenOffice and transfer ownership of the project to the Apache Software Foundation. Apache continued to develop and release new versions of OpenOffice for several years, but in 2016, the project was officially sunsetted due to a lack of active development and a declining user base.

For OpenOffice, there were additional factors that came into play. Back in 2010, when Oracle acquired Sun Microsystems, there were concerns about Oracle's commitment to the open source community. A group of developers created a fork of OpenOffice called **LibreOffice** that year, where most of the active community development and energy around an open source office productivity suite went to. We discussed forks in *Chapter 2, What Makes a Good Open Source Project?*, where we saw that when a project fork and the forks don't merge back into one project, one project tends to survive because of the lack of resources one fork receives compared to the other. With the community's energy effectively shifted to LibreOffice, OpenOffice was a prime candidate for sunsetting.

The next part of the open source sustainability cycle is **Products** – let's look at signs of a project approaching being sunsetted there.

Products – technology space in decline

If you've been around the tech industry for many years, like I have, you've seen lots of technology trends come and go. Remember **Personal Digital Assistants** (**PDAs**), such as the Palm Pilot? These were supplanted by devices combining the PDA and the smartphone into one. One of the earliest and most popular smartphones was the Blackberry, which is now completely extinct thanks to the Apple iPhone and the ecosystem of Android devices. Thousands of open source projects were tied to the Palm Pilot and Blackberry ecosystems. When those ecosystems fell apart as the technology became irrelevant, even the most active open source community could no longer sustain itself.

If the project is based on outdated technology or is no longer compatible with newer platforms or systems, it may be more practical to discontinue the project and start a new one from scratch. The Camino Web Browser (`https://caminobrowser.org/`) somewhat fell into this category because while it used the same Gecko rendering engine used by Mozilla Firefox, it used the Mac-native Cocoa API for the user interface, which made it seamlessly fit into the Aqua Desktop environment in the early versions of Mac OS X. As the Cocoa APIs used by Camino became discontinued, combined with the fact that the Mozilla Firefox browser became much more native-feeling and performant on Mac OS X than it had been in late 2001 when the project started, the project decided to sunset. Though instead of starting a new one from scratch, the project started working more in the upstream Mozilla Firefox project to continue improving the support of Firefox on Mac OS X.

Here are two additional examples of open source projects sunsetting due to a decline in their technology space:

1. **MeeGo**: MeeGo was an open source operating system for mobile devices, tablets, and netbooks that was developed by Nokia and Intel. However, with the rise of iOS and Android in the mobile market, interest in MeeGo declined, and the project was eventually sunsetted in 2011.

2. **Google Wave**: Google Wave was an open source collaboration platform that was designed to bring email, instant messaging, and document collaboration into a single platform. However, despite early excitement, interest in Google Wave declined, and the project was eventually sunsetted in 2012.

The last part of the sustainability cycle for open source projects is **Profits** - let's look at how, when the investment and funding dry up, it becomes harder and harder to keep a project going.

Profits – funding and investment dry up

Open source projects often rely on funding from donations or grants to support their development and maintenance. That funding might be pure cash funding, but it could also be funding in terms of developer and engineering resources, marketing support, and hardware and collaboration infrastructure – these types of funding are often more crucial to an open source project's success. Simply put, if funding dries up, sustaining the project over the long term can become difficult or impossible.

OpenSolaris was a popular project that attracted a large and active community of developers and users. However, after Oracle acquired Sun Microsystems in 2010, the company discontinued OpenSolaris and announced that it would no longer be releasing updates or new versions of the operating system.

The decision to sunset OpenSolaris was controversial, and it led to the formation of several community-driven efforts to continue developing the code base, such as the Illumos and OpenIndiana projects. However, despite these efforts, the OpenSolaris project as it was originally conceived is generally considered to have been sunsetted.

The sunsetting of OpenSolaris highlights some of the challenges that open source projects can face, particularly when they are tied to a particular company or organization that may be subject to an acquisition or other changes in direction. Despite these challenges, however, many open source projects continue to thrive and make important contributions to the development of software and technology.

Often, funding and investment dry up as a result of changing marketing conditions, but sometimes, it's related to legal issues that arise that make it difficult or impossible to continue developing and distributing the project. An example is CyanogenMod, a popular open source operating system for Android smartphones and tablets offering features and customizations not available in the standard Android operating system. Android enthusiasts and developers widely used it to create custom ROMs for their devices.

However, in 2016, Cyanogen Inc., the company behind CyanogenMod, announced that it was discontinuing the project and would no longer provide updates or support for the software. The decision was reportedly made due to a dispute between the company and its hardware partners and concerns about potential legal issues related to the use of proprietary software and APIs.

Following the shutdown of CyanogenMod, the community of developers and users who supported the project continued to work on a new open source Android operating system called LineageOS, which aims to provide similar features and customizations while remaining fully open source and community-driven. Today, LineageOS is widely used by Android enthusiasts and developers and continues to receive updates and improvements from its community of contributors.

Now that we've looked at the signs of a project slowing down and on the path to sunsetting, let's look at how to sunset a project.

The sunsetting process

Sunsetting an open source project is a difficult decision for a community. Making that decision requires the involvement of all active community participants, from maintainers to end users. In this section, we will look at the steps leading up to sunsetting; then, we will look at the step after the sunset officially happens.

Let's get started with the first step in sunsetting a project: making sure everyone agrees it's the right idea to do so.

Aligning on sunsetting in the community

If the project has a community of developers, it's important to involve them in the decision-making process and to encourage them to take on the responsibility of maintaining the project or forking it to create a new project. This can help ensure that the knowledge and expertise invested in the project are not lost.

Sometimes, a community gets small enough that aligning on sunsetting isn't hard. Getting the remaining community members together and discussing the state of the project and their interests can resolve things easily. I went through this while president of the OpenSocial Foundation back in 2014; at that time, with just SugarCRM, IBM, and Jive Software as members, they saw that their product directions weren't aligning with the work happening in the related projects and were able to quickly decide when to sunset the foundation and work (transitioning what was left into standards work in the W3C) made the most sense. That is a smooth sunsetting process… haha.

Not all sunsetting processes are smooth, especially when there might be competing interests or developers finding personal attachment to their work or the project itself. An example of this is the Ubuntu Unity desktop environment, a **Graphical User Interface** (**GUI**) developed by Canonical, the company behind the Ubuntu Linux distribution. It was designed to provide a modern and user-friendly desktop environment for Ubuntu users, with features such as a launcher and dash for accessing applications and files.

In 2017, Canonical announced that it was discontinuing Unity and shifting its focus to other areas, such as cloud computing and the Internet of Things. While Canonical pledged to continue providing security updates for Unity for several years, the discontinuation announcement was met with resistance from some members of the Ubuntu community. A group of Unity users and developers formed a community-driven project called Unity8, which aimed to continue developing and improving the Unity desktop environment as an open source project. However, despite the efforts of the Unity8 community, the project has struggled to gain traction and attract new contributors. The project was renamed Lomiri and is trying to regain community momentum as of this writing. This is a great example of the challenges that are faced when the business interests in sunsetting an open source project aren't considered alongside the community interests and the wider impacts on the community around the project.

Once a project community aligns on sunsetting, the next step is to announce that sunsetting is going to take place. Let's look at that now.

Announce intent to sunset

When a project is sunsetting, the project maintainers must communicate this decision to the community. This can involve announcing the decision on the project's website, mailing list, or social media channels. While there are multiple ways to provide notice, two primary considerations should be part of any intent to sunset announcement:

1. **Provide ample notice**: As soon as the decision to sunset the project has been made, you should provide ample notice to end users. This will give them plenty of time to plan for the transition and find alternatives.

2. **Communicate clearly**: When communicating with end users, it's important to be clear and transparent about the reasons for the sunset and what they can expect in the coming months. It can also be good to provide regular updates and answer any questions or concerns from end users; often, a project doesn't consider all the impacts sunsetting might have on a community, and being able to address those concerns helps make the process smooth.

An example of a project doing a great announcement of its intent to sunset was Firebug, which was an open source web development tool that allowed developers to inspect and edit HTML, CSS, and JavaScript code in real time. Web developers and designers widely used it to debug and optimize web pages.

In 2017, the developers of Firebug announced that they would be discontinuing the project and recommending users switch to the built-in web development tools provided by modern web browsers. *Figure 14.3* illustrates them updating their website to announce the project's sunset:

Thank you, Firebug. You made the web amazing for all!

The story of Firefox and Firebug are synonymous with the rise of the web. We fought the good fight and changed how developers inspect HTML and debug JS in the browser. Firebug ushered the Web 2.0 era. Today, the work pioneered by the Firebug community through the last 12 years lives on in Firefox Developer Tools. Switch to the latest version of Firefox and see the very latest devtools updates.

Tips on making the switch   Firebug Releases   Firebug Source   Blog

Figure 14.3 – Firebug home page announcing it's been sunsetted (https://getfirebug.com/)

The Firebug announcement is good; it's clear and appreciative of the community's support and helps direct users to projects and tools that they should consider migrating to. This leads to the next part of the sunsetting process: helping end users transition.

Work with end users on transitioning

Looking at the Firebug project, part of informing the community of the intent to sunset is to provide guidance on how they can continue to use the project or migrate to alternative solutions. Even though a project is sunsetting, that doesn't preclude users still using it and maintaining it themselves; as we said at the beginning of this chapter, once code is out under an open source license, that is a permanent move. But more often than not, end users will want to move to a different solution.

Here are a few steps that you can take to work with end users during the sunset process:

1. **Offer alternatives**: As the sunset process progresses, work with end users to identify alternatives that they can use to replace the project. This may involve recommending other open source projects or commercial offerings.

2. **Provide migration support**: Depending on the complexity of the project, end users may require support with migrating their data and workflows to a new solution. Work with them to provide documentation, tools, and resources to help with this process.

Firebug primarily directed their users to the Firefox Developer Tools, which heavily borrowed from the concepts used in Firebug. Firefox created a wiki page guide to help users with the migration, mostly helping the end users find the features they used in Firebug in the Firefox Developer Tools:

⌂ / Migrating from Firebug   Report an issue / View page source

Migrating from Firebug

When migrating from Firebug to the Firefox Developer Tools, you may wonder where the features you loved in Firebug are available in the Developer Tools. The following list aims to help Firebug users to find their way into the Developer Tools.

For the latest developer tools and features, try Firefox Developer Edition.

Download Firefox Developer Edition

General

Activation

Firebug's activation is URL based respecting the same origin policy. That means that when you open a page on the same origin in a different tab, Firebug gets opened automatically. And when you open a page of a different origin

Figure 14.4 – The Migrating from Firebug guide in the Firefox Source Code Tree documentation (`https://firefox-source-docs.mozilla.org/devtools-user/migrating_from_firebug/index.html`)

Firebug provided a clear path for users to migrate to alternative tools while ensuring that the project's code and documentation remained accessible to the wider community.

Once a project has been sunsetted, there is work to do when closing shop for the project. We'll look at this in the next section.

What comes after sunsetting?

Post-sunsetting, the primary responsibility is to make it clear that the project is no longer maintained and ensure the project's assets have a long-term home. Sometimes, we see projects come out of being sunsetted or parts of the code base being incorporated into future projects or used when legacy applications need to be ported to new platforms in the future. We'll look at what a project should do in this section.

Mark code repositories and issue trackers as archived

Right after sunsetting a project, it's crucial to clarify the project's status. This involves archiving the project's code and documentation in a public repository so that users and developers can still access it in the future. This can be especially important if the project significantly impacts the open source community.

Here are some best practices for marking code repositories when sunsetting an open source project:

1. **Add a notice to the repository's README file**: The README file is often the first thing that users and contributors will see when they visit your project's code repository. Adding a notice to this README that explains that the project is no longer being actively developed or maintained can help to prevent confusion.

2. **Use a "deprecated" or "archived" label**: Many code hosting platforms, such as GitHub, allow you to mark repositories with labels that indicate that they are no longer being actively developed. Using labels such as "deprecated" or "archived" can help make it clear that the project is no longer being actively maintained.

3. **Add a note to the repository's description**: Adding a note to the repository's description that explains that the project is no longer being actively developed or maintained can help prevent confusion.

4. **Consider redirecting users to alternative solutions**: If there are alternative open source projects that users can use instead of your project, consider adding links to those projects in your repository's README or other documentation. This can help users find alternative solutions that meet their needs.

Note that this doesn't have to be complicated for a project to do, but as we stated earlier in this chapter, it should be clear. Let's look at the **SceneJS** project (`https://github.com/xeolabs/scenejs`) and how it makes it clear the project has been sunsetted:

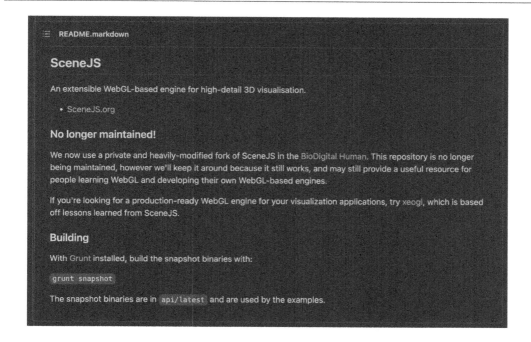

Figure 14.5 – The SceneJS README file announcing the project is no longer
maintained (https://github.com/xeolabs/scenejs#readme)

Here, you can see that all the key pieces of information were conveyed; that it's no longer maintained, why it was sunsetted, and where users can go for a similar solution.

In addition, a project should ensure any related tools or services are shut down. Here are some things to consider:

1. If the project had any associated services, such as a website, social media accounts, or discussion forum, make sure to deactivate them or redirect them to an alternative solution.

2. If the project received funding, close down any accounts or arrangements associated with that funding. If funds are left over, consider donating them to one of the projects that was recommended end users migrate to.

After sunsetting, the project having a long-term home is important from both a user support perspective as well as a historical one. Let's look at that now.

Find a home for asset ownership

Open source projects usually have two types of assets: the code and documentation, and the project's name and logo (known as the *marks*). For code and documentation, many of the open source code hosting platforms have archiving programs and policies for open source projects; GitHub has its Archive Program (`https://archiveprogram.github.com/`), which is a good example here.

For a more comprehensive solution, several organizations can serve as neutral third parties for open source project trademarks, including the Software Freedom Conservancy, the Free Software Foundation, The Linux Foundation, and the Open Source Initiative. It's crucial that when an open source project sunsets, the trademarks associated with the project can be managed consistently with the project's goals and values. Organizations such as those just mentioned are well known as stewards of open source projects. Additionally, they can manage the hosting of websites and credentials to code repositories in case the last maintainers cannot be reached.

Transferring the trademarks to a third party ensures that they are not used in ways inconsistent with the project's open source principles or could harm its reputation or legacy. For example, if the trademarks associated with an open source project were transferred to a for-profit company that did not share the project's values, the company could use the trademarks in ways that were not in the best interests of the project or its community.

The goal when handling open source project assets after sunsetting should be to ensure that the work is preserved for future use and that users and contributors are informed of the project's status and any alternative solutions that may be available.

While sunsetting is the last stage in the life cycle of an open source project, that doesn't mean it's the end. Projects can come back from being sunsetted; let's look at how.

Can a project come back from sunsetting?

Yes, an open source project can come back after it has been sunsetted, although it depends on the reasons why the project was discontinued in the first place. If the project was sunsetted due to a lack of funding or developer interest, it might be possible for new funding or developers to come forward and revive the project. In some cases, the project may be forked by other developers or organizations who want to continue its development under a new name or with new features. This can result in a new community forming around the project, with new contributors and users.

Generally, there are two paths to a project coming back from sunsetting:

1. Handing over the project to a new maintainer who can continue to develop and maintain it
2. Forking the project to create a new project that can continue to evolve and meet users' needs

However, it's important to note that bringing back a sunsetted project can be challenging, especially if the original project had a large and active user base that has moved on to other solutions. The new project must demonstrate its value and relevance to the community, and it may take time to rebuild momentum and attract new contributors. The Unity8/Lomiri project story discussed earlier in this chapter is a good example of the challenge of bringing back a project from being sunsetted. While a sunsetted open source project can come back, it's important to carefully consider why the project was discontinued in the first place and have a clear plan for how to address those challenges if the project is revived.

Summary

In general, the decision to sunset an open source project can be a difficult one, and it is important for the project maintainers to communicate the decision clearly and to provide guidance to users on how to migrate to alternative solutions. However, in some cases, sunsetting a project may be necessary to ensure that resources are used effectively and that the project's legacy is preserved.

Do note that sunsetting an open source project doesn't equate to the failure of an open source project; when we looked at many of the project examples in this chapter, we saw they all had a significant impact in their primes, but conditions changed, which led to a sunset. And note that even though a project was sunsetted, it doesn't mean it didn't impact the future. For example, despite its eventual sunset, OpenOffice was an important open source project that helped promote free and open source software in the office productivity market. The project also inspired the development of several other open source office suites, such as LibreOffice and Calligra.

It's fitting that we close this book by talking about sunsetting an open source project. But as we covered, putting code out under an open source license is a permanent action; having an open source project isn't. I hope this chapter showcased that while projects can end, the code and work can continue to live on.

Index

W

Z

Packtpub.com

Subscribe to our online digital library for full access to over 7,000 books and videos, as well as industry leading tools to help you plan your personal development and advance your career. For more information, please visit our website.

Why subscribe?

- Spend less time learning and more time coding with practical eBooks and Videos from over 4,000 industry professionals

- Improve your learning with Skill Plans built especially for you

- Get a free eBook or video every month

- Fully searchable for easy access to vital information

- Copy and paste, print, and bookmark content

Did you know that Packt offers eBook versions of every book published, with PDF and ePub files available? You can upgrade to the eBook version at Packtpub.com and as a print book customer, you are entitled to a discount on the eBook copy. Get in touch with us at customercare@packtpub.com for more details.

At www.Packtpub.com, you can also read a collection of free technical articles, sign up for a range of free newsletters, and receive exclusive discounts and offers on Packt books and eBooks.

Other Books You May Enjoy

If you enjoyed this book, you may be interested in these other books by Packt:

Build Your Own Programming Language

Clinton L. Jeffery

ISBN: 9781800204805

- Perform requirements analysis for the new language and design language syntax and semantics
- Write lexical and context-free grammar rules for common expressions and control structures
- Develop a scanner that reads source code and generate a parser that checks syntax
- Build key data structures in a compiler and use your compiler to build a syntax-coloring code editor
- Implement a bytecode interpreter and run bytecode generated by your compiler
- Write tree traversals that insert information into the syntax tree
- Implement garbage collection in your language

Packt is searching for authors like you

If you're interested in becoming an author for Packt, please visit `authors.packtpub.com` and apply today. We have worked with thousands of developers and tech professionals, just like you, to help them share their insight with the global tech community. You can make a general application, apply for a specific hot topic that we are recruiting an author for, or submit your own idea.

Share Your Thoughts

Now you've finished *Open Source Projects - Beyond Code*, we'd love to hear your thoughts! Scan the QR code below to go straight to the Amazon review page for this book and share your feedback or leave a review on the site that you purchased it from.

`https://packt.link/r/1837636885`

Your review is important to us and the tech community and will help us make sure we're delivering excellent quality content.

Download a free PDF copy of this book

Thanks for purchasing this book!

Do you like to read on the go but are unable to carry your print books everywhere? Is your eBook purchase not compatible with the device of your choice?

Don't worry, now with every Packt book you get a DRM-free PDF version of that book at no cost.

Read anywhere, any place, on any device. Search, copy, and paste code from your favorite technical books directly into your application.

The perks don't stop there, you can get exclusive access to discounts, newsletters, and great free content in your inbox daily

Follow these simple steps to get the benefits:

1. Scan the QR code or visit the link below

https://packt.link/free-ebook/9781837636884

2. Submit your proof of purchase
3. That's it! We'll send your free PDF and other benefits to your email directly

Made in the USA
Las Vegas, NV
05 June 2023

72990219R00136